The New Agrarian Mind

The Movement Toward Decentralist
Thought in Twentieth-Century America

Allan Carlson

Transaction Publishers
New Brunswick (U.S.A.) and London (U.K.)

Second printing 2012

Copyright © 2000 by Transaction Publishers, New Brunswick, New Jersey.

This book is printed on acid-free paper that meets the American National Standard for Permanence of Paper for Printed Library Materials.

Library of Congress Catalog Number: 99-056518
ISBN: 1-56000-421-5 (cloth); 0-7658-0590-1 (paper)
Printed in the United States of America

Library of Congress Cataloging-in-Publication Data

Carlson, Allan, 1949-
    The new agrarian mind : the movement toward decentralist thought in twentieth-century America / Allan Carlson.
        p.   cm.
    Includes bibliographical references and index.
    ISBN 0-7658-0590-1 (alk. paper)
        1. United States—Intellectual life—20th century. 2. Country life—United States—Philosophy. 3. Agrarians (Group of writers). 4. Sociology, Rural—United States. I. Title.

E169.12.C276   1999
305.5'52'09730904—dc21

                                                                    99-056518

The New Agrarian Mind

Contents

Acknowledgements

The staff of the University of Wisconsin-Madison library system, particularly at the Steenboch Agriculture Library, gave me considerable assistance, as did the archivists at Marquette University , home of the papers of Luigi Ligutti.

A special grant that gave me the time and resources to complete the needed research and to draft the manuscript came from The Earhart Foundation of Ann Arbor, Michigan.

As before, very special help came from my long time associate, Heidi Gee, who managed the word processing chores with skill and patience.

For helping me to understand better the modern agrarian problem, and for inspiring me to complete the project, I need to thank the good folk at Heritage Homesteads, on the Brazos de Dios River in Texas.

For reading the manuscript and saving me from errors of language and interpretation, I am grateful to Michael Jordan of Hillsdale College, James Schall of Georgetown University, and Bill Kauffman of Batavia, New York. For the errors that remain, of course, I alone am responsible.

Finally, I thank my wife, Elizabeth, and my children—Anders, Sarah-Eva, Anna, and Miriam—for the gift of a canvas wall tent. Placed in a grove of trees on my wife's family farm in Owen Township, Winnebago County, Illinois, it served as the place where this manuscript took form in the delightful summer of 1998.

To Elizabeth Cecelia, my garden friend

Introduction: The New Agrarians

The year 1900 was the watershed in American farm and rural life.

The agrarianism woven into the very fabric of the new American republic was, in one sense, still strong. As Thomas Jefferson had made the argument in a 1785 letter to John Jay: "Cultivators of the earth are the most valuable citizens. They are the most vigorous, the most independent, the most virtuous, and they are tied to their country and wedded to its liberty by the most lasting bonds."[1] Similar early celebrations of the yeoman farmer came from the pens of Jean Hector St. John de Crevecoeur (*Letters from an American Farmer*) and John Taylor of Caroline (*Arator*), sentiments that echoed across the nineteenth century.

Despite federal investments in the National Road and the wide promotion of canals, it would still have been possible, circa 1840, to imagine decisions that could have preserved the yeoman subsistence farmer as the normative American. New transportation routes could have been denied on public lands. Or the use of the power of eminent domain might have been curtailed. Or joint-stock companies might have been denied. Or preference could have been given, in various ways, to local and regional, rather than national and international markets. But the monocrop South, using agrarian rhetoric, pushed for open international trade, the better to market its cotton, while new settlers in the Mississippi Valley demanded internal improvements for access to the markets of the East and Europe.

Meanwhile, the industrial process resting on the joint-stock corporation and an extensive division of labor grew to rival, then surpass the home economy. Before 1840, homespun cloth, homemade clothes, hand wrought furniture, domestically produced candles, and home educated children were the rule, in city and countryside. After that year, industrial processes pressed into a rapidly growing number of product lines and the modern salesmen emerged, radically changing American household life. A highly integrated home economy, involving the altruistic, non-monetary exchange of goods and services by family members, gave way to heightened individualism, consumerism and other signs of economic modernity. The factory system also spread into education, with the state taking the lead in shaping public schooling as a collective, industrialized enterprise run by professionals, leaving the family as an institution again in retreat.

Partisans still debate the question of whether the Civil War was primarily over the issue of slavery or a contest between an agrarian civilization in the South and a rival industrial civilization in the North. Whatever the interpretation one might choose, it is undeniable that after 1865, there would be no holding back on the rapid, heavily subsidized spread of the railroads, on the quick settlement of the Plains states and the West, and on the expansion of industry and commercial agriculture to every corner of the nation. Even so, it was unclear for a time how this might affect the rural-urban balance. The Homestead Act of 1862 opened to farming vast tracts of essentially free arable land, and drew millions of new European immigrants, particularly from Germany and Scandinavia, to the Middle and Far West. The unsettled corners of Iowa, Minnesota, Wisconsin, Nebraska, and Kansas filled up quickly, followed by a rush to claim land in the Dakotas, Montana, Colorado, and finally Oklahoma. Meanwhile, Mormon leaders guided the settlement of the intermountain basin.

In the 1890s, the American frontier was declared closed, and the last skirmishes with the decimated Indian tribes occurred. Still, the census of 1900 showed that the farm population of the United States had grown by 20 percent during the prior decade, reaching 29,875,000. There were nearly 6 million farms in 1900, over _four times_ the number counted in the antebellum year of 1850. The vast watershed of the Mississippi River—including the great farming regions drained by the Ohio, Tennessee, Missouri, and Arkansas Rivers—was now fully peopled by yeoman farm families. At the heart of this informal agrarian empire was the state of Iowa, a new political powerhouse where corn and farmer were kings and from which would issue a string of U.S. secretaries of agriculture.

Yet the same turn-of-the-century census betokened trouble for the Agrarian Republic. To begin with, calculations showed that, in spite of the continued growth in rural numbers, people in urban America now outnumbered their country cousinss: 30,160,000 city dwellers versus 29,875,000 on the farm. For the first time, farmers had become an American minority. Moreover, the momentum of growth had shifted strongly in favor of the cities. (It would not be until later that rural partisans would learn that the farm population had ceased to grow in absolute, as well as relative terms, peaking in 1917 at 32.5 million. As late as 1940, though, the farm population numbered 30.5 million, still above the level recorded in 1900.) Analysis of census numbers also showed that American cities had followed their European counterparts in fostering low, below-replacement birth rates and mounting family instability. By way of contrast, rural America remained remarkably vital, with birth rates 75 to 100 percent higher than those found in cities and with abundant fertility recorded especially in the Plains states and the Southern highlands.

The prior two decades had brought new signs of rural stress, as well. Huge increases in the number of acres put to grain and the ubiquitous presence of the railroads created a true national agricultural market, sharply reducing the importance of local economies and driving down prices. Indeed, serious depressions in commodity prices shook farmers in the late 1860s, the early 1880s, and again in the 1890s, bringing the first waves of foreclosures and the abandonment of homesteads. The Patrons of Husbandry, or the Grange, emerged in the 1870s and 1880s as a social-political movement to advance the interests of farmers, above all to protect them from the "depredations" of the railroads and the banks. The Farmers Alliance followed in the 1890s. Henry George's volume, *Wealth and Poverty*, advanced the idea of a "single tax" on the development value of property, partly to protect the land tenure of farmers. Steam-powered threshers made their appearance about this time, marking the first direct challenge by power machines to the domain of the horse and mule and also bringing early examples of the displacement of human farm labor by technological advance. With the appearance of the machines, the man-hours needed to produce 100 bushels of wheat fell from 152 in 1880 to 108 by 1900. For corn, the decline was from 180 to 147. The Populist Party drew heavily on the votes of discontented farmers in 1892, and the Presidential campaign of William Jennings Bryan four years later rested on the anger and energy of a troubled agricultural sector.

So, as the twentieth century dawned, new questions faced rural America. How would the agrarian sector adjust to the farmers' new minority status? Should the innovations of science and the new machine technologies be welcomed on the farm? How could America hold onto the next generation of farmers? Was commercial farming compatible with strong family life? How could the nation insure continued enjoyment of the socially conservative gifts delivered by a rural populace: a sense of independence, commitment to democracy, an abundance of children, stable community life? Could the nation even survive without a vital farming populace rooted in productive working homes?

This volume examines the development of one distinctive set of answers to these questions, provided by a series of writers and thinkers spanning the whole of the twentieth century: botanist and country life advocate Liberty Hyde Bailey, rural sociologist Carle Zimmerman, economist Ralph Borsodi, novelist and public farmer Louis Bromfield, the "Twelve Southerners" of Vanderbilt University, American historian Herbert Agar, Iowa priest and rural activist Luigi Ligutti, and the poet-novelist-essayist Wendell Berry. They came from different backgrounds: Protestant, Catholic, Jewish, and atheist; Northerners, Southerners, and sons of the Border States; native and foreign born. In different times and voices, they called their work the "country life" campaign, "agrarianism," "traditionalism," "distributism," "decentralism," "anti-urban," and "anti-industrial." They are collectively labeled here the New Agrarians, a phrase borrowed from Herbert Agar, both to set them apart from the simpler Jeffersonianism born in the nineteenth century and to emphasize their deliberate grappling with the forces of modernity. Unlike the politics-of-interest of the Grange, the Populists, and the Bryanites, the work of the New Agrarians was intellectual, literary, and academic. Starting with Liberty Hyde Bailey, there was a coherent and often direct transfer of attitudes and ideas among this body of writers and across the whole century. These bonds are strong enough to bear the label, "movement."

Appropriately, the New Agrarians shared a coherent set of goals that were at once socially conservative and economically radical. They sought to preserve the family unit as the foundation of society. They worked to encourage and protect the high fertility of rural Americans and the place of the countryside as the nursery of the nation. They promoted the economic democracy that would be derived from a wide and fairly equal distribution of land and other productive property. And they stressed the vital importance of the working home on the farm as the primary social integrator. As the following analysis will show, they also tended to hold other, more curious shared assumptions: a deep faith in technology as the friend of the subsistence farmer and smallholder; hostility to organized religion in general, and to fundamentalist and sectarian Christianity in particular; faith in the power of progressive social engineering; and full support for mass education, from the grade school through the university and beyond.

Their story remains significant in several ways. The New Agrarians represented the one serious attempt in modern America to create a "third way" in politics, one not easily fit onto the conventional liberal-conservative, or left-right spectrum. While considerable attention has focused on each of these writers as individuals, through books, dissertations, and articles, no systematic attention has been given to their essential unity and the durability of their campaign between the century's beginning and end. Moreover, their work has had practical consequences, affecting many millions of lives, including the grand mobilization of rural leadership in the 1920s, the flowering of subsistence homestead communities in the 1930s, the crafting of the American "conservative mind" in the 1950s, the forging of the environmental movement in the 1960s, the founding of rural communes in the 1970s, the creation of a "pro-family" movement in the 1980s, and the discovery of the secrets of the Plain People such as the Amish in the 1990s. All these results might be seen as shards of the New Agrarian project, incomplete fragments of a program that could never claim victory as a unitary cause.

A few comments should be offered about those prominent writers and public figures associated with decentralist and agricultural questions, but not included in this book. For example, Henry Wallace of Iowa, publisher of *Wallace's Farmer* and U.S. secretary of agriculture, was a famed farm spokesman in the early twentieth century, an "agrarian" in mind and habit. Yet his prominence lay in the fields of politics and journalism, his thought was largely derivative, and he was rarely mentioned in the work of the New Agrarians. Louis Mumford, critic of the modern city and advocate for a "bio-technic" civilization, called himself a "decentralist" and would be cited with some frequency by several of the New Agrarians. However, this disciple of John Dewey held a principle focus on _urban_—not rural—renewal, through the promotion of the garden-city suburbs. On those matters that were close to the New Agrarian project, his arguments were actually anticipated by Ralph Borsodi. Architect Frank Lloyd Wright also celebrated decentralism and rural locales as values to be preserved. Yet his core concerns were aesthetic and regional, rather than truly agrarian in nature. Artists of the regional revival, such as Iowa's Grant Wood, were in most respects in harmony with the New Agrarian ideas. Yet, by definition, their focus was on the visual, rather than the printed word. Finally, Russell Lord was a versatile agrarian writer and editor who openly confronted modernity and consciously sought to define a "new agrarian" tradition. He also had direct contact with most of the cast: from Bailey and Bromfield to Agar and Ligutti. Yet as such, his work was derivative, more that of commentary and history than original thinking. Indeed, he served as a sort of Boswell to the New Agrarian collective.

The organization of chapters follows the temporal flow of the New Agrarian project. It took shape shortly after 1900 in the fertile mind of Liberty Hyde Bailey. During the 1920s and 1930s, the second generation of writers—Zimmerman, Borsodi, Bromfield, the Vanderbilt Agrarians, and Herbert Agar—lifted the agrarian project to the apogee of its influence. Father Ligutti carried the cause through the troubled 1940s and 1950s. Wendell Berry brought the New Agrarian campaign, battered and near death, to the century's end.

In what follows, the reader should recognize this author's sympathy for the primary goals of the New Agrarians and his delight in much of their work. At the same time, the reader will find criticism, sometimes sharp in nature, of the missteps taken by this Agrarian band along the way, particularly where their own biases or arguments undercut the very goals that they claimed to pursue. Some of these errors were born of prejudice; others came from a failure of observation or analysis. The final chapter summarizes reasons for the apparent failure of the New Agrarian project. Yet it also suggests that the core purpose of the New Agrarians—the recreation of working homes on subsistence farms as incubators of family solidarity and social health—actually has found some success, in wholly unexpected places, even as the new century and millennium dawn.

Note

1. Letter, Jefferson to Jay, 23 August 1785, in *The Best Letters of Thomas Jefferson*, ed. J.G. de Roulhac Hamilton (Boston and New York: Houghton Mifflin, 1926): 15.

1

Toward a New Rural Civilization: Liberty Hyde Bailey

As America's best-known plant scientist and as an innovative university administrator, Liberty Hyde Bailey left a large mark on his nation. In addition, for a critical twenty-five years of his life, Bailey focused his energies on building an Agrarianism fit for the twentieth century. From 1903 to 1928, he campaigned to craft a new rural civilization, one that could weather the economic and social storms that had shaken American agriculture during the prior thirty years. With a remarkably fertile mind and a prolific pen, Bailey created the Country Life movement. While many other well-known Americans—from Theodore Roosevelt to Henry Wallace—joined in this campaign, its leading historian concludes that Bailey "looms largest...during the opening decades of the twentieth century."[1] Moreover, he crafted a set of goals, themes, and arguments that would, at once, guide and haunt this New Agrarianism as an intellectual movement for the remainder of this century. He redefined the agrarian mind in progressive, forward-looking ways. But ironically, Bailey would also guide this pattern of thought into paths that rejected the only forms of rural community and home reconstruction that proved able to meet the modernist challenge.

The "Outlook"

Liberty Hyde Bailey was born in western Michigan on the Ides of March, 1858, to a father bearing the same name and to a mother from the prominent Harrison family of Virginia. She died when young Liberty was six years old, and the elder Bailey became the shaping force in his son's life. A large man, powerful and rugged, who clung to homemade candles and homespun cloth long after they had disappeared elsewhere in their Michigan township, Bailey senior was the quintessential Yankee. Reared in Vermont, he was a strident abolitionist, known for his temperance, quiet strength, and simplicity. While of Congregational religious antecedents, Bailey senior found his spiritual home among the Freemasons. He would pass the Masonic vision of spiritual unity and universal brotherhood on to his son, with significant results.

The Bailey family planted and operated a large apple orchard in southwestern Michigan. According to his biographers, young Liberty absorbed here the lessons of nature and gained his deep love for the flora of North America.[2] Gaining stature at a youthful age for his skills at grafting apple trees, young Bailey began to intellectualize his work as well. At age fifteen, he read a paper on "Birds" to the South Haven [Michigan] Pomological Society, leading to his election as ornithologist of the society. Four years later, he entered Michigan Agricultural College in East Lansing, as a student of horticulture and agriculture. He became fascinated by the Rubus genus of blackberries and other brambles, and produced a string of attention-getting academic papers.

On graduation, Bailey chose not to return to the family orchard, viewing such work as intellectually confining. Instead, he became a newspaperman for a year, until receiving an offer to enter Harvard University as special assistant to the famed botanist, Asa Gray. In 1884, Bailey also joined the editorial staff of the *American Cultivator*. The next year, with some graduate education under his belt, he accepted an offer from Michigan Agricultural College to return as its first professor of horticulture. Full of energy, Bailey set out to transform the field from mere gardening into something more grand. As he explained, "Horticulture the art is old; horticulture the science is new."[3] Books began to appear in amazing profusion, eventually including his magisterial *Cyclopedia of American Horticulture* (four volumes), *Cyclopedia of American Agriculture* (four volumes), *The Annals of Horticulture* (five volumes), *Botany, Principles of Agriculture*, and *The Plant Life of North America*. In 1888, the offer came to assume the Chair of Practical and Experimental Horticulture at Cornell University.

Bailey became a legend and institution-builder at the Ithaca, New York campus. In an 1893 address to the university's Agriculture Association, he called for a state-fostered agricultural school that was "free from bigotry and convention and inspired with patriotic hope," adding: "Let that institution be Cornell!"[4] With state grants in 1894 and 1897, he created "experiment stations" for horticultural investigations and a model program of "extension agents," who would carry research results directly from the University to New York's farmers. He called these innovations "a plain, earnest and continuous effort to meet the needs of the people on their own farms."[5] Bailey authored monthly nature-study leaflets for children (e.g., "How a Squash Plant Gets Out of Its Seed," "A Child's Garden") that went to 3,000 New York grade school teachers, and he spoke to hundreds—eventually thousands—of rural audiences. He was founding editor of the journals *Country Life in America* (1901) and the *Cornell Countryman* (1903). In 1904, with a grant of $250,000 from the New York Legislature, he created the College of Agriculture at Cornell, becoming its first dean. By 1913, student enrollment had climbed from 100 to 1,400, the faculty had grown from eleven to 100, and Cornell stood as the preeminent agricultural school in the country. He retired that year, to become a private scholar, a "separate soul," and to accelerate his work on social and political questions.

While part researcher and scientist, Bailey was also poet and metaphysician. He wrote hundreds of poems, some of them collected into volumes of verse (e.g., *Wind and Weather*). He saw poetry as "prophecy," a way to gain hold of aspirations that were "elemental and universal."

At the turn of the century, Bailey turned increasingly to philosophy, an emphasis that would flower into his Country Life campaign. In an 1899 essay for the *Independent,* a magazine of "free opinion," entitled "An Evolutionist's View of Nature and Religion," Bailey laid out for the first time his personal world view and the role of evolution as a. new, progressive faith.[6] He expanded these arguments into a 1905 book, *The Outlook to Nature*, which he dedicated to his ninety-year-old father. Early portions of this extended essay bore a Whitmanesque quality in their lyrical praise for the commonplace:

> I would preach the surface of the earth, because we walk on it....I would preach the sky....One must have a free vision if he is to know the sky....I preach the mountains, and everything that is taller than a man.[7]

However, at the core of the book lay a discussion of evolution and Christianity, where the author cut to the heart of human purpose and meaning. Bailey began with a compelling distinction, using Scripture to deny that faith and science were in conflict. "I find nothing in Scripture to make me disbelieve evolution," he wrote. "Strictly speaking, evolution does not attempt to explain creation, but only the *progress* of creation. Whatever its form, it begins where Genesis does—'In the beginning, God.'" He saw the whole scheme of evolution as "a design," arguing that "the fact that we have only now been able to apprehend this scheme is all the more proof that it is divine."[8]

Yet from this relatively benign start, Bailey moved on to jettison, with subtlety and wit, virtually the whole of Christian doctrine. He noted, for example, that "the evolution philosophies" altered one's point of view toward "all problems of life and destiny." Evolution demanded "that we be willing to free ourselves from every bondage of doctrine and dogma, from traditions and superstitions, from 'authority' and prejudgments." Evolution bid us "to a high place." It magnified individual effort, kindled the inner light of conscience as opposed to authority, lessened belief in "mere wonders," stimulated reason, and emancipated the man. "It asks us to lay aside prejudice and small dogmatisms."[9]

Lest the reader not understand, Bailey specified the sort of "small dogmatisms" that ought to be put away. "Salvation is *not* the highest goal of religion," he explained. "[T]he emphasis is being transferred from salvation to service," and from blind obedience to "observation" and "study," where man became "a partaker" in the evolutionary process. Indeed, Bailey praised the changes already occurring among leadership elites in the Protestant churches: "[T]he layman...may be little aware of the progressive attitude of the church as a whole, of its *full* acceptance of the results of scientific research, its growing spirit of freedom from the non-essentials on which men differ, the new leadership that it has acquired." Equally promising, in his view, was the budding *ecumenical* spirit, the tendency "for men to determine wherein they agree rather than wherein they differ."[10]

Bailey concluded that the "supernatural" had been over-emphasized in the old faith. "Religion," he explained, "is as natural and normal as other human activities and aspirations." It was "an evolution" itself, where "our conception of God will enlarge as our horizon enlarges." At the same time, he implied, the supernatural had been under-emphasized in nature. As Bailey wrote: "Evolution implies that God is not outside nature, *but in nature*, that he is an indwelling spirit in nature as truly as in man." Accordingly, the study of evolution would "impel us to a new and great reverence for The Power," one that bound all humanity and one that resided in the natural world.[11]

This celebration of God as the unifying force of human brotherhood, this injection of divine force into nature, this affirmation of ecumenism, and this dismissal of the "small dogmatisms" of Original Sin, the Incarnation, the Atonement, the miracles of Jesus, and the Trinity were all consistent with the Freemason creed. In a 1911 poem, also bearing the title, "Outlook," Bailey honed and elevated this post-Christian world view into a celebration of Nature as God:

> They [aspects of nature] teach that all the world is good.
> Alike for man and brute and wood
> All set in one vast fellowhood
> Nor innate guilt appears....
>> And I blaspheme not
>> The perfecting works of God;
>> And I build my holy fires
>> Where every living thing aspires.
>> And I am I.
>> Dominion unto me is given
>> As my fertile years go by
>> To win my way to heaven
>> Myself I must redeem –
>> All nature helps me on
>> And all good saints of here and yon –
> My soul must be supreme.
> Within myself my kingdom lies
> Nor any fatal faiths shall blind my eyes
> When my soul would take its wings and rise....
> From first unto the last
> Some mighty essence runs
> It moveth in the worlds and riseth in the suns:
> Its scheme I would forecast....
>> When I consider the heavens, the stars, and the moon
>> My spirit out wings its small forenoon
>> With pride of master and man
>> To partake in the plan.
> We helpless gaze unto the stars:
> But some great day we shall in signal be with Mars
> And in a twinkling shall sense a wider brotherhood
> Than any man hath ever understood –
> A kinship that encompasseth the universe
> Wherein will all our feeble cults disperse
> And all the worlds our neighbors be
> In one vast fraternity.[12]

This spiritualized ecological approach would animate and guide the Country Life movement then taking form. As such, its precepts—hostility to the Christian faith found among the country people, the celebration of science and technology, progress through education by elites, and the worship of Nature as God and God as Nature—would echo through New Agrarian circles for decades to come, with ironic and disturbing consequence.

Agrarianism Re-Formed

But this could not be seen as the Country Life campaign began, full of solid goals and energy. As articulated by Bailey, the new Agrarianism of the Twentieth Century sought:

1. *To preserve the family.* Bailey emphasized that the family was the fundamental, and irreplaceable social unit. In a remarkable break with other turn-of-the-century progressive thinkers, he wrote: "even with all the beautiful social schemes, we have not yet found a substitute for the family. The effort to let the school take the place of the family has failed." Bailey argued that the very nature of the farm strengthened families, for "the farm is a cooperative enterprise in which every member of the family has a stake; every boy and girl has actual (not make-believe or time serving) duties and responsibilities." Only farm homes stood as "real houses, with room for children and the storage of liberal supplies." At the same time, farming sustained working homes; it was "a co-partnership business...between a man and a woman....The home is on the farm and part of it." Posing the central agrarian question, Bailey asked: "Do those prophets who would industrialize all production really wish to take the farm out of the family?"[13]

2. *To sustain an adequate fertility.* Bailey charged that it was necessary "to sustain the spirit of the farmer" because "the maintenance of fertility, and therefore the welfare of future generations, is in his keeping."[14] As he explained more fully in the volume, *The Training of Farmers*:

> In as much as the city...has not yet solved the problem of permanently providing a growing population, the farm home assumes a most important relation to civilization. It is charged with the duty not only of maintaining the open country but of contributing population to the city.[15]

3. *To produce moral men and women.* The Cornell professor saw the industrial city as the great corrupter of human potential. "The city sits like a parasite," he wrote, "running out its roots into the open country and draining it of its substance. The city takes everything to itself—materials, money, men—and gives back only what it does not want."[16] The urban world produced "eight-hour men and managed men...clock watchers and irresponsible gang-servers." Factory work was "nerve exhausting" and "impersonal."[17] In contrast, the farm home bore the ability "to maintain the quality of the population. It is a preservator of morals, and it is well, therefore, that the farming people is conservative."[18] This meant that rural America's task was

> to supply the city and metropolis with fresh blood, clean bodies and clear brains that can endure the strain of modern urban life; and to preserve a race of men in the open country, that, in the future as in the past, will be the stay and strength of the nation in time of war, and its guiding and controlling spirit in time of peace.[19]

4. *To preserve democracy.* Along with the whole line of nineteenth-century agrarians, Bailey held that nearness to the soil made persons fit for self-rule. "Any close and worthwhile contact with the earth tends to make one original or at least detached in one's judgments and independent of group control,"[20] he wrote. The founders of the American Republic were mostly farmers, and the farmer remained "the fundamental fact in democracy" because he had been granted "the keepership of the earth." Political progress still required "a body of unattached laborers and producers" who could form "a natural corrective as against organization men, habitual reformers, and extremists."[21] Bailey pointed to predictions about a future marked by corporate farms of 5,000 or more acres, and responded,

> Perhaps; this prophecy regards farming only as an industry. If so, the world will be ruled entirely by corporations, agriculture, industrial, commercial, professional, for the corporations would control government: we shall have a government of corporations rather than of persons.

Without the survival of farms as "separate patriarchal units of importance," there simply could be no democracy.[22]

5. *To build a rural civilization.* In all this, Bailey sought to preserve, renew, and redirect the distinct rural culture that he had known as a child. There was a "world-motive" to equalize matters "as between

country and city," an international movement to be found in Russia, Eastern Europe, India, and North America to preserve the ways of the farm. Bailey denied that his campaign was part of a romantic "back-to-the-land" movement. More than once, he would complain about schemes to place the urban unemployed back on farms, asking how they could be expected to make a living on places where experienced farmers had given up? Instead, the goal was to hold on to those who were already on the land, to stop "unmaking" farmers, and to rely on the natural fertility advantage of country people to sustain "a real rural society that shall rest directly on the land." Where "the past century belonged to the city," Bailey opined in 1911, "the present century should belong also to agriculture and the open country."[23]

To this great vision of a vital and socially conservative Rural Civilization, Bailey brought certain other assumptions that shaped his subsequent work. To begin with, as a committed scientist, Bailey refused to become a latter-day Luddite, hostile to the economic and scientific forces unleashed over the prior hundred years. Industrialization was inevitable, he wrote, with "[i]ndustry of every kind…taking the place of the older order." Such industry need not have "a sordid and commercial end," but could in fact "grow into perfect flower." Indeed, industrialism was "The glory of our time," the sign that civilization "has entered on a new epoch." Economic laws were not at war with the farmer; for the laws of supply and demand were "natural." Indeed, he argued early on that "[t]here cannot be permanent overproduction," for society was a "self-sustaining organism" to which agriculture would necessarily adjust. The economic task was for the farmer "to contribute his share to the evolution of an industrial democracy." There could be no turning back to a subsistence-styled agriculture. Rather, he endorsed "modern diversified and intensive farming" and specialized, one-crop farmsteads such as dairying and orchards as in harmony with the spirit of the times.[24]

In a related vein, Bailey viewed science and technological advance as unquestionable goods. Science enjoyed the qualities of openness, straightforwardness, and integrity. There were no parties in science, only truth and the progress that came from truth. In contrast to the "outlook of helplessness" which had characterized the farmer of the past, the countryman could now turn to "the power and courage of science." Where agriculture had once been viewed as art, it would now be transformed into science.[25]

The real problem facing American farmers, Bailey concluded, was social, not economic. Rural life had certain deficiencies. It was "in a state of arrested development." The "nativeness of rural institutions" had died out, and the countryside had been "socially sterilized." Social conditions in the open country, he argued, "are far short of their possibilities," which was the real reason for the accelerating abandonment of farms. Rural people were saddled with inadequate institutions, were ignorant of the qualities of nature, and were abused by urban-dominated legislatures. Bailey was breezily confident that the rural population would never decline in absolute terms, arguing that while "the ratio of farmers to the whole population may still decrease, the actual number of farmers will increase. The rural districts will fill up." Again, the real challenge was social: "A new social order *must be evolved* in the open country, and every farmer of the new time must lend a strong hand to produce it."[26]

At century's end, it is easy to see the objective problem implicit in these operational assumptions. Industrialism, in one sense, means harnessing technology to capital in order to reduce the amount of labor applied per unit produced. Growth in the number of farmers and the unlimited application of science to farm production could be reconciled only through two additional assumptions: demand for farm products would have no effective limits; and technological advances would be slow. There is evidence to suggest that Bailey held both views. Natural growth of the American population and the opening of foreign markets, he suggested, would provide ample opportunity for the sales of America's farm produce.[27] Meanwhile, his relatively rare discussions of specific farm technologies usually implied that future changes would be modest. For example, he declared in 1907: "Few implements are more perfect than the present-day plow in the application of mechanical principles and in workmanship."[28] Perfection, by definition, could not be surpassed.

The Country Life Campaign

Bailey's campaign to build a new rural civilization took a large step forward in his 1907 speech, "The State and the Farmer." Delivered in East Lansing, Michigan, before a distinguished audience that included President Theodore Roosevelt, Bailey called for "a radical revivifying and redirection of all rural institutions." As he stated, "the great rural movement of the future is to be the evolving of a new social economy."[29]

The president left impressed. In August of the following year, Roosevelt summoned Bailey to a late-night White House meeting and urged him to become chairman of a new National Commission on Country Life. Roosevelt's motives appear twofold. At the political level, the commission would give a useful boost to Vice President William Howard Taft's campaign for the presidency against rural populist William Jennings Bryan.[30] At the conceptual level, Roosevelt shared many ideas with Bailey, including concerns over family deterioration and fertility decline and faith in the progressive spirit. Indeed, in his book on *The Country-Life Movement*, Bailey would praise Roosevelt's rallying phrase, "the fighting edge," and call for farmers to "conquer" their farms in the same spirit of "fine social brotherhood" seen in the building of the Panama Canal.[31]

Bailey agreed to head the Commission, provided that his friend Kenyon Butterfield, president of the Massachusetts Agriculture College and leading critic of the rural church, also be appointed. Roosevelt concurred. Others named to the panel included Gifford Pinchot, chief forester in the U.S. Department of Agriculture and an ardent conservationist, and Henry Wallace of Iowa, the editor of *Wallace's Farmer*.

The Commission's Report, issued in 1909, was largely Bailey's work, having been thoroughly revised by him no less than five times. It carried an introduction by President Roosevelt, who reasoned,

> We were founded as a nation of farmers, and in spite of the great growth of our industrial life it still remains true that our whole system rests upon the farm, that the welfare of the whole community depends on the welfare of the farmer. The strengthening of country life is the strengthening of the whole nation.

The report concluded that "[t]he work before us...is nothing more or less than the gradual rebuilding of a new agriculture and a new rural life." It specified that "guidance" was the greatest need. This implied that only new leaders and redirected education could meet the challenges facing the farm population. At the practical level, the report called for adoption of the Extension System, which Bailey had partly pioneered, at the national level. Working through the agriculture colleges, the USDA should seek to place a trained extension agent in every American county, to coordinate direct education for men (in the latest agricultural techniques), for women (in home economics), and for youth (as future farmers and homemakers). Other portions of the report called for the renewal of rural churches and schools, with the emphasis again on new ideas and new leaders.[32]

Rural education "freed from the conventionalisms of mere educational traditions" and "relieved from all narrow estimates of its scope and value" was the common imperative, Bailey insisted. "It is perfectly apparent," he continued, "that the fundamental need is to place *effectively educated* men and women into the open country. *All else depends on this.*" Agriculture was not "a technical profession or merely an industry, but a civilization." The farm home was the very pivot of this civilization. As such, "the homemaking phase of country life" was as important as "the field-farming phase." While extension programs would work with the existing farm population, the long-term object must be to integrate fully farm and university: "In the future only the well-informed and efficient-thinking man can succeed; that is, only the educated man....It seems to me that, by the very nature of the progress we are making, the college man must go to the farm."[33]

A concrete result of Bailey's agitation and the Commission's Report was passage by Congress of the Smith-Lever Extension Act on May 8, 1914. It provided for cooperative agricultural extension work between the agriculture colleges of the various states and the U.S. Department of Agriculture. Extension agents would fan out across the countryside. Instruction would embrace practical demonstrations in agriculture and home economics (through Homemaker Clubs) and also involve the uplift of rural youth (through what would become the 4-H Movement).

For Bailey, though, this was only the start. A grander movement had to be built. As he had commented on the release of the Commission's Report:

We must in some way unite all institutions, all organizations, all individuals, having any interest in country life into one great campaign for rural progress....We must picture to ourselves a new *rural social structure*, developed from the strong resident forces of the open country; and then we must set at work all the agencies that will tend to bring this about. *The entire people* need to be roused to this avenue of usefulness. Most of the new leaders must be farmers....who will throw themselves into the service of upbuilding the community. A new race of teachers is also to appear in the country. A new rural clergy is to be trained. These leaders...will work, each in his own field...for the one goal of a new and permanent rural civilization.[34]

It was clear to Bailey that such a movement would require a manifesto, a compelling philosophical vision that could inspire and motivate. This he would provide in his 1915 tract, *The Holy Earth*. The summer before, he had embarked on a lecture trip to New Zealand. On board ship, in the intense heat of the equator, Bailey drafted this volume. While drawing heavily on the themes of his 1905 book, *The Outlook to Nature*, the author was more circumspect here. The rejection of Christian doctrines such as Atonement and Original Sin became muted and indirect. Instead, Bailey offered a positive alternate vision of mankind's place on the planet, of human purpose.

Written in sometimes vivid prose, *The Holy Earth* celebrated "the mothership of the earth." Evolution was the way in which humans could understand the process of creation, and in fact take part in it. It was "the philosophy of the oneness in nature and the unity in living things," a system guided by the Great Patriarch, God the Father:

> Verily, then, the earth is divine, because man did not make it. We are here, part in the creation. We cannot escape. We are under obligation to take part and do our best living with each other and with all the creatures. We may not know the full plan, but that does not alter the relation.

Indeed, the earth was *good*, every man knowing "in his heart…that there is goodness and wholeness in the rain, in the wind, the soil, the sea, the glory of sunrise, in the trees, and in the sustenance that we derive from the planet." Accordingly, it was a mistake to view evolution as a process of ruthless competition. Rather, the primary qualities were cooperation and procreation: "The dependence of one being on another, success in leaving progeny—how accurate and how far seeing was Darwin!"

The farmer, Bailey insisted, was always the key to this bond with the earth. The Creation was "biocentric," with forms of life proceeding upward and forward in a mighty plan of sequence. The true husbandman understood this. He had a strong moral regard for his land, animals, and crops. He was the agent of society in guarding and subduing the surface of the earth. In consequence, the public must bear as part of its "duty to the race" the costs for "the special education of the man on the land." More importantly, the farmer was also the agent of God, called now to be like God in the care of the earth. As Bailey summarized, "A man cannot be a good farmer unless he is a religious man."[35]

In its core passages, *The Holy Earth* was a powerful testament to Nature as God and to the farmer as acolyte and collaborator in the ongoing process of creation. It stood as a metaphysical justification for the special status that Bailey demanded for the farmer. And it served as a blueprint for the movement that Bailey would seek to build.

New, reliable leadership was also central to the plan. To advance that goal, Bailey undertook the massive task of compiling and privately publishing *RUS*, or *The Rural Uplook Service*. First published in 1918 (and appearing through 1930), the volume was intentionally a kind of rural *Who's Who*. It provided curriculum vitae for 2,746 Americans who were "now contributing through their achievements to the betterment and advancement of rural life."[36] There were, however, two peculiarities about the volume. First, "successful farmers" were consciously excluded from the book (unless they came in under another category), Bailey arguing that such an effort "would have made a book of far different intention" and greater bulk. Instead, "rural leaders" were defined as teachers, researchers, businessmen, ministers, lecturers, extension agents, authors, editors, rural organizers, and administrators. Moreover, unlike the *Who's Who* volumes which he used as his model, Bailey neither solicited nor reported the church memberships of his subjects.

Necessary to the plan as well would be "the holding of local, state, and national conferences on rural progress, designed to unite the interests of education, organization, and religion into one forward movement for the rebuilding of country life."[37] Toward that end, Bailey helped convene the First National County Life Conference in Baltimore in 1919. Several of the founders paid deference to England's Sir Horace Plunkett, whose work on rural reorganization in his land they hoped to emulate. The event actually marked a fundamental break in American rural organization. Going the direction of "agriculture as a business" were those who would organize the American Farm Bureau Federation the following year. Joining Bailey in the Country Life Association were those who, while acknowledging the need for rural "economic justice," placed their emphasis on uplifting the family on the farm. As the Association's first President, Kenyon Butterfield, explained the difference:

> The Country Life interest is, we believe, the supreme rural interest....[W]e want to make it clear to everybody, certainly to ourselves, that the end of all of these efforts for economic effectiveness is human welfare, and not the possibilities of still more profit, not merely ease and comfort, but the choice things of the spirit.[38]

The ultimate test of economic success would be "a high quality of people upon the land," a goal best achieved by efforts "to stimulate, inform, and develop the people themselves."[39]

The New Agrarian Mind

The National Country Life Association remained an influential presence in American rural affairs into the 1950s, and in existence for another two decades. But this was not Bailey's real legacy. Rather, it lay in the new themes and direction that he crafted out of his outlook and work, themes very different from those found in agrarian thought in the two prior centuries. In various combinations, they would define the twentieth-century agrarian mind in America in ways both novel and troubling. These were:

1. *Technological innovation is friendly to the family farm.* As a scientist and a progressive, Bailey raised no questions over the results gained by invention. Regarding the home, he declared that "[e]very advance in the management of the household contributes to the general welfare: it sets new ideas under way."[40] The farmer on the tractor, still unusual in the 1920s, became for him the prototypical modern yeoman.[41] The policy agenda of the National Country Life Conference embraced "good roads," rational transportation planning, the extension of phone lines into rural areas, rural free delivery, and bus lines as "essential to better country life."[42] Capitalization of farm production must be accelerated; "the necessity of economizing human labor must itself force the use of gasoline and other engines, small water power, electrical power, and others...on thousands and millions of farms... [W]e must...train up a race of mechanic-minded farmers."[43]

2. *Decentralization is the natural and beneficial result of technological innovation.* While strongly in favor of centrally guided education for farmers, Bailey was in most other matters a firm believer in decentralization. And he held that the natural result of new technology would be to break large agglomerations of economic and political power into smaller parts. "There is every indication," he wrote in 1927, "that decentralization must grow. The motor car and the truck and the constructed roads make it possible; the rural free delivery, the telephone, the radio, portable lighting outfits, heating devices, adaptable machinery, also makes it possible."[44] In addition, he saw, and praised, "the decentralization of cities." As early as 1908, he identified "a new species of rural drainage," specifically the movement of rural folk into small, rather than large urban locales. "This condition is

being aided from the city itself in the rapid growth of suburbanism. These new conditions constitute one step toward vitalizing the open country."[45] In *The Holy Earth*, Bailey took a more radical step, looking toward the day when "we shall take down the wonderful towers and cliffs in the cities, in which people work and live...but in which they have no home." In that end time, "the great city expansion will be horizontal rather than perpendicular. We shall have many knots, clustered about factories and other enterprises, and we shall learn how to *distribute* the satisfactions in life rather than merely to assemble them."[46]

3. *Peasant models of rural existence are dehumanizing and to be deplored.* Balancing their preference for a "cultured, progressive, liberal-minded people" on the land or in the suburbs, Country Life advocates held in scorn a "peasant-minded people whose interest in life, aside from the instinct of acquisition, is bounded by three elementary wants—hunger, thirst, and sex."[47] Bailey himself disliked the living in "hamlets" and other signs of peasant life brought over to America by German and East European immigrants. He also cast scorn on suggestions that "handicrafts" be introduced in the open country as a means of supplementing income. While employing economic arguments ("It is very doubtful whether such handicrafts...could compete in the markets"), his distaste for the very idea is clear.[48] His views were reinforced by a 1917 visit to China, where he was repelled by the reprocessing of human waste back into the soil and by the assiduous care taken to recover every bit of fiber and root for human use. "I have never seen such sacrilege of the earth," he opined. "If the agriculture of China is permanent, then there is no outlook for the Chinese people except that they shall remain what they are."[49]

4. *The farmer and the farm family must be reengineered.* Despite his praise for American farm families as the source of fresh blood, the generators of morality, and the guarantors of democracy, Bailey actually held the existing rural population in a certain kind of contempt. Women needed to be pulled out of their farm homes, so they might come together "to discover woman's work" and "to form intelligent opinions on farming questions in general." The rural population needed "to be livened up." A "radical overhauling of the political organization of rural life" was essential. Indeed, indigenous rural forces seemed

incapable of doing anything right. In his book, *The Training of Farmers*, Bailey complained that "the current country movement to revive sports and games" had gone badly. The tendency, he reported, was "just...to introduce old folk-games" from the old countries, peasant-like rituals that "represent the life of other peoples," "are not adapted...to our climate," and "[t]o a large extent...are love-making games" (in a way, Bailey's harshest form of condemnation). Indeed, Bailey deemed even the existing county fairs to be misguided: they must turn from a focus on commerce and cheap amusement toward the purposes of "education" and "recreation."[50] In discussing the work of his experiment stations, Bailey—almost unwittingly—revealed his true estimation of the authentic farming class, as at once ignorant, prejudiced, and childlike in demeanor, a class of savages:

> The farmers, who comprise the bottom factor in any democracy, have been among the most prejudiced of men....Slowly but certainly we are placing before him a new way of approach to the problems of life, an inspiring and authoritative example in the conquest of his conditions. At first perhaps rebellious, then tolerant, then curious, then cautious, he now accepts the new way and begins to demand exact reasons for everything he does.[51]

The very language of action to be pursued—"a radical revivifying and redirection of all rural institutions"; "stimulation and reconstruction"; cutting farmers loose "from the slavery of old restraints"—would mark a hitherto unprecedented level of social engineering in America, a deep intrusion into all aspects of rural life: Something like "Ma and Pa Kettle Meet the Social Workers." The inaugural National Country Life Association conference caught the spirit. While acknowledging "the life of the family in the home" as of "distinctive value" to rural life, democracy was not fully "experienced in the home, between father and mother, parents and children." The "despotism" often shown by farm fathers was "out of harmony" with new realities, and should be supplanted by a fresh "division of rights and responsibilities" among family members. If farm families were recalcitrant, then the women's movement should be called in to forge attitudes of change. Revealingly, the Conference Report also targeted those rural communities which had "too many" social organizations "in proportion to their population and leadership." In place of ethnic-based forms of socialization, rural life must be made democratic. Parochial and communal social groups should be broken down and replaced by "inter-neighborhood" and "inter-community" groups. New leaders must be found "who will promote inclusive rather than exclusive sociability."[52]

Ideally, these new leaders would be college-trained social workers who would also become farmers. Bailey already saw positive signs: "From some of the [agriculture] colleges, the young men and women go back to the country thoroughly alive to the necessity of organizing the social forces there....Something like the student volunteer movement will eventually come out of this rising sentiment."[53] Government by the old politics of "influence" must and would go, and "government by merit must come," where experts with democratic values and authentic motivation could create the "new social economy,"[54] one with "the right sort of rural community and the right sort of people in that community."[55]

5. *Education by enlightened experts is the key to rural survival.* Bailey and others in the Country Life movement held quasi-religious faith in the transforming power of state guided education. As the Cornell professor wrote in 1903, "the power that moves the world is the power of the teacher."[56] The task of education was not to communicate information:

> Facts are trivial as facts. They do not open the eyes of the blind, nor kindle the soul with enthusiasm. We are slaves to facts. Wake a man up. Shake out localisms and prejudices. Inspire him. Set him at work. Send him on a mission with joy.[57]

True education meant the suppression of inherited ways, and the substitution of progressive ways. In particular, the reformed state College of Agriculture represented a new civilization, one where a young man or woman would be lifted up to awareness "that he or she is part of a world movement."[58] This new school would be one "that is capable of redirecting rural life." Country Life leadership "should be entrusted only to persons who see the whole problem of rural life," who have been invested in the special wisdom of the emerging movement.[59]

Indeed, Bailey's faith in state education was so deep, and his confidence in progressive governance so great (e.g., "The United States Department of Agriculture [operates]...with remarkable effectiveness"),[60] that he was moved to an extraordinary proposal:

> It occurs to me that there should be just one more department represented in the [Federal] cabinet, and it should be of a nature that it can contain within itself all questions that will have to do with the general public welfare...and this should be a [U.S.] Department of Education.[61]

6. *Christianity is an obstacle to rural reconstruction.* While normally cautious in his choice of phrases, Bailey saw Christian doctrine as a problem to be overcome. "The rural church is largely inert or lost," he reported in *The State and the Farmer*, and he quoted from an anonymous letter complaining about denominational rivalries, "petty" squabbles over church affairs, and the misguided clergy: "One...can hardly imagine the littleness of the superannuated gospel-splitters who are often sent to such outlying parishes."[62] Elsewhere, he noted that many believed "that the usefulness of the country church is passing," and added: "This may be true to some degree if the church is to hold merely to the kind of work that has been done in the past." However, if the church were to become "a much more energetic engine for the public good,"[63] it could extend itself beyond "gospel work" and become a real force for renewal.

These arguments would be more fully and completely developed at the early Country Life Conferences. Association President Kenyon Butterfield repeatedly charged that "the country church is the least alive, the most lagging of all our rural institutions," and so a special target for reform.[64] The Report of the Committee on Morals & Religion at the 1919 Baltimore NCLA meeting offered an unusually candid and depressing portrait of existing rural religion. Everywhere, the Committee fretted, denominationalism remained strong: "The Protestant, Roman Catholic and Jewish religious organizations are still far apart....The only thing peculiar to rural religion is the more complete predominance there of the denominational form." While a few groups such as the YMCA drew praise for their "service in rural moral propaganda," their modest gains were quite overwhelmed by a force running opposite to the needed ecumenical "realignment":

> It is represented by the growth of the Holy Rollers, Pentecostal Nazarenes and other Separatist religious societies in all parts of the country. These societies are characterized by pietism and inwardness in religion. They take special satisfaction in living apart from the religious bodies which discuss federation and union and from one another. They invent their own religious expressions and cherish their own peculiar religious experiences. Probably no other religious feature of the country has grown so fast in the past ten years as these forces opposed to union, federation, comity and cooperation.[65]

Yet the Committee was optimistic about the long-term future. "Federation of the religious forces" through ecumenism had value primarily as a "restraint upon denominational zeal." And less zealous churches could be more easily turned toward socially constructive ends. For example, Bible studies could be reconfigured toward "the study of problems of child welfare," with emphasis on combating "the social evil" (in this context, extramarital sex) with materials to help parents "in the teaching of sex hygiene to their children." And Sunday Schools could be integrated into the county extension programs, with Sunday classes taught by "the national and state agents of agriculture" on farming, home economics, and health. It seems notable that this report by the Committee on Morals and Religion also concluded with a call to the U.S. Congress for passage of Senate Bill 4897, "for the creation of a National Department of Education" providing federal funds for rural education, "health education," and "the education of the illiterate."[66]

7. *Economic forces should and will give way to the spiritualizing of agriculture.* While spirit must diminish within the Christian and Jewish faiths, it must grow within the human understanding of Nature. Bailey's call for a Society of the Holy Earth rested on this effort. "We shall put our dominion into the realm of morals," Bailey explained. "It is now in the realm of trade."[67] This meant that the real solution to the agricultural problem was to give the countryman "a vital, intellectual, sympathetic, optimistic interest in his daily life." Bailey concluded: "For myself, if I have any gifts, I mean to use them for the spiritualizing of agriculture." Indeed, as the twentieth century opened, he saw signs of a great spiritual awakening. "One sign of this awakening is the outlook nature-ward," he wrote. "The growing passion for country life is a soul movement."[68] Conflicting economic forces, he assumed, should and would give way.

8. *There must be a "new economics."* In the latter years of his Country Life work, Bailey grew increasingly schizophrenic over the economics of agriculture. His denial of the possibility of "over production" gave way to an effort to justify special treatment for farmers. Writing in *What Is Democracy?*, Bailey argued that while the farmer raised supplies for the world through individual effort, he brought his supplies from collective enterprises: "He deals with the earth open-handed; he deals with commerce with his hands tied." Accordingly, the "ordinary philosophy of unrestrained competition" as society's

regulator did not reach the farmers' essential situation. "We need a different order."[69] By 1927, with American agriculture in its eighth year of a serious depression in prices, Bailey grew almost frantic. He accepted the reality of "overproduction," relative to market price. Balancing two possible responses—fewer farmers and farm families or restraints on technology or production—he reluctantly and revealingly opted for fewer farmers and undiminished technological advance: "If there is consistent over-production of agricultural supplies, then there are too many farmers, not too much production to the acre or to the man." Bailey decried any teaching that discouraged production by the individual farmer as "weakening and devitalizing."[70] But the strain on his own philosophical premises began to show. Even "progress" came into question. "We are blinded by the rapidity of discoveries and by the material additions to life," he wrote. "But scientific discovery, material goods, and what we ignorantly call 'progress' are not part of civilization until they are incorporated in the soul."[71]

From this, Bailey toyed with a more radical economics. He proposed a new kind of money, one based on "energy expended toward a result." He suggested that agricultural transactions be pulled altogether out of markets. While corporatizing agriculture may make sense from the perspective of the ledger, it made little sense relative to the environment, "for fertility [of the soil] must be maintained, and this requires something in the nature of diversification...and close adaptation to local conditions."[72] Bailey also hearkened back to the more radical rhetoric of *The Holy Earth*: about "a communism" attached to the "proper use and partitioning of the earth"; about the transformation of land ownership into a limited life trust; about the "right" of "every person" to the personal use of some part of the earth; about a fair and just "redistribution of lands", and a parallel redistribution of capital; about the taking down of "the wonderful towers and cliffs of the city"; about the elimination of products "that nobody should ever want."[73]

Retreat to the Brambles

Yet just as he careened close to the radical solutions of agrarian communism, he drew back and quietly abandoned the cause. In 1930, a disciple and protégé, Russell Lord, interviewed Bailey for the *Cornell Countryman* and found him "serenely unperturbed as to agricultural organization or organization of any kind."[74] Pulling out of his Country Life obligations in the early 1930s, Bailey turned instead to scientific inquiry, with attention divided between intensive study of palm plants (involving considerable travel in the tropics) and a return to genus Rubus, where he had begun (he published a 200-page book on dewberries in 1943, and a 932-page work on blackberries, raspberries, and related brambles three years later).

All the same, his influence on modern American agrarianism remained strong, even determinative. It would surface in the work of subsequent writers, ranging from Ralph Borsodi and Louis Bromfield to Wendell Berry, so that the broad New Agrarian themes that he had pioneered would echo for another sixty years. So too would the inherent contradictions of his work:

• *The revealing resistance of real farmers and rural people to the Country Life campaign.* Not only did country folk cling to their old-time, gospel-thumping faiths; they also opposed other forms of New Agrarian social engineering, such as school consolidation plans, causing Kenyon Butterfield to conclude woefully that "agricultural prosperity in itself...is no guarantee of a satisfying and permanent country life."[75]

• *The nearly complete misunderstanding of the operative economic forces.* Unless countered by something more real and potent, the thrust of the industrialization of agriculture was simply too powerful to overcome.[76] As in all other forms of production, the consequence of technological innovation and capital investment was to reduce the contribution of labor to production. For farming, that meant fewer farms and farm people. Country Life advocates, most especially Liberty Hyde Bailey, never grasped the significance of the support that their "Extension program" drew from prominent business interests. The latter plainly understood that the Extension process would inevitably expand corporate markets and reduce the economic independence of farmers. In making country life more modern, more urbane, more differentiated, and—despite the rhetoric—more material, the Country Life movement doomed an autonomous agrarian sector, and culture.

• *The reliance on state-schools to achieve family reconstruction.* It had been the industrialization of family functions that had produced the weak and disordered homes in urban areas that Bailey deplored. Corporate businesses now provided the food, clothing, light, housing, and transportation of urban dwellers, while industrially organized state entities had taken over the discipline and education of children. Bailey understood that true working homes were those that had avoided the industrialization of a significant share of their work, and he called for the defense of such homes in the countryside. Yet his core solutions involved the zealous application of state education, from the kindergarten through the extension agent, for their success. Put another way, he relied on industrialized state education to produce anti-industrial results in other areas of life, an implausible strategy even on the surface, and one fated to failure. Indeed, modern evidence would show that mass state-education was a principle cause—demographer John Caldwell would say the principle cause—of family weakness and fertility decline.[77]

● *And the quiet war conducted on the only force that proved capable of preserving communal rural life in the modern age*, namely "gospel-splitting," separatist Christian faith. Whether motivated by Freemasonry, by anti-immigrant (and especially anti-German) sentiments, by revulsion against peasant communalism, or by a simple failure of scientific observation, Liberty Hyde Bailey and colleagues set themselves against the only intellectual and social experiments in rural life that would survive—even "beat"—modernity in this century, groups such as the Hutterites and the Old Order Amish. Long after the Country Life campaign and the desired New Rural Civilization had died, these sturdy, God-fearing, German peasants would steadily spread across the American soil.

Notes

1. William L. Bowers, *The Country Life Movement in America, 1900-1920* (Port Washington, NY: Kennikat Press, 1974): 45
2. The two principle biographies of Bailey both lean toward hagiography: Philip Dorf, *Liberty Hyde Bailey: An Informal Biography* (Ithaca, NY: Cornell University Press, 1956); and Andrew Denny Rodgers III, *Liberty Hyde Bailey: A Story of American Plant Sciences* (New York, and London: Hafner Publishing Company, 1965 [facsimile of the 1949 edition].
3. Quoted in Dorf, *Liberty Hyde Bailey*, p. 59.
4. "Agricultural Education and Its Place in the University Curriculum." Address to the Agricultural Association of Cornell University, Ithaca, NY, January 31, 1893.
5. Quoted in Dorf, *Liberty Hyde Bailey*, p. 108.
6. Liberty Hyde Bailey, "An Evolutionist's View of Nature and Religion," *Independent* 51 (Feb. 2, 1899): 335-339.
7. L. H. Bailey, *The Outlook to Nature* (New York: The Macmillan Company, 1905): 50, 54, 56.

8. Bailey, *The Outlook to Nature*, pp. 277-78, 283.

9. Ibid., pp. 286, 293.

10. Ibid., pp. 287-290.

11. Ibid., pp. 292-293. Emphasis added.

12. Reprinted in Rodgers, *Liberty Hyde Bailey*, pp. 481-484.

13. L. H. Bailey, *The Harvest of the Year to the Tiller of the Soil* (New York: The Macmillan Company, 1927): 55, 82-83, 85; and L.H. Bailey, *The Country-Life Movement in the United States* (New York: The Macmillan Company), 1911): 85.

14. Bailey, *Harvest*, p. 81.

15. L. H. Bailey, *The Training of Farmers* (New York: The Century Co., 1909): 71.

16. Bailey, *Country-Life*, p. 16.

17. Bailey, *Country-Life*, p. 50; Bailey, *Harvest*, p. 62.

18. Bailey, *Training*, p. 71.

19. Quotation from Rodgers, *Liberty Hyde Bailey*, p. 373.

20. Liberty Hyde Bailey, *The Holy Earth* (Ithaca: New York State College of Agriculture, 1980 [Reprint of 1915 edition]): 87.

21. L.H. Bailey, *What is Democracy?* (Ithaca, NY: The Comstock Publishing Company, 1918): 95-96, 99; Bailey, *Holy Earth*, pp. 87, 91; and Bailey, *Harvest*, pp. 52-53.

22. Bailey, *Harvest*, p. 83.

23. Bailey, *Country-Life*, pp. 1-3, 6-8, 32; and Dorf, *Liberty Hyde Bailey*, p. 145.

24. Bailey, *Country-Life*, pp. 8, 55-57, 98, 116; Bailey, *Outlook*, p. 20; Bailey, *Training*, p. 69; and Rodgers, *Liberty Hyde Bailey*, p. 355.

25. L.H. Bailey, *Ground Levels in Democracy* (Ithaca, NY: Privately published, 1916): 8, 11, 13, 15; Bailey, *Training*, p. 72; and Rodgers, *Liberty Hyde Bailey*, p. 21.

26. Bailey, *Country-Life*, pp. 8, 41, 56, 63, 105; L.H. Bailey, *The State and the Farmer* (New York: The Macmillan Company, 1908): 15.

27. Bailey, *Training*, p. 17.

28. Bailey, *State*, p. 11.

29. Bailey, *State*, pp. 111-113.

30. Dorf, *Liberty Hyde Bailey*, p. 150.

31. Bailey, *Country-Life*, pp. 57-59.

32. U.S. Congress, Report of the Country Life Commission (Senate Doc. 705, 60th Congress, 2nd Session, 1909).

33. Bailey, *Country-Life*, pp. 61, 64, 77-78; Bailey, *Training*, pp. 188-89, 238.

34. Quoted in Rodgers, *Liberty Hyde Bailey*, p. 372.

35. Bailey, *The Holy Earth*, pp. 5-6, 10, 13-14, 18, 23-24, 59.

36 L.H. Bailey, *RUS: Rural Uplook Service. A Preliminary Attempt to Register the Rural Leadership in the United States and Canada* (Ithaca, NY: Privately published, 1918): 3-5.

37. Bailey, *Country-Life*, pp. 10-11.

38. *Proceedings of the First National Country Life Conference*, Baltimore 1919 (Ithaca, NY: National Country Life Association, 1919): 26.

39. *Rural Organization. Proceedings of the Third National Country Life Conference* (Washington, DC: American Country Life Association, 1921): 4.

40. Bailey, *Country-Life*, p. 86.

41. Bailey, *Harvest*, p. 53.

42. NCLA, Proceedings, p. 23.

43. Bailey, *Training*, pp. 239-240.

44. Bailey, *Harvest*, p. 54.

45. Bailey, *State*, p. 17.

46. Bailey, *Holy Earth*, p. 44.
47. Quoted in Bowers, *The Country Life Movement*, p. 24.
48. Bailey, *Country-Life*, pp. 100-101, 116; also Bailey, *What Is Democracy?*, p. 105.
49. Quoted in Dorf, *Liberty Hyde Bailey*, pp. 172-173.
50. Bailey, *Country-Life*, pp. 90-92, 107, 109, 169; and Bailey, *Training*, pp. 8-9.
51. Bailey, *Ground Levels*, pp. 23-24.
52. NCLA, *Proceedings* [1919], pp. 16, 18, 118.
53. Bailey, *The State and the Farmer*, pp. 88-89.
54. Ibid., pp. 91-92, 111.
55. *Rural Organization*, p. 5.
56. Liberty Hyde Bailey, *The Nature-Study Idea: Being an Interpretation of the New School Movement to Put the Child in Sympathy with Nature* (New York: Doubleday, Page & Company, 1903), p. 88.
57. Quoted in Rodgers, *Liberty Hyde Bailey*, p. 356.
58. Bailey, *Country-Life*, pp. 94, 218-219.
59. Bailey, *The Training of Farmers*, pp. 79-80, 148.
60. Bailey, *Holy Earth*, p. 94.
61. Bailey, *The State*, pp. 108-109.
62. Ibid., pp. 17-18.
63. Bailey, *Training*, p. 77.
64. *Rural Organization*, p. 1.
65. NCLA, *Proceedings* [1919], pp. 33-34.
66. Ibid., pp. 85, 87-88.
67. Bailey, *Holy Earth*, p. 13.
68. Bailey, *Nature*, pp. 82, 87-88.
69. Bailey, *What Is Democracy?*, pp. 104-105.
70. Bailey, *Harvest*, p. 66.
71. Ibid., p. 75.
72. Ibid., pp. 71, 76, 84.
73. Bailey, *Holy Earth*, pp. 31-32, 34, 44-46, 51.
74. Quoted in Dorf, *Liberty Hyde Bailey*, p. 197.
75. *Rural Organization*, p. 5.
76. On this point, see Bowers, *The Country Life Movement*, pp. 133-134.
77. See John C. Caldwell, *Theory of Fertility Decline* (New York: Academic Press, 1982), chapters 4 and 10; and Avery M. Guest and Stewart Tolnay, "Children's Roles and Fertility: Late Nineteenth Century United States," *Social Science History* 7 (1983): 355-380.

2

Building a Science of Rural Society:
Carle C. Zimmerman

At the First National Country Life Conference, held in Baltimore, the Committee on Rural Sociology reported that "America's thinking on rural social questions" was still mired "in the first stage." As the University of Wisconsin's C.J. Galpin, chairman of the committee, explained, statistical measures were flawed, the field work being done was "fragmentary and uncorrelated," and the discipline had failed to provide "sufficient scientific basis for social action." The committee called for a new commitment to an applied rural social science.[1]

Emerging over the next two decades as the leading American figure in the construction of this distinctive rural sociology would be Carle C. Zimmerman. As co-author of *Principles of Rural-Urban Sociology* (1929) and *A Systematic Source Book in Rural Sociology* (1930-32), he was a vital part of "the finest synthesis of the field of rural sociology achieved to date."[2] Zimmerman was also a founder of the Rural Sociological Society, and later its president, and he placed one of his doctoral students in the post of managing editor for the new journal, *Rural Sociology*. Named a professor of sociology at Harvard University in 1931, he would from that prestigious post further shape the discipline of rural social investigation in America.

Zimmerman acknowledged Liberty Hyde Bailey's inspiration and shared with him a passion for the preservation of rural life. The sociologist celebrated the social gifts of the countryside, including stronger families, higher fertility, and a more stable and independent political order. Yet in significant ways, he parted company with the Country Life movement. Where Bailey's project involved the "reconstruction" and effective de-Christianization of the rural churches, Zimmerman defended their integrity and value. Where most Country Life advocates scorned the term, peasant, as well as the reality of peasant-life (subsistence agriculture, handicrafts, hamlet—or village—living), Zimmerman embraced them with a kind of enthusiasm. And where Bailey revealed a fatal ignorance of home or family economics, Zimmerman worked relatively sensitive economic analysis into his work. The source of these differences probably lay in Zimmerman's own background and in the strong influence of two European intellectual traditions on his work.

To begin with, Zimmerman was born to German Lutheran parents in Cass County, Missouri. Growing up in a village of 300, he developed an appreciation for the German-American communities, Catholic and Lutheran, that had settled and still dominated the Upper Mississippi Valley. Where Bailey, as Anglophile and Yankee, saw a dangerously unassimilated foreign presence in this region, Zimmerman saw a sturdy peasantry who had brought solid virtues with them from Europe.[3]

Moreover, Zimmerman was a Christian, a student and admirer of figures such as Augustine, Erasmus, and Luther, and a defender of doctrinal integrity. Even in his scholarly works, he would take to task "many ministers of various 'Christian denominations' who in their sermons and ideologies, *in spite of their professions of Christianity*, have very little, if anything, from Christianity as it existed historically, and practically deny its fundamental dogmas." Without naming names (but with Butterfield and Bailey apparently in mind), Zimmerman also chided the " 'enlightened scientific suggestions' of many of the rural sociologists" and rural reformers who held that the rural church "is decaying because it is not 'keeping step' with the progressive changes" in the urban churches. In fact, Zimmerman replied, "the real menace" to Christianity lay in this very urbanization of rural institutions, adding:

> The "small" churches, "underpaid" ministers, [and] "inadequate" organization of rural religious life is, from the standpoint of preservation of this historical Christianity, the greatest bulwark.[4]

Zimmerman also drew deeply on recent European sociological work. The most important influence here was his close friendship and early collaboration with the Russian-educated sociologist, Pitirim Sorokin.

Eight years senior to Zimmerman, Sorokin had been born in Yarensky County, Volgoda Province, Russia, in 1889. His ethnic Russian father made a living as an itinerant repairer of religious icons. His mother was of the Finno-Ugric people called the Komi. Although she died in 1892, her Komi sisters gave shelter to Sorokin after he fled the alcohol-induced tantrums of his father. Here he found a *gemeinshaft* community which stoked his passion for village life. Already a skilled icon-maker as a child, Sorokin was self-taught to age fourteen. In 1909, he entered the Psycho-Neurological Institute in St. Petersburg as a student of sociology, and transferred to the University of St. Petersburg the next year, where he studied the sociology of law. By 1917, he had emerged as a young leader of the peasant political movement taking form in Russia. A revolutionary, he served in the government of Kerensky, only to be jailed by the successor Bolsheviks in 1918. Barely escaping execution, he later wrote a paper indicting the Communist regime for the deaths of millions of rural people in the famine of 1920-21. Arrested again, Sorokin accepted banishment over death.[5]

The émigré eventually came to the United States, eager to pursue his own sociological vision, one that could be summarized as positive, moral, linear, Christian, and scientific. He also hoped "to study American peasants." In 1924, the University of Minnesota teamed him up with the young instructor, Carle Zimmerman, to teach a seminar on rural sociology. They soon became fast friends and close collaborators, first at Minnesota, and then at Harvard.[6]

Sorokin reinforced for Zimmerman an appreciation for the universal nature of the farmer-peasant, the view that there were few significant differences between the independent American yeoman in Bailey's beloved "open country" and the Russian peasant in the collective *mir*. As they would write in the joint work, *Principles of Rural-Urban Sociology*, "both [authors] are from the farmer-peasant class."[7] The truly important social distinction, they said, was the division between urban and rural:

> Quite different is the environment of the cultivator. If he lives on an open farm he is nearly all the time in the bosom of nature. If he lives in a small village or hamlet, he is in a similar condition. Only the thin walls of his farmhouse or hut separate him from nature when he is indoors.[8]

Reflecting his affection for peasant exuberance, Zimmerman came to delight in the story once told by Benjamin Franklin, "The Strange

Case of Polly Baker." Hauled into a Massachusetts court for bearing four fatherless children, Polly Baker made an impassioned speech, denouncing the lack of marriage ideals among the colonial Bostonians, and defending herself as a good mother, furnishing children for the settling of America. The judge declared her not guilty, married her, and together they set out for the frontier, where they had many more offspring. Zimmerman also recounted Franklin's praise for the "Palatine Boor" types of people, German peasants who lived simply in America and had broods of children.[9] In addition, Zimmerman attributed the relative health of America's countryside primarily to the fecundity of the Highland Celts who had settled in Appalachia and the Ozarks, and to the "Catholic and Lutheran immigrants" who had come after 1840. Indeed, he praised the family-strengthening effects that derived from immigration. Decrying "the anti-familism" of the Eastern establishment, he added that only when "the doors of immigration were closed (first by war, later by law, and finally by the disruption of familistic attitudes in the European sources themselves)" did "the anti-familism of the old cultured classes" finally begin to have corrosive effect.[10]

Looking to the communal quality of peasant life, Zimmerman defined the *family farm* as "an organization of agriculture in which home, community, business, land and domestic family are institutionalized into a living unit which seeks to perpetuate itself over many generations."[11] He dismissed fears of an American "descent" into peasantry through the spread of small holdings with a call for the "thoughtful subsidy...of part-time agrarianism as a way of life for the masses of our rural people not on farms and as an increasingly prominent practice on so-called commercial farms."[12] He drew hope from the surge in the number of peasant farms in Central and Eastern Europe after World War I, and expected the same for America.[13]

Zimmerman also drew heavily on the insights and work of the French sociologist, Frederic LePlay. While discussed in more detail later in this chapter, LePlay's use of the detailed case study, his deep appreciation for the complexities of the home economy, and his focus on the "stem family" as well suited to the modern world had positive effects on Zimmerman. Where Bailey and the Country Life movement found themselves in a hopeless quagmire whenever family economics reared its head, Zimmerman gained a valuable dual understanding of the family standard of living: "The material [side LePlay] called *the daily bread* and the non-material he called the Decalogue or the moral law."[14] From this followed a focus on the value of noncash "home production" to the family's life, and on the power of moral forces to shape and influence economic and social change. Zimmerman also used LePlay's term, "the stem family," to explain the unusual reproductive success of Celtic families in America's Appalachian-Ozark region, which would become a major theme of his book, *Family and Society.*

Two other overarching themes in Zimmerman's work deserve note. From the mid-1920s through the mid-1950s, Zimmerman held to a fervent anti-urbanism. "[A]ccording to all evidences," he wrote, "the urban family is in decay; and this decay has some causal relationship with the process of urbanization itself." Weak marriages, an enormous increase in divorce, tumbling family size, the spread of sexual freedom, the "emancipation of women," and the disorganization of the family as a social, religious, economic, and educational unit were all products of urban life and "its mental, moral and physical poisons."[15] Sorokin and Zimmerman's portrait of the psychological weakness of "the urban man" ably captures this view:

> He is in a very unsafe position and the ground under his feet is less stable. He is crushed as soon as some slight wind blows. To whom or to what may he go for consolation in such a misfortune? He does not as often believe in God, or when he believes it is less dogmatically and in a less proportion. He has lost his traditions....His sophistication and scepticism have made him relatively free from any "duty" or "obligation" and have stripped these from their "sacredness" to his eyes. His fellows are "strangers"; .... He either does not have children or a wife, or a community of co-living with these or similar persons.[16]

Zimmerman's paramount concern was the birth rate. He held that "the basic function of the family is reproduction and the maintenance of population." All other functions, including marriage, were subordinate to this purpose.[17] By definition, he continued, "familistic societies are those in which the birth rate is high." Conversely, family decline could best be documented through a decline in the birth rate. Importantly, Zimmerman also held that "basic changes in the family are functionally related to changes in the birth rate." On the farm, increases in family size were associated with larger areas of cultivated land and less involvement in nonfamily life, in America as in peasant Europe.[18] More broadly, the study of other family systems confirmed the same point: family functions such as feeding, education, and development of the personality were "closely related" to the birth rate.

Indeed, "[m]ost of them imply parent-child relationships by their very name."[19]

Accordingly, the marital birth rate became for Zimmerman the thermometer measuring family health. The "family" question and the "population" question were in most respects identical, he argued. In his book, *Family and Society*, Zimmerman called "an absolutely stable or decreasing population...*unthinkable* for the survival of a nation." In his *Family and Civilization*, he defined the bases of "familism" as fidelity, childbearing, and "indissoluble unity" (meaning no divorce), and concluded that hope for the future rested on "the making of *familism* and *childbearing* the primary social duties of the citizen."[20] Zimmerman's very attachment to rural life and agrarianism rested on their fecundity. As he wrote regarding the family farm: "These local family institutions feed the larger culture as the uplands feed the streams and the streams in turn the broader rivers of family life."[21] Or as he explained in another context: "If a positive population policy is developed in America it will probably apply with greater stringency and effectiveness in the rural districts."[22] Revealingly, when Zimmerman grew convinced in the mid-1950s that American rural life was in irreversible crisis and retreat and that urban areas had found a way to become biologically "self-regenerating," he turned on the former, even renouncing country life and—implicitly—most of his earlier work.

Crafting a New Discipline

Such an end could not have been foreseen by any reader of Zimmerman's *Principles of Rural-Urban Sociology*, co-authored with Sorokin and appearing in 1929. While claiming to be purely "scientific," without bias or preaching, the volume was in fact a basic and lengthy New Agrarian tract, the marshalling of a vast array of research evidence to affirm the health and value of farm life, and the corrupting qualities of the city.

The "fundamental task" of a rural sociology, the co-authors said, was "to describe the relatively constant and universal traits or relations of the rural social world as distinct from the...urban social universe." Sorokin and Zimmerman defined "rural" fairly strictly, as meaning persons "actively engaged in an agricultural pursuit, such as collection and cultivation of plants and animals, and the totality of their children." This occupational focus was supplemented by other key distinctions. The rural cultivator worked out-of-doors, where he knew the weather, "breathes cleaner air, and consumes more of the sunlight." The urban person, by contrast, was "wrapped in a thick blanket of artificial culture," where no "free wind refreshes him but a draft of the electric fan," where no sunlight greets him "but the artificial gas or electric light." Rural society was also more homogeneous, in virtually every respect, from race and religion to economic status. Moreover, farming was a relatively "closed class": its doors opened to the children of farmer-peasants, but largely closed to those whose fathers were in other occupations. This transformed a rural people into a special inheritance deserving unusual recognition and protection. For once lost, a rural peasantry could not be easily reconstructed. Rural life knew less mobility as well. If the city could be seen as "a fast river in which the particles of water move intensively," then rural life was "a pond with tiny streams of influx and outflux." Relative to urban life, the rural world was also one of "ownership," with "the bulk of the farmer-peasant class" being "a proprietor class, *par excellence*." Finally, where urban people lived lives of "conspicuous and wasteful consumption," rural folk secured goods "more from nature." Family life and work life were in fact "an undifferentiated unit" on the farm, the natural locale of the working home.[23]

Turning to a synthesis of the available research, their conclusions were—without important exception—all favorable to rural life and farm. The only areas where they found no significant differences between rural and urban life were those of skin pigmentation and head size (or the so-called "cephalic index"). To the undoubted disappointment of the academic racists prominent at the time, Sorokin and Zimmerman reported no uniform results.[24]

In all other areas, the clear advantage lay with rural life. Worldwide, the health and acceptance rates of army recruits was higher for rural than city youth. So too for most other indices of health: farm people had lower rates of tuberculosis, venereal disease, alcohol and drug addiction, insanity, heart disease, arteriosclerosis, and cancer. The sole consistent exception was pellagra, which the authors called "relatively unimportant." Rural intelligence was high (normally at the level of "skilled craftsmen") and increasing, while rural folk were more "persistent" in school and over-represented in high-schools and colleges. Regarding suicide, rural areas showed dramatically "greater forcefulness, vitality, and love for...life." Sorokin and Zimmerman explained this as a consequence of the countryman's immersion into a web of community, belief, and custom: "a man born and reared in a rural environment is bound to his neighbors by thousands of social ties much stronger than the city man with his occasional bed-fellows." There was much less crime in rural areas, as well, when calculated on a per-capita basis. And the nature of crime was different: in cities, it was directed heavily toward property, involving premeditated calculation; in the country, crime was more commonly directed at persons, ranging from assault to murder, and usually a crime of passion. This reflected, in turn, the farmer-peasant's greater respect for private property: the "farmer-peasant is imbued incessantly with the sense of the value of private ownership and...his senses of individual responsibility, independence, and self-reliance." These qualities helped account for the deeper attachments also held by country people to their homes, their native land, and their national cultures.[25]

The authors gave considerable attention to the distinctive family virtues of rural life. "Rural people have greater vital indices than urban people," they coyly reported. Cities were not reproducing themselves, meaning that "the rural biological stock of to-day tends to form the basis of the urban biological stock of to-morrow." Moreover, these were children born into marriages, with illegitimacy rarely found in the country. In explaining the rural advantages, Sorokin and Zimmerman turned first to the influence of religion. In America, the biblical doctrine of "multiply and replenish the world" held more sway in the countryside; in other nations, "the cult of the family" found expression in ancestor worship and household gods. Turning to economics, they noted that there were "few women's employment agencies in the rural districts." Rather, women married at a younger age, and immediately formed a vital part of the household economy on the farm. Children, moreover, became economic assets early on in rural districts, and were readily welcomed into the working home. And the spread of birth control propaganda and devices was much more heavily concentrated in the cities.[26]

Not coincidentally, marriages were also much stronger in the countryside. They came earlier, lasted much longer, and were more universal. The early appearance and greater number of children were partial explanations. So too was the finding that "the religious organization of country life *is more about the family* than in the cities." Added to this, the very nature of agricultural production encouraged a family to thrive. "About every farm there are tasks peculiarly fitted to a man and to a woman," meaning that marriage "is a positive economic asset for both parties." Unlike the city, a rural marriage allowed people "to get ahead" economically. The authors emphasized how this made rural men and women "partners in the best sense of word," with "identical" economic interests. Co-living for twenty-four hours a day created "a community of feeling, believing, rejoicing, suffering, [and] thinking" that was much stronger than in cities. Following an extensive analysis of rural beliefs and behaviors regarding sexual equality, Sorokin and Zimmerman concluded that rural folk were no less egalitarian than those in the city. Rather, "the rural family shows more *unity* and *mutual attachment* and *engulfment of the personality* of the partners into one 'union of body and soul,' while the urban family is marked by a much higher atomization."[27]

However, into this celebratory analysis of rural life crept one dark theme, which the authors label "Rurbanization." In this volume, they saw this process as largely negative, defining it as the intrusion of city ways and attitudes into the countryside, and "a weakening of rural-urban differences," with all the give coming from the rural side. The "'[m]echanization of agriculture tends to stamp the farmer-peasant mind with the same stigmata as the urban mind": it became deterministic and materialistic. To survive in "the wide ocean of the world money economy," the commercial farmer had to plan rationally, discard "the ways of his...forefathers," embark on "an incessant process of modification," and begin to borrow, invest, and speculate. The social consequences of *rurbanization* included a lower birthrate, a shrinking of the economic functions of the family, the weakening of the "community of co-living," and more divorce.[28]

All the same, they did not see this process as inevitable or irreversible. Overall, *Principles of Rural-Urban Sociology* stood as a testament to the continued vitality and irreplacability of rural life.

The three-volume version of *Principles* appeared in 1930-32, under the title *A Systematic Source Book in Rural Sociology*, and with Country Life veteran Charles J. Galpin joining Sorokin and Zimmerman as the third co-author. The co-authors dedicated the work to Theodore Roosevelt, Sir Horace Plunkett, and "Also to Liberty Hyde Bailey, Chairman of the Country Life Commission, whose deep insight into the life of the American farmer shaped the report of the Country Life Commission into a Document of Principles out of which has developed Rural Sociology in the United States."[29] Taking the one-volume and three-volume versions as a whole, no other American work of rural sociology would match their sweep, breadth, and positive thrust.

In 1935, Zimmerman played a central role in creating the Rural Sociological Section of the American Sociological Association. While the society's new journal, *Rural Sociology*, found its institutional home at Louisiana State University, Zimmerman was one of five members of the board of editors and he arranged for his doctoral student, T. Lynn Smith, to become managing editor. Galpin welcomed volume 1, number 1 of the journal by summoning the spirits of "those virile, early protagonists of an abounding rural life"—notably Country Life leaders Kenyon Butterfield and Sir Horace Plunkett—and by calling for "a better day in American agriculture," one based on "the spirit of rural truth-finding."[30]

A Time of Optimism

For the balance of the decade, Zimmerman grew in optimism that a rural renaissance in America was at hand. Writing in 1935, he saw the Great Depression—despite its traumas—as driving home certain truths. There appeared to be "human limitations upon the size of the city," including traffic congestion and the rising relative cost of resources such as water. The division of labor seemed to have gone too far, descending into a bewildering complexity, while the spread of social isolation or *l'anomie* also left persons looking for more meaning in their lives. "High capitalism," the 1930s had taught, "does not appear to work." All these trends led him to conclude that America "may have a cyclical reversal in which the lack of security in the industrial system will be compensated for by a greater development of agriculture and rural life." He looked to "an economy which is simpler, but which offers more safeguards for the family and living," and "an increase of part-time farming."[31]

In a contribution to that end, Zimmerman co-authored with Merle Frampton of the Westminster Foundation the volume, *Family and Society*. Subtitled "A Study of the Sociology of Reconstruction," the book was "a brief for the application of theories similar to those held by [Frederic] LePlay to the study of social facts" and to the "problems of reconstruction now facing America." The co-authors attributed a good share of America's social turmoil to the corruptions born of material prosperity: "When men are prosperous, they tend to become careless." The growth in government welfare programs and the rise in taxes to pay for them were symptoms of the emergence of a disturbing "new type" of humanity: persons "depending for their living upon the public and semi-public agencies." To counter this, Zimmerman and Frampton looked to the farmer. Although he faced "the treacherous forces of nature," the cultivator was still able to secure "at least a minimum for existence" from his efforts, and so avoid a crippling dependency.[32]

Zimmerman took special inspiration from LePlay's concept of the "stem-family" (*famille-souche*). The Frenchman had discovered this family form during his 1836 investigation of foundry methods in the British Isles. He found there the "seven essential elements of a prosperous society," above all, *fecundity*, regardless of whether the subjects were English, Welsh, or Scot, Presbyterian, Quaker, Catholic, or Unitarian. Briefly, LePlay saw the family as the basic social unit, one which "by a remarkable favor of Providence has within its very structure the beneficial qualities of the individual and those of association." Analysis, however, revealed three types of families: patriarchal, unstable, and "stem." Only the latter, under modern conditions, allowed for reasonable order, authentic progress, and true prosperity. A "stem" family united one married child to the paternal household. In turn, this adult maintained the ancestral homestead and supplied all other siblings with a "state of independence." Being "home-centered," the "stem" family could maintain "a reasonably high birth rate." According to LePlay and Zimmerman the "stem" family also united "the useful traditions of the family ancestors" with "strong habits of work," the collective needs of the family with individualism, and liberty with restraint. Zimmerman stressed that the stem family was not given to only one time period, but was a choice available to all eras. It "develops among all people who combine the benefits of agriculture, industry, and settled life with the common sense idea of defending their private life from the domination of legislators, from the invasion of bureaucrats, and [from] the exaggerations of the manufacturing regime."[33]

Zimmerman emphasized that efforts to restore part-time subsistence farming were fully in the spirit of LePlay. Both in the country and on the outskirts of cities, "stem" family.dwellings had "vegetable and fruit gardens as natural appurtenances,...a few outbuildings for the use of domestic animals....[and] [w]hen the household crafts require it the home is completed by a work-shop."[34]

Zimmerman and Frampton proceeded to apply LePlay's techniques in a study of "a prosperous, stable Ozark Highland family," circa 1932. With character types that, in different ways, would also surface in the work of Frank Owsley, Andrew Lytle, and Wendell Berry, the co-authors described a rural family of mainly Celtic blood, with nine children. The father was "the most successful farmer in the county," showing an ability to make and save money. Strongly religious, the family regularly attended church and Sunday School, and all revival services and camp meetings, and sang hymns together at home. "Most of the early home teaching is done by the father, who tells stories of young men and women who have gone astray and explains the cause of their downfall. The evening hearth is the classroom." This "family hearth is supplemented by the work of the school," so that the education of the children remained home centered. All family members worked on the farm, with the women carrying their own distinctive tasks. As Zimmerman and Frampton concluded:

> This family...is strikingly similar to a number of families described by Frederic LePlay for the various "Cases of Prosperity" in Western Europe. The family has sufficient food, clothing, and shelter for all basic needs. They have little money from our commercial standards and purchase few goods. It is strongly familistic and highly integrated....They observe local customs rigidly. The home and the hearth are the center of their familistic enterprises....[The family's] members have not been a burden on the relief funds of county, state, or federal agencies. On the contrary, it stands ready to help its absent members.[35]

Implicitly, at least, this Ozark family was held up for admiration and replication. The co-authors concluded the book with an extensive look at one active effort to restore subsistence gardens in "a stranded industrial town,"[36] part of a contribution to the "subsistence farming project."

Zimmerman's investigation of *Rural Families on Relief* for the Works Progress Administration reinforced his Depression-induced optimism. Overall, he found, the rural population remained biologically "prolific," when compared to the troubled cities. In particular, rural folks on subsistence farms of the Appalachian-Ozark region and the German- and Scandinavia-Americans of the "Spring Wheat" Belt on the Upper Plains had the most stable families and the highest fertility of all Americans. These were also the families least likely to receive public assistance, turning instead to extended kin and voluntary sources when needing help. The only disturbing note for Zimmerman was the behavior of the relatively rich farmers of the Corn Belt, where "the tendency toward a small family system is evident."[37]

In another 1938 book, *The Changing Community*, Zimmerman grew almost euphoric over the possibility of rebuilding family solidarity and raising the birth rate through re-ruralization. The detailed study of one rural region, called "Milkville" here, found "that family solidarity has increased since the disappearance of the industrially-minded population of fifty years ago." Under conditions in the 1930s, farm life had become "a dominant bond in family organization," a bond that "has undoubtedly been strengthened since farm incomes have been reduced by lowered prices." Indeed, the Depression seemed to have the unexpected effect among those farm families of making recreation once again subservient to family needs:

> For example, not only is there no organized outdoor sport in the community, but such informal and less time-consuming diversions as hunting, hiking, and even pitching horse-shoes, are rarely followed by young people; it would appear that they willingly regulate their lives by family requirements and family loyalties.

In all this, Zimmerman took heart. Indeed, he even predicted "that in the near future, out-of-town opportunities will still be unable to break down the present contentment with family farm life."[38]

Rural Failure and Despair

Less than a decade later, though, Zimmerman had basically lost hope in rural revitalization. He was aware of the consequences of World War II in the countryside: a sharp reduction in the number of active farmers and farm laborers; an acceleration in the introduction of complex farm machinery; the consolidation of farms into ever larger units; and the virtual disappearance of the experimental subsistence homesteads. The promises of the 1930s had been dashed by the war-induced acceleration in social and economic change.

Quiet pessimism and despair haunt Zimmerman's 1947 *magnum opus*, *Family and Civilization*. Adapting themes from both Sorokin and LePlay, he developed in this book his own categorization of family types. Earlier efforts, he maintained, had been inadequate, failing to describe how the family functioned relative to other institutions in society. His new typology contained: (1) *the trustee family* (corresponding to LePlay's patriarchal family), where the clan exercised considerable social, economic and political influence, held the unquestioned loyalty of its members, and gained an aura of immorality; (2) *the atomistic family* (corresponding to LePlay's "unstable" family), where marriage was reduced to a weak contract, where "the individual becomes sacred," where illegitimacy vanished as a concept, and where antagonism between husbands and wives and parents and children grew; and (3), the *domestic family*, where the extended family receded in importance, where a balance of power existed between the married-couple family and other social agencies, where the old religion struggled to hold the moral order together, and where families bore at least three children each, to insure the reproduction of the nation.[39] At times, Zimmerman suggested that the *domestic family* was more of a transition phase, particularly for highly dynamic societies. But at other times, he maintained that it was closest to the dictates of human nature, the most common of family forms, and the basic type found in "all developed civilizations."[40] In any case, the bulk of the volume traced and analyzed the changes in family system experienced by the world's great civilizations, past and present.

Relative to American agrarianism, Zimmerman declared that "our farm and rural families are still to a large extent the domestic type."[41] But he drew little solace from this. While a "familistic remnant" could become "an influence or vehicular agent in the reappearance of familism," he did not see that happening. Rather, he agreed with Westermarck regarding the likelihood of a "disappearance of marriage" and with Sorokin that the main family functions "will further decrease until the family becomes a mere incidental cohabitation of male and female while the home will become a mere overnight parking place mainly for sex relationship."[42] Zimmerman saw change accelerating, in part, because the family was "already so completely atomized that it produces no stable social body in which to solidify." Children, called the family's "human parts," were simply not sufficient to reproduce the society. With a longing but sad look at rural America, he concluded that "[o]utside of a few limited circles, there simply seems to be no strong established systems of social belief." The family "cannot and will not" stand still: "That the family of the immediate future will move further toward atomism seems highly probable."[43]

In other works from the late 1940s, the same pessimism reigned. Zimmerman's *The Family of Tomorrow: The Cultural Crisis and the*

Way Out appears to have been the consequence of the first "Kinsey Report" on *Sexuality in the Human Male,* which at once affirmed his worst fears and spurred him on to action. Zimmerman offered a summary of his main themes in *Family and Civilization* and a policy agenda to change direction. Tellingly, he admitted to the ruin of his hopes for rural America: "There is no longer the possibility of feeding our social system from a constantly replenishing stream of 'honest and sturdy peasants.' We now have no hinterland or unspoiled Lutheran and Catholic Europeans, from which to feed our cities and our clamorous industries." Even his deeply admired "stem" family exemplars, the Celtic-American hillbillies, were failing: "Our Appalachian-Ozark people...[who] furnished much of the 'native' blood of the country, due to their high birth rates and their quick migration during times of need...soon will no longer have a family system materially different from that in the rest of the United States."[44]

In an extended tirade, he railed against the "well-to-do farmers" who now had high incomes and relative security, but who failed to have children. "It is common knowledge," he wrote in disgust, "that in the wealthy corn-belt counties of the United States—the best agrarian land in the world—a very high proportion of the wealthiest farms will be sold at auction," because there were no heirs. Farmers with state-guaranteed prices on top of widespread food scarcity now clamored for "free housing" or "free medical treatment" during their wives' pregnancies. In an amazing rejoinder (albeit similar to Bailey's chiding), Zimmerman declared: "Offhand one should say that what this class needs most of all is *a system of values*—a general realization as to what the rural family should mean for the recreation of our culture." In short, the peasantry were no longer acting like peasants, to Zimmerman's agitated sorrow.[45]

In his 1949 presidential address to the Rural Sociological Society, he offered similar judgments. "The latifundia [large corporate estates] have ruined us," he stated, using a term echoing from ancient Rome. "We have not yet found a way to make the family system of our cities self-regenerating," while "we are consciously introducing these anti-family and anti-family-farm movements into the countryside." If the number of family farms fell in absolute number, then the rural family dissolved "and the whole cultural movement toward atomization of family relationships has no limiting factor." So it was happening, as "independent and culturally stable people" fled from the countryside, to be replaced by "corporate, capitalistic and non-family forms of agriculture." The whole situation was "a menace to the level of life," but he saw no way out.[46]

The Deceptive Suburban Miracle

Except in two small observations. In his "Family Farm" address, he briefly returned to the concept of "rurban" people, first used in his 1928 book, *Principles of Rural-Urban Sociology*. In the latter, it was a negative term, a sign of the urbanization of country people. But in his 1949 address, it now represented people who split their year between city and country and who "are tending to merge with the familistic segment of the country people," unconsciously creating "a new social class." Zimmerman saw this as "a very hopeful" sign.[47] In *The Family of Tomorrow*, meanwhile, he commented on the uptick in the fertility rate in 1946-47. "On the surface, all seems fine," he reasoned, but underneath he saw the still growing popularity of the one- and two-child family system. "Sooner or later we must exhaust the particular 'life extension' given by the unusual number of war and postwar marriages and the great number of first and second births culminating in one year."[48]

Only a few years later, though, disciples of Zimmerman begun to suspect that something more important was happening: that they might be witnesses to the emergence of "a variant type of urban family," one "able to maintain sufficient fertility and integration to satisfy the Zimmerman requisites and yet function adequately in the urban community." In 1949, in fact, "for the first time" in U.S. demographic history, the number of children under age five per 1,000 women was higher in "rural non-farm" areas than in either urban or rural-farm regions. The suburban family had become the new incubator of family values, and most especially of fertility.[49]

Several years later, with evident relief, Zimmerman joined in the celebration of the family reborn. In the 1960 volume, *Successful American Families*, he reported on his Ford Foundation-backed investigation into the phenomenon of "best-friend families." Using a sample of 60,000 U.S. families from eight American cities, Zimmerman identified those that succeeded. Family "success," he indicated, could be judged by three criteria: (1) avoidance of family disruption (divorce or desertion); (2) avoidance of contact with police; and (3), keeping the children in school until graduation. Those families that succeeded, he reported, had surrounded themselves with "a new social invention": the use of "friendship groupings" or "friend-families," who shared values with parents and helped to shield the young from the vicissitudes and corruptions of life.[50]

"Our study shows that out of the present social situation has come a capacity for the onward march of the American people into the new technical world of the Atomic Age," Zimmerman jubilantly concluded. Not only were one-third to one-half of these "friend-families" found to be kin, suggesting the astonishing rebirth of the extended family in the suburbs. More importantly, "most of them are, or are becoming, adequate biologically in that they are 'reproducers.'" In a fairly bizarre, almost unthinking act of self-criticism, he celebrated the new found ability of urban America to produce a three-child normative family system, stating: "Somehow or other our sociology has given us a false picture of the fundamental and lasting social processes found in these cities." Zimmerman simply could not get over the wonder of it, repeating over and again the significance of the miracle: "This Twentieth Century...has produced an entirely new class of people, neither rural nor urban. They live in the country but have *nothing* to do with agriculture....[T]hese constitute a new class...neither peasants, proletariats, nor capitalists," but suburbanites. He added: "Never before in history have a free urban and sophisticated people made a positive change in the birth rate as have our American people this generation."[51]

By 1967, still holding to the idea that "the urban population is biologically reproductive," Zimmerman would dismiss the whole of agrarian fundamentalism. The modern farmer "cannot afford to be a family farmer," he wrote. The rural community on the Plains had "lost its place as a home for a folk." The old image of "rural goodness and urban badness" had properly been forgotten. City people predominated now, and "they do not feel that they are less virtuous than country people." There was no linkage between "farming" and "democracy," and probably never had been. And finally: "The new image of the countryman as only due standard treatment as a citizen, and not the preferred type, is a natural development."[52]

If this sounded like a funeral sermon for rural sociology as a whole, there was good reason, for the discipline had clearly entered a time of crisis. In the early 1960s, the journal *Rural Sociology* almost ceased publication, for lack of a university sponsor. The U.S. Department of Agriculture, which during the 1940s had assembled dozens of sociologists in the Farm Population and Rural Life Branch of the Bureau of Agricultural Economics, dismantled the program over the following two decades. By 1970, only one part-time rural sociologist remained in the USDA Social Science section, and there was little concern for the program's future. Indeed, as a leading rural sociologist would later report: "[a]s a result of internal problems, coupled with the continuing decline in rural population and the changing character of rural life, serious questions were even being raised about the appropriateness of a separate sociological society called 'rural.'"[53]

Lulled into complacency by a "baby boom" in the suburbs that would soon prove to be ephemeral, the scientific defenders of rural America abandoned the stage.

Ongoing Themes

Under the influence of Sorokin and LePlay, and through his own identification with German-America and denominational Christianity, Carle Zimmerman avoided several distracting strains of the New Agrarianism: notably, the war on Christian orthodoxy and the opposition to a peasant way of life. Yet in other ways, he was in full harmony with the principle themes of the Country Life, or New Agrarian campaign:

Technological Advance is a Unchallengable Good

In their *Principles of Rural-Urban Sociology*, Sorokin and Zimmerman openly acknowledged that as "more farm machinery is developed...fewer workers are needed on the land." Although resolutely seeking to keep farm people on farms, for social and demographic reasons, they praised technological innovations for lessening "the irksomeness of farm labor" and raising yields. They provided a positive account of the new machines—the "combine" harvester-thrasher, corn harvesters, four-row cultivators, trucks, and tractors—and denied that their use represented an untoward "mining of the soil."[54] In a 1946 manuscript, Zimmerman labeled as "positive influences" in the rebuilding of rural life: highways, automobiles, radio, television, the spread of electric power, plastics, the electric freezer, and automatic washing machines.[55] In some respects, Zimmerman's enthusiasm for technological advance knew no bounds. As late as 1949, while woefully complaining about the dire consequences of rural depopulation, he also praised the rapid displacement of horses by tractors and celebrated the Rural Electrical Administration, "automobiles, good roads, and radio" for making "rural living culturally and temporally instantaneous with urban life." While acknowledging in a footnote that the Brannan Plan, then under debate in Congress, would favor "the farm family and a national family policy," he implicitly deplored the favoritism it showed to small holdings. A true "familistic policy," he said, would in fact "aid the rapid forward movement of the three agrarian revolutions now under way—Mendelian (hybridization), Chemurgical (i.e., use of 2-4-D and DDT, etc.) and soil treatment (the multiple factor attack)."[56]

Decentralization shall mark the future

In *Principles*, Sorokin and Zimmerman argued that the special nature of farming would prevent further centralization and consolidation of land: "thanks to the peculiarities of agriculture, a large enterprise there does not have and cannot have many profitable preferences in comparison with small farms owned by farmers, which large enterprises have in other industries." Momentarily forgetting such prominent examples as the rise of the *latifundia* in ancient Rome, they wrote that all history showed a "progressive increase" in the number of farmer-peasant enterprises. Mechanization would make no difference.[57] Nearly two decades later, Zimmerman declared that the "day of the great city centers seems over." He described the "great place" that rural life would play "in the America of the future" as "a haven of refuge or familistic way of life for millions who do not care to keep up with the ever increasing complexity of our cities." Urban centers would be displaced by "great regional aggregates, semi-urban, semi-rural, where living as a 'way of life' would predominate." Modern communication made this decentralization possible, and even inevitable. In the "rurban" suburbs, American families would find their salvation.[58]

The Farmer and Farm Family Should be Re-Engineered

Sorokin and Zimmerman, in *Principles*, acknowledged the value of a well-informed "applied rural social technology." And although less explicit than Bailey and the Country Life leadership in their embrace of social work and rural uplift, their call for deep social-political intervention was real. As they concluded: "attempts to prevent the spread of urban birth control, family disorganization, epicureanism, and cynicism to rural districts may be of considerable value"; and "an improvement of economic, educational, cultural, political, and other conditions of the rural world is dictated by the vital interests of the urban world itself."[59] In the 1940s, Zimmerman largely abandoned his earlier view that the family had a relatively fixed nature, varying only in degree of strength and weakness. Instead, he suggested that "the finite cause of the family lies in cultural need—nothing else," leading him to look for—indeed, to seek to create—a new family form. If the emerging social polarization could be made to be "a short day," he wrote, then "a beautiful sunset [of the old family], a warm night and an early dawn" would follow, where "we shall see a new family system arise similar to the best product of the Industrial Revolution, but adjusted to the atomic age."[60] Later, he openly joined the ranks of the progressive social engineers, declaring that the "new age demanded a stronger, more resolute and better equipped individual." To "produce such persons will demand a reorganization of the present family system and the building of one that is stronger educationally and morally." Curiously, he maintained that Soviet Russia had realized the same lesson in 1936, leading Joseph Stalin to implement certain pro-family reforms. Later, suburban Americans had stumbled onto the truth that "the world needs a new person who is both learned and familistic." Where "Russia discovered this the bloody way," he concluded, America "had discovered this the peaceful and intellectual way."[61]

The Necessity of Progressive Public Education

In their discussion of the functions of the traditional rural family, Sorokin and Zimmerman borrowed a line from historian J.M. Williams: "Until the establishment of the common school system, children got their education in the home."[62] But they failed to see the import of this observation, possibly due to Zimmerman's personal enthusiasm for the common schools. Both of his parents were public school teachers, and he never had observable doubts over the value of the system. Indeed, in his frequent criticisms of "the loss of function" school of family sociology (usually associated with William Ogburn),

Zimmerman simply denied that schooling and other "lost" functions were all that important. Even in cities, he maintained, parents "still have ten times more influence upon the value behavior of the young" than all the new agencies put together, including public education. Despite their many negative influences, the industrial revolution, the rise of cities, and the displacement of family-centered education by state education "still has not destroyed the real meaning of family functions in the parent-child unit."[63] When measuring family success, Zimmerman instinctively turned to increased schooling: "we consider education in a special sense to be socially creative. We are seeking to evaluate families on their responsiveness to the general American and world situation, and one indication is a willingness to seek increased education."[64] The common school, not the parochial family, was the appropriate teaching vehicle for social renewal.

America's First "Sickness"

Zimmerman shared another quality with Bailey and the Country Life advocates: few real farmers and rural folk paid him much attention. Zimmerman's core concern was to maintain a relatively high fertility in the United Sates; to this, all else was subordinate. But it seems unlikely that many "little Carles" were conceived and borne by grateful country people, eager to do their part for social reconstruction. Rather, farm folk followed the economic signals they received from their work, the social signals they picked up from schools, the print media, and the radio, and the moral signals they culled from their churches, and—to borrow a modern phrase—made their reproductive choices.

While avoiding some of the more interventionist aspects of the Country Life campaign, Zimmerman still viewed rural people and farm life as means to an end. In some respects, he was prescient. It would be American "peasants" of the "Palatine Boor" type—persons who also viewed agricultural life as a means to an end—who would at century's end be the only rural group still bearing large families in America. The difference, though, lay in their respective "ends": Zimmerman wanted numbers; the American peasants sought obedience to God's will, from which the numbers would follow.

In his conclusion to *Family and Civilization*, Zimmerman predicted that the United States and "the other countries of Western Christendom" would reach the last phase of a great family crisis between 1947 and the year 2000, a crisis identical to that experienced by Greece and Rome in earlier millenia. He added: "The results will be much more drastic in the United States because, being the most extreme and inexperienced of the aggregates of western civilization, it will take its first real 'sickness' most violently."[65] In his euphoria over the suburban Baby Boom of the 1950s, Zimmerman forgot about this prediction. Yet in wake of the collapse of the peculiar and short-lived social conventions of that decade and in light of the consequences—a plummeting marital fertility rate, a rising level of "out of wedlock" births, and ubiquitous divorce—his initial read of the situation now seems much more valid, and his abandonment of religiously infused rural life premature.

Notes

1. C.J. Galpin, "Report of Committee on Rural Sociology in Schools and Colleges," in *Proceedings of the First National Country Life Conference* , Baltimore (Ithaca, NY: National Country Life Association, 1919): 124-126.
2. T. Lynn Smith, "Rural Sociology in the United States and Canada: A Trend Report," *Current Sociology* 6 (1957): 12.
3. See: T. Lynn Smith, "The Life and Work of Carle C. Zimmerman," in *Sociocultural Change Since 1950*, eds. T. Lynn Smith and Man Singh Das (New Delhi: Vikas Publishing House, 1978): 1-3.
4. From: Pitirim Sorokin and Carle C. Zimmerman, *Principles of Rural-Urban Sociology* (New York: Henry Holt and Company, 1929): 427, 442.
5. From Carle C. Zimmerman, *Sorokin, The World's Greatest Sociologist: His Life and Ideas on Social Time and Change* (Saskatoon: University of Saskatchewan, 1968): 1-2, 14-19.
6. Smith, *Sociocultural Change*, pp. 2-3.
7. Sorokin and Zimmerman, *Principles*, p. vi.
8. Ibid., p. 17.
9. Carle C. Zimmerman, *Family and Civilization* (New York and London: Harper & Brothers, 1947): 691.
10. Zimmerman, *Family and Civilization*, p. 692.
11. Carle C. Zimmerman, "The Family Farm," *Rural Sociology* 15 (Sept. 1950): 211-212.
12. Carle C. Zimmerman, *Outline of American Rural Sociology* (Cambridge, MA: Phillips Book Store, 1946): 42.
13. Sorokin and Zimmerman, *Principles*, pp. 68-69.
14. Carl C. Zimmerman and Merle E. Frampton, *Family and Society: A Study of the Sociology of Reconstruction* (New York: D. Van Nostrand Company, 1935): 91.
15. Sorokin and Zimmerman, *Principles*, pp. 345, 180.
16. Ibid., p. 179.
17. Carle C. Zimmerman, *Consumption and Standards of Living* (New York: D. Van Nostrand Company, 1936): 200.

18. On this point, Zimmerman refers to: C.P. Loomis, "The Growth of the Farm Family in Relation to Its Activities," *North Carolina Experiment Station, Bulletin No. 298* (June 1934); in *Consumption*, p. 202.
19. Zimmerman, *Consumption*, pp. 201-202.
20. Zimmerman, *Family and Society*, pp. 6, 10; Zimmerman, *Family and Civilization*, pp. 697, 810.
21. Zimmerman, "Family Farm," p. 211.
22. Zimmerman, *Outline*, p. 42.
23. Sorokin and Zimmerman, *Principles*, pp. 8, 16-17, 26-28, 63, 75.
24. Ibid., pp. 125-35.
25. Ibid., pp. 156-157, 169, 177, 259-261, 399, 409, 519.
26. Ibid., pp. 215-220; 338-339.
27. Ibid., pp. 228-229, 348-49, 353-365. Emphasis added.
28. Ibid., pp. 620-625.
29. Pitirim A. Sorokin, Carle C. Zimmerman, Charles J. Galpin, *A Systematic Sourcebook in Rural Sociology, Volume I* (New York: Russell and Russell, 1965 [1930]): v.
30. "Greetings from Charles Josiah Galpin," *Rural Sociology 1* (March 1936): 3-5.
31. Zimmerman, *Family and Society*, pp. 11-13.
32. Ibid., pp. 73-74, 83.
33. Ibid., pp. 77, 95, 121-133.
34. Ibid., pp. 130, 137.
35. Ibid., pp. 211-237.
36. Ibid., pp. 323-335.
37. Carle C. Zimmerman and Nathan L. Whetten, *Rural Families on Relief.* Research Monograph 17, Works Progress Administration, Divison of Social Research (Washington, DC: U.S. Government Printing Office, 1938, reprint by New York: DaCapo Press, 1971): xvi, xx, 4, 60, 66-68.
38. Carle C. Zimmerman, *The Changing Community* (New York and London: Harper & Brothers, 1938): 441-442.
39. Ibid., pp. 124-130; 732-736.
40. Ibid., pp. 130, 732, 742.
41. Ibid., p. 130.
42. Ibid., pp. 794, 796.
43. Ibid., p. 806.
44. Carle C. Zimmerman, *The Family of Tomorrow: The Cultural Crisis and the Way Out* (New York: Harper and Brothers, 1949): 214.
45. Zimmerman, *Family of Tomorrow*, p. 248.
46. Zimmerman, "The Family Farm," pp. 212-214, 218-219.
47. Ibid., pp. 219-220.
48. Zimmerman, *Family of Tomorrow*, p. 242.
49. See E. Garty Jaco and Ivan Belknap, "Is a New Family Form Emerging in the Urban Fringe?" *American Sociological Review* 18 (Oct. 1953): 551-557. Also: Silvia Fleis, "Suburbanism as a Way of Life," *American Sociological Review* 21 (Feb. 1956): 34-37; and Wendell Bell, "Familism and Suburbanization: One Test of the Social Choice Hypothesis," *Rural Sociology* 21 (Sept.-Dec., 1956): 276-283.
50. Carle C. Zimmerman and Louis F. Cervantes, *Successful American Families* (New York: Pageant Press, 1960): 7, 14-16.
51. Zimmerman and Cervantes, *Successful American Families*, pp. 17, 41, 45, 116, 207, 208.

52. Carle C. Zimmerman, "Socio-Cultural Changes in the Plains," in *Symposium on the Great Plains of North America*, eds. Carle C. Zimmerman and Seth Russell (Fargo: The North Dakota Institute for Regional Studies, 1967): 198-209.
53. Sheldon G. Lowry, "Rural Sociology at the Crossroads," *Rural Sociology* 42 (Winter 1977): 463.
54. Sorokin and Zimmerman, *Principles*, pp. 535-537.
55. Zimmerman, *Outline of American Rural Sociology*, p. 49.
56. Zimmerman, "Family Farm," pp. 215, 220.
57. Sorokin and Zimmerman, *Principles*, p. 626.
58. Zimmerman, *Outline*, p. 49.
59. Sorokin and Zimmerman, *Principles*, p. 635.
60. Zimmerman, *Family of Tomorrow*, pp. 60-61, 213-214.
61. Zimmerman, *Successful American Families*, pp. 12, 217-218.
62. Sorokin and Zimmerman, *Principles*, p. 366.
63. Zimmerman, *Family and Civilization*, pp. 698-704.
64. Zimmerman, *Successful American Families*, p. 8.
65. Zimmerman, *Family and Civilization*, p. 798.

3

Crafting a Decentralist Economics:
Ralph Borsodi

Gathering September 15, 1943, in Manhattan's historic Aldine Club, five hundred "Friends of the School of Living" listened to economist Ralph Borsodi address the question, "What Americans Can Do About the Postwar Collapse." The dinner crowd included novelist and Nobel laureate Pearl S. Buck, director of the American Civil Liberties Union Roger Baldwin, an impressive share of the Columbia University faculty, members of the prestigious Farm Club of Manhattan, and an array of America's leading editors and thinkers.

Borsodi's answer to the problem posed was simple and direct:

> Look within...[S]top looking to Washington for salvation....[Advance] a nationwide back-to-the land movement...[so] we can individually raise food and livestock, erect shelters and houses, cut wood for fuel, and produce other necessaries for ourselves....[W]e should buy either a farm or subsistence homestead *now*, or organize a self-liquidating homestead association *now*....[Those] who do not already know how to live in the country should start their education in gardening and productive country life *now*.[1]

This speech, in some respects, marked the high water mark of Borosodi's career as a public philosopher. For fifteen years, he had exercised a considerable influence on the course of mainstream American ideas, authoring several best-selling volumes on the perils of urban life and the promise of country living and inspiring thousands of his fellow citizens to return to a family-centered life on the land. More than any other agrarian writer of the twentieth century, Borsodi aimed at creating a systematic economic theory of decentralism, one including a compelling integration of home production into calculations of economic gain. His ultimate failure rested in part on his own personal weaknesses, in part on World War II which leveled the mid-century homestead revival, and in part on assumptions that he shared with other New Agrarians. Included in the latter category were his undiluted enthusiasm for technological innovation, his belief that the force of history was naturally moving toward decentralization, and a deep hostility toward revealed religion.

On Advertising and Distribution

Borsodi was born in New York in 1888 to parents of Jewish-Hungarian origin, and grew up on the Lower East Side. His father, William, was active in the Single Tax movement built on the ideas of Henry George. Ralph Borsodi joined the movement as well, and, in 1918, became chairman of the New York State Committee of the Single Tax Party.[2] By all accounts, he was a man of iconoclastic ideas and grand visions, highly independent and very self-assured. Those who came to know him personally usually became either strident opponents or devoted followers.[3]

He began his career as a consulting economist for several of America's leading corporations and trade groups, including R.H. Macy & Company, the Spool Cotton Company, and the National Retail Dry Goods Association. His attention focused especially on marketing problems, where he grew increasingly disturbed over the changes that he saw.

In a story that would become famous, he told of his family's move in 1920 from New York City to an abandoned seven-acre homestead to the north, in Rockland County. During the first summer there, his Iowa-born wife canned tomatoes. When she proudly presented them to her husband, the economist in him thought: "Does it really pay?" Was home production of this sort really efficient, particularly when time or labor was factored in? He began his calculations and, to his surprise, found that it *was* efficient: the cost of the homemade product was 20 to 30 percent lower than the price of the factory-made product. The result violated every prevailing assumption about the nature of industry. How could this be?[4]

To answer this question, Borsodi wrote a series of books in the 1920s, including *National Advertising* and *The Distribution Age: A Study of the Economy of Modern Distribution*. He identified a transition among reputable American corporations, from a focus on making products that met consumer needs toward an economy of "distribution," resting on high-pressure marketing, the manipulation of emotion, and heavy consumer debt. Nearly 70 percent of a product's cost, he found, was now comprised of advertising, transportation, and storage expenses. From this, Borsodi posited a new economic law: "Distribution costs tend to move in inverse relationship to production costs."[5] This explained why gardening, food preservation at home, and a range of other "old fashioned" activities had now become economically rational.

While an acknowledged expert on advertising, Borsodi deplored the new model of "national advertising" for other reasons. Not only did it represent a vast waste of human talent and energy on Madison Avenue. It was also, at root level, immoral:

> The object of national advertising is to create desire. It ignores the question of the necessity for the goods and tries only to succeed in persuading the public to buy what the advertiser offers...[The advertiser] creates...a necessity in the lives of the people that has no economic or moral basis in fact.[6]

Borsodi argued as well that the American economy of the 1920s was no longer a competitive market system. Using language similar to that later employed by "public choice" economists, he wrote: "As a matter of fact, it has become more truly *a competition to secure privileges* which enable their possessors to operate *outside* of the competitive market." He indicted not only *state*-granted franchises and subsidies, but also licenses, tariffs, special tax breaks, and nationally advertised trade-marks, which conspired to *raise* prices, *crush* diversity, *handicap* the small producer, and *favor* extreme centralization.[7]

Artificial Factories, Natural Families

In the late 1920s, Borsodi began to expand these themes into a fairly complete philosophical system, through the best-selling books *This Ugly Civilization* (1928), *Flight From The City* (1933), and *Prosperity and Security: A Study in Realistic Economics* (1938). His argument rested on three historic and economic premises:

1. *The Artificial Status of Corporations.* Borsodi argued that the large, joint-stock business corporations of his time were neither a natural nor an inevitable development. Instead, he saw them as the consequence of a grant by governments of legal privileges, ones de-

nied to families and individuals. These privileges included limits on liability, so that in the case of disastrous loss, corporate investors and managers would lose only the amount of their direct investment; perpetual life, insuring the corporation against the hazard of death (and inheritance taxes) to which personal or family enterprises were inevitably subject; and the ability to issue a variety of stocks, bonds, and debt instruments, which gave the corporation considerable advantages in securing capital. Indeed, Borsodi considered corporate charters as "veritable letters of marque," granting corporate leaders freedom from criminal responsibility: "short of actually taking money out of the treasury of the company (a foolish proceeding when there are so many ways of appropriating it legally), ...the charter which the state grants to the organizer of a corporation is a commission to embark upon the adventure of *doing* the investing public with impunity." Elsewhere, he described Acts of Incorporation as a "bargain for privilege" between corporate organizers and the state, one made by its very nature to the disadvantage of small, family-based enterprises. Accordingly, he emphasized the deep tension between the "unnatural corporation," resting on an "ideology of infinite debt," and the "natural family," with its grounding in the non-monetized household economy.[8] "No wonder corporate enterprises have prospered," Borsodi concluded, "while private and personal enterprises have declined."[9]

2. *The Artificial Nature of Large Industry.* Just as the large corporations themselves enjoyed success primarily through state privilege, so did the regime of centralized factories rest on state subsidies, tax privileges, and legal favoritism. Borsodi, it must be emphasized, was neither anti-machine nor anti-technology. The real enemy, he stressed, was the factory. As explained in a long diatribe in *This Ugly Civilization*:

> It is the factory, not the machine, which is reducing all men and all commodities to a dead level of uniformity because the factory makes it impossible for individual men and individual communities to be self-sufficient....

> It is the factory, not the machine, which destroys both the natural beauty and the natural wealth of man's environment; which fills country and city with hideous factories and squalid slums....

> By destroying the economic foundations of the home [the factory] has robbed men, women and children of their contact with the soil; their intimacy with the growing of animals, birds, vegetables, trees and flowers; their familiarity with the actual making of things, and their capacity for entertaining and educating themselves.[10]

Crafting a revisionist economic history that anticipated several themes adopted by Lewis Mumford, Borsodi argued that the early Industrial Revolution, resting on application of the steam engine, had given a natural economic advantage to the central factory only for a short, if critical, time. He said that subsequent inventions—especially the small electric engine and the internal combustion gasoline engine—had restored the natural productive advantage in many cases to homes and small shops. Controlled experiments, matching modern decentralized tools with large machines, showed that family-scale production was, circa 1930, the most efficient form of production for nearly 70 percent of the goods and services consumed by the average family.[11] However, effective political control of the state by industrial corporations insured their continued domination, through subsidies direct and indirect.[12]

As Borsodi explained: "The huge factory is a steam-age relic rendered obsolete by the electrical age," yet sustained in the twentieth century by the power of government.[13] In capitalist countries, "well-meaning persons, appalled by the horror of industrialism, have joined hands with the vested interests...and are trying to subsidize the factory system into decency, and to protect it from the competition of its more efficient but smaller rivals." Cartels, tariffs, patents, quotas, and the New Deal's National Recovery Administration codes all contributed to this. In socialist countries, the whole system rested "upon the illusion that the factory system is itself a good thing," in agriculture as well as in the making of other products.[14]

The problem, Borsodi emphasized, also extended to heavily subsidized transportation networks, such as canals, railroads, and highways, which were the very lifeblood of mass industry: "Every time a distant factory destroys the market of a local producer, it is in part due to the fact that the distant factory enjoys this [transportation] subsidy on the goods which it manufactures." In the absence of government-financed transportation systems, Borsodi argued, "production would still be largely local."[15]

He noted as well that "the factory system dominates modern methods of education. The system began at the nursery school level. It ended in the university, preparing young people to be cogs in the industrial machine, and leaving them incapable of independent living on the land. The modern school was notable "for its efficient equipment, efficient methods, and efficient personnel." Specialization spread among teachers along with standardized curricula. Students "go to school en masse, they play en masse, they think en masse." While knowing more abstract facts than the child of the pre-factory age, they "do not understand their environment as well" and they were incapable of feeding, sheltering, and clothing themselves.[16]

3. *The Misleading Premises of Modern Economic Thought.* Borsodi held that the "apologists for capitalism," the "advocates of communism," and "the protagonists of fascism"—whatever their other differences—were united in their theory "that mass production is the most efficient of all methods of production."[17] This defense of centralized factories began with Adam Smith; Karl Marx had expanded on it; and the matter reached complete scientific exposition in the early twentieth-century work of Frederick Winslow Taylor. The problem, Borsodi insisted, lay in the assumption posited by Smith, and accepted by all his successors, that humans actually obtain what they want and satisfy their desires only through exchange. In fact, he argued, there were four ways that humans met their needs:

(a) *They make what they want for themselves*, usually within the household in a *non*-monetized process of family production;

(b) *They get what they need by gift, charity, or beggary*, on a non-monetary or altruistic model within a family, and on a monetary basis outside it;

(c) *They take what they want from others*, through criminal theft or through *legal* theft (such as redistributive taxation, trade privileges, or subsidies direct and indirect), a process employing "mainly politicians, lawyers, and the officials who execute the orders";

and (d), *They trade what they have earned or produced for what they need or desire*, using barter or money.[18]

Classical economic thought, Borsodi showed, focused exclusively on the latter aspect of economic life, ignoring the other three. This created in turn vast distortions in analysis, and misleading accounts of "growth" that masked the importance of the family. For example, when an activity formally done through the home economy, such as vegetable gardening, gave way to the purchase of vegetables in the marketplace, a formerly uncounted activity now leaped onto the books. A liberal economist would claim this whole amount as "economic growth." Borsodi saw it as a shift from one form of production to another, probably less efficient, form, a loss rather than a gain in the overall effectiveness of the whole economy.

Borsodi insisted on viewing families as economic enterprises: "small groups of persons, living together, usually related to one another by marriage or ties of blood, pooling and sharing in some degree their incomes, and dividing what they purchase or acquire or produce on their farms and in their homes among their members according to their respective needs and requirements."[19] In his accounting of economic enterprises in the United States, circa 1929, he numbered 36,402,000 of these families, compared to 427,515 "privileged corporations," 194,000 governments, and 100,000 "criminal enterprises." To give families their due, he demanded a wholly new and accurate form of accounting, one that moved beyond the cabal of government and privileged corporation.

Within families, Borsodi gave especial attention to the work of the homemaker. Ignored by the classical liberal economists, and deemed a parasite by the Marxists, the woman in the home drew Borsodi's praise for her vast economic contribution through: cleaning and washing; cooking, baking, and serving foods; canning and preserving; butter-making, chicken-raising, and gardening; sewing and dressmaking; bearing, nursing, and raising babies; and teaching children.[20] All of these actions, he noted, generated important economic gains, and defined the working home. Using simple (but, as more recent work suggests, highly accurate) calculations, Borsodi showed that *even* in 1929-30, when industrialization was ubiquitous, the value of the food, clothing, and other goods and services produced by families exclusively for their own use nearly equaled the combined value of all factory-produced goods, all agricultural products offered for sale, and all the distribution services rendered by merchants. In short, the shadow, uncounted family economy was just as large as the money economy.[21]

The Family Crisis and the Homestead Renewed

Borsodi attributed the mounting family crisis of his age—fewer and later marriages, more divorces, plummeting fertility, and the disappearance of the three-generation household—exclusively to the economic distortions caused by the artificial dominance of modern industry and the progressive abandonment of the land. In *This Ugly Civilization*, he wrote:

Against the family...the factory wages a ruthless war of extermination....Industrialism seeks to root out individual devotion to the family and the homestead and to replace it with loyalty to the factory....The factory has pretty well succeeded in dissolving the family into its constituent parts and in transforming the individuals thus produced into malleable mobs who produce and consume, work and play, live and die, all for its glory.[22]

The factory system distorted the natural foundations of marriage, as well. The individual was "biologically incomplete," Borsodi wrote, "male or female halves of personality subject to an imperious mandate that we mate and consummate our beings in the reproduction of our own kind." Yet industrialized education delayed marriage and encouraged sexual promiscuity, so tending "to pervert our entire life."[23] Contacts between men and women in office or factory settings encouraged other rounds of nonmarital sex.

Problems became more acute among those who still managed somehow to marry, for the factory system had transformed children into "economic catastrophes," putting "a blight upon parenthood." A growing number avoided children altogether, and entered a lifetime of promiscuity. The others married late, and had few or no children, because a decent standard of living could be maintained only if they sacrificed their normal lives as mates and parents, and, "for all practical purposes," sterilized themselves. He added: "So we turn to contraception and even embrace abortion, with all its risks, rather than burden ourselves with the economic handicap of children."[24]

The "modern" family of two careers, fragile marriages, and few children was "manifestly abnormal," he concluded, the sad product of a dehumanizing order. Gone too were family dancing, folk singing, and native art, all "systematized out of existence," additional sacrifices to a coercively sustained, falsely justified system of centralized production.

The only solution to this social catastrophe, Borsodi insisted, was widespread decentralization *and* restoration of the working home. Ideally, this meant a return by as many as possible to small farms, the natural setting for family living. As he argued: "Man, no matter how often he has tried to urbanize himself, can only live *like a normal human being* in an essentially rural place of residence."[25] The commercialization of agriculture had upset the foundations of national life. Agriculture was a way of life, and "it is no more possible to treat agriculture as a business (without utter disregard of its intrinsic nature) than to treat art and religion in that manner."[26] While the isolated

American farm of 160-acres had clear advantages over the city, Borsodi favored the peasant-like village or rural community as more humane and satisfying. Family by family, community by community, people must "return to the land."[27] Where not wholly possible, the home must still be reconstructed as "an economically creative institution," reclaiming many of the functions already lost to industry. Each family must begin "an adventure in home production," rooted in "true organic homesteads...organized to function not only biologically and socially but also economically."[28] Gardens, chicken coops, a few cows and pigs, carpentry workshops, loom rooms: all were necessary in real family homes. When fully engaged in home production, the wife and mother could save more of her husband's salary through such activities than she could earn as an office worker.[29]

Turning to education, Borsodi recounted the experience of his family, after leaving the city. Finding the local rural school "impossible" for their two sons, he looked to his own wife and, "[w]hen I compared Mrs. Borsodi to the average school-teacher in the public schools, I saw no reason why she could not teach the children just as well, if not better." Working out an arrangement with the county school superintendent, the Borsodis simply brought their children home. Once again, their "experiment in domestic production" proved its superiority over a mass system of production. Two hours a day of course work, it turned out, was all it took for the Borsodi boys to keep pace with their public school counterparts, reflecting the great waste of time in group education. They also found that the remaining hours could be filled with reading and creative activities in the garden, the kitchen, and the workshop. Moreover, home schooling taught the Borsodis that true education "was really reciprocal; in the very effort to educate the boys, we educated ourselves."[30]

Out of these principles and lessons, Borsodi crafted a broad decentralist agenda, resting on his vision of a totally free market, a pure political and economic anarchy. He called for legislation to end the special tax breaks, subsidies, and public monopolies through which he believed economic centralization was able to survive. The special privileges for joint-stock corporations "must be changed into [a program] which will gradually eliminate *every* and *any* form of political interference with social and economic life."[31] Borsodi also believed that ordering economic life on a fair, level playing field would eliminate the social ills on which the welfare state rested: "Such grave problems as unemployment, old age, and mental and physical sickness...would cease to be major problems in a society in which the family, country life, and private property functioned effectively."[32]

Borsodi urged that capital be redirected into "home-making and home-producing channels." Building and loan associations, land and agricultural banks, and installment finance corporations needed to emerge to finance and build new homes, equipped with modern domestic machinery.[33] Widespread rural electrification and application of the electric motor and the compact gasoline engine to tasks would then make it possible "for local producers and private families to utilize the power which the steam-engine had restricted to the four walls of great factories."[34]

For the countryside, Borsodi looked not just to the spread of small homesteads, but to the virtual elimination of commercial farming. He argued that the average farm family of the 1930s was "farming too much." These "industrialized" farms, tied perilously to manipulated, insecure markets, should reduce their operations simply to meet their own needs, which Borsodi called "a comparatively easy road to follow." Meanwhile, the nonfarming family should farm or garden enough to supply itself with the essentials of life: "This is the road to economic freedom and economic freedom is essential to the conquest of comfort." As a rule of thumb, each family should produce two-thirds of its needed goods and services in the home or on the land owned by the family. Only one-third should be purchased. Borsodi held that animal husbandry and the care of pet animals were essential to "normal" existence: "Just as every family must surround itself with growing things, so it must equip itself with living things." Love, to be complete, required both human and animal objects, while the latter also furnished a "natural method" of introducing children to sexuality and birth and death.[35]

More than comfort and economic security were at stake here. Borsodi insisted that national survival and the preservation of liberty were in question as well. Industrialized families, with their reliance on "earning-and-buying," were shifting with ever greater frequency "the maintenance of their children, their aged, and even their mature members when unemployed or otherwise faced with misfortune" to government social agencies and public relief. The public school system took over "more and more of the burden" of raising their children: "it even furnishes them with their luncheons." The huge costs, waste, and inefficiencies of "this substitution of government for family maintenance" would, if not reversed, inevitably produce "fiscal disaster."[36]

Embracing an old agrarian theme, Borsodi also claimed that free democracy still rested on the autonomous homestead. The truly free person was not "merely the man who has the infinitesimal fraction of the political power represented by a vote." Rather, the free man was one "so independent" that he could "deal with all men and all institutions, even the State, on terms of equality." This agenda alone, he held, would allow humanity to escape from the modern tyranny of politicians, advertisers, and "even industrial engineers."[37]

He also insisted that this was the formula to restore the true democracy of the original American Republic, where the large majority of families were farmers and artisans, on rural homesteads of fair size, combining the crafts of field, shop, and household. Drawing on the work of historian Charles Beard, Borsodi emphasized how this community of families had provided food in abundance, built good and substantial houses, and crafted their own furniture and implements. Such a community had no state schools, but all its members could read and write, had books, and sustained academies for higher study through private donation. No one was rich; but no one was poor, and no member of this community ever doubted his or her access to all the food, clothing, and shelter necessary to life. All persons, both men and women, were artisans, and made their home products with joyful expression. In this life of self-sufficiency, they found security:

> It is a matter of incontestable historical fact that these families had, largely as a result of their own labor without the boasted advantages of contemporary technology or foreign trade, an abundance and variety of food stuff far beyond the budget of the overwhelming majority of American farming and laboring families today, and they enjoyed a continuing security in economy vouchsafed to none of the one-crop farmers and industrial workers in the contemporary order of things.[38]

Borsodi's vision was to restore this pre-industrial world, circa 1830, using the appropriate modern technologies to remove the drudgery while saving the essence of the good agrarian life. He ended *This Ugly Civilization* with a pleasant description of his goal: "A comfortable home in which to labor and to play, with trees and grass and flowers and skies and stars; a small garden; a few fruit trees; some fowls, some kine, some bees; and three big dogs to keep the salesmen out— and I, at least, have time for love, for children, for a few friends, and for the work I like to do."[39]

The School of Living

Borsodi recognized the great difficulties of rebuilding a world such as this. Under the regime of centralized industry, the continuity of persons educated to liberty had been broken. Whole American generations had been reared without knowledge of the ways to live in independence and family-centered security. Modern city dwellers, even if provided "with all the tools and implements which the Swiss Family Robinson providentially found," would in fact "die of exposure, of sickness, and of hunger" before they could use them, so "pathetic" was their dependence on factory-made necessities.[40] Borsodi concluded that men and women would have to be retrained to live in the new agrarian order. Accordingly, he retired as a consulting economist in 1933, and at the foot of the Ramapo Mountains, Borsodi created The School of Living. Built within the Bayard Lane Community, a private, restricted homestead cooperative, the School of Living sought to save civilization through re-education and practical research that would show "the scientific validity of decentralization."[41]

The School of Living operated through several departments. The Homemaking Division conducted elaborate tests of home production, particularly in the areas of cooking, preserving foods, and laundering. It issued scientific papers on the relative gains in efficiency found between home and factory production. The cultivation of kitchen gardens and training in the care of poultry and dairy animals came under the Agricultural Division. The Craft Division taught small-scale woodworking, furniture production, and home spinning and weaving for family use, while the Building Division offered training in the construction of a home. Finally, the Division of Applied Exchange studied the problems of independent small business and, through its *Newsletter of Small Business*, urged steps to decentralize "wasteful central industries." Frequent lectures "on the philosophy of the homestead way of life" featured Mr. Borsodi, himself. The School of Living offered four academic terms each year; "[y]oung couples planning for homes of their own are good prospects for entrance."[42]

The most complete expression of Borsodi's work appeared in 1948, under the title *Education and Living*. The volume summarized his philosophical and historical arguments, and included the results of years of applied research on the efficiency gains achieved through home production.

Education and Living also featured his most complete description of the Natural Family. In an explicit break with American liberal thought, Borsodi emphasized that a true democratic community rested on families, not on individuals; particularly on those families which owned a homestead and so contributed to the community's health and security. He stressed that the mid-twentieth-century "nuclear" or "companionate" family, composed of husband, wife, and two children, fell far short of the "natural" label. Normal living, Borsodi insisted, meant being a "corporate member" of a true family, defined to include three generations, tied to a hereditable estate, and bearing a corporate name, values, history, traditions, and customs.[43] The Natural Family must also be fully functional, in eleven distinct areas: maintenance for survival, meaning food and shelter; protection against the vicissitudes of life; the endowment of children, so they might start off with a leg up in life; the discipline of wayward family members; work or "the vocational function"; recreation for the revival of spirit; the provision of rest and recovery from exertion; education for character; "their sexual and genetic needs," or "the *eugenic* function"; their need for love; and their need for association. Any family which failed to fulfill *any* of these functions by transferring it to "business, school, church, or state" made itself "abnormal," and had fundamentally failed.[44] Unfortunately, several of the terms used in this list—specifically "eugenic" and "church"—betokened the more troubled aspects of his evolving philosophical scheme.

Common Agrarian Themes

A militantly independent thinker, Borsodi separated himself from some aspects of the Country Life campaign. Through his appreciation of household production, handicrafts, and the small village, Borsodi effectively endorsed the traditional peasant style of life. Indeed, he placed a modern, highly educated peasantry restored at the center of his own project. Unlike Liberty Hyde Bailey and the other Country Life progressives, Borsodi held a refreshing distrust of the state and of governmental solutions to moral problems. Indeed, he properly indicted government policy for aggravating and, in some respects, creating the current agrarian crisis. He insisted that social reconstruction of any sort would have to be the result of private endeavor, not state subsidy or coercion. Borsodi also brought to his philosophy an in-

formed and valuable emphasis on the economics of household production and a call for a new form of public accounting that fully recognized
the contribution of families to their own and to the public well-being.

Yet in other ways, Borsodi was firmly in the camp of the new
Agrarianism. These shared themes counted:

1. *Hostility to revealed religion in general, and American Christianity
in particular.* Where Bailey was cautious and often indirect in his
critique of the historic faiths, Borsodi was militantly atheistic. Modern
religion, he insisted, was part of the industrial problem, with churches
seeking to transfer to themselves the devotion that should go to the
homestead and with churchmen eager to create "mobs of herd-minded
worshippers." In *This Ugly Civilization*, Borsodi called religion (defined as "the theology of the various churches") a solace for the fearful, a habit for the unthinking, and an escape from the realities of life.
Religion was "nearly all snare and delusion," a collection of "pseudo-
answers" with little more than antiquity to recommend them. Borsodi
was brutally blunt: "Until we utterly and completely exorcise all religion
from our being; until we drop all fears, superstitions, rituals, [and] habits
which spring from religion, no true spiritual comfort is possible." Declaring that "we must be atheistic" in denying "any of the gods which man up
to the present time has evoked," the author specifically denounced the
Jehovah of the Old Testament and the "triune god of Father, Son and
Holy Ghost." He condemned the doctrine of immortality as "a crime
against the sacredness of this life," as well as the ideas of heaven and
hell, the Ten Commandments, and even the moral law.[45] He concluded
that if "we must have the psychic release of genuine religious experience," then it would be best to "devise a new worship of the *lares* and
penates—of the spirit of the home, the family and the fireside," things
"at least...worthy of consecration at our hands."[46]

Borsodi's views on religion appear to have derived from his own
devotion to the work of the post-Christian philosopher Friedrich
Nietzsche. Direct quotations from the German nihilist laced *This Ugly
Civilization* (e.g., "There is no sorer misfortune in all human destiny,
than when the mighty of the earth are not also the first men"[47]), as did
indirect incantations of "the superior man," "moral values of our own
devising," and "the transvaluation of values," the Nietzchean means
by which Borsodi would construct a new order.

2. *The farmer and the farm family must be re-engineered.* While un-
willing to use government as his tool of social reconstruction, Borsodi

was not going to leave agricultural America alone. He summoned the "superior men" who had shaken free of the old religions to challenge and defeat "the ruthless, acquisitive and powerful types" who now ran things, and then go on to build a new civilization. Existing farm families were "farming too much" while everyone else was "farming too little." Superior men would guide both groups to the proper mean. The whole of American life had been corrupted, not only by factories but by false traditions of much greater age. All would have to be swept away. But that would just be the beginning, for "the only convention to which we who aspire to the superior life can freely commit ourselves is the convention of perpetually revaluing all the customs, traditions, and ideas which we adopt." This was the "adventure in the transvaluation of values," a task fit only to "sensitive non-conformists."[48]

In *Education and Living*, he spelled out quite precisely what the end should be. If a community was "to justify its existence," merit the devotion of its members, and "make them cheerfully willing to sacrifice time and money for its support," then "it needs the leadership of a genuine *elite*...,a *nobility*. It needs...*quality-minded people* to lead and inspire it; it needs *quantity-minded* people to administer its enterprises and institutions; and it needs *common people* if its work is to be done."[49] In place of a flawed and false democracy, Borsodi would create a class-oriented, elite-driven human order composed of three classes: the intellectual nobility; managers; and a mass of simple workers.

3. Education must be guided by enlightened experts. While crafting a powerful case for the decentralization of virtually every aspect of human life, and while in some ways actually the "discoverer" or "inventor" of modern home schooling, Borsodi betrayed both principle and experience on this crucial point of his argument. Instead of calling for the broad application of home schooling at all levels and by all people, he became fixated on the School of Living idea. He appears to have concluded that not every family could do what the Borsodis had done, that home education was only for the children of the "quality-minded." Instead of a "church-centered, bank-centered, government centered" *and* family-centered society, Borsodi wanted "a school-centered and university-centered society."[50] The intellectual nobility must teach the "quantity minded" and the "common." These views appear to be a consequence of his Nietzchean reliance on "superior men," who would control education in a rightly ordered land. As he explained in *This Ugly Civilization*: "In a society in which the press, the stage, and *the class-room* were controlled by the quality-minded, leviathan would be reduced to normal dimensions."[51] Or as he wrote later, civilization could be saved "only...if dedicated educators take the lead in saving it."[52]

4. *Technological innovation is friendly to the family homestead.* More so than for any other modern Agrarian, this was a primary truth for Borsodi. The whole of his experimental investigations at the School of Living and the central thrust of his interpretation of history were to underscore the artificially sustained dominance of the big factory and "the revolutionary cultural potentialities of cheap, flexible, and small unit power."[53] While the technologies of 150 years ago, focused on steam, favored the factory, all innovations since worked to the benefit of small-scale producers. If government favoritism for the old and the large could only be overcome, he anticipated that the technological future would be the same, and favorable to the productive homestead.

5. *Decentralization is the natural future.* This, again, was a central belief for Borsodi, one shared with Bailey and Zimmerman, but held by the first all the more firmly. Absent government regulation, subsidy, and intervention, Borsodi insisted that economic forces would naturally push toward the decentralization of society. Small communities, small shops, small farms, and large families would thrive.

From Prophet to Crank

During the 1930s, Borsodi's reputation and influence grew large. His major work, *This Ugly Civilization,* had appeared in 1928. As the Great Depression settled over America during the next five years, Borsodi's indictment of industrial civilization gained wide attention as accurate prophecy. His books drew extravagant praise in the *New York Times*, the *New Republic*, the *Nation*, and other leading periodicals. From the *Cincinnati Enquirer* came this not atypical review of *Flight from the City*: "The most heartening book we have ever read, bar none! Points out a means of adopting a way of life for which most readers have longed hopelessly." When the federal government created the Division of Subsistence Homesteads in 1933 as a New Deal response to the Depression, an early grant went to a thirty-five-home project in Dayton, Ohio. The local organizers had already called in Ralph Borsodi as consulting economist to guide the effort. He immediately set out to create productive homes, involving gardens, looms, handicrafts, and "education." Although obstructions from Washington, DC bureaucrats led to his angry resignation after only a year, Borsodi's views seemed at once avant garde and prescient.[54] After learning how to forego his denunciations of Judaism and Christianity, he became a leader of efforts during the mid- and late-1930s to unify the Agrarian movement (see chapter 6). He was one of the few Agrarians, moreover, who could claim to have a national following. Uncounted thousands of Americans reordered their lives as part of the Borsodi Homestead movement, and returned to the land, committed to gardening, weaving, wood working, animal husbandry, children, and the three-generation family.

By the late 1940s, however, Borsodi was "drifting." His School of Living had shut down earlier in the decade, and financial pressures and managerial problems led Borsodi to sell the facility. His wife died in 1948, and he was soon "moving about the country and visiting with old friends." A new opportunity came up when three women instrumental in the 1933 Dayton project—Virginia Wood, Elizabeth Nutting, and Margaret Hutchison—purchased land in Florida to build a Borsodi-styled community. Incorporated as the American Homesteading Foundation, they established Melbourne Village, featuring homesteads with subsistence gardens, handicrafts, and other forms of "production for use." Borsodi arrived in 1949 as the philosopher-in-residence (one subsequent village news release would promote "'Borsodics'—Gems of Wisdom from 'The Brain'"), and soon embroiled himself in contentious debates within the village.

Like other secular attempts in constructing a homestead community, this one had a relatively short and troubled life. After a promising start, subsistence gardens grew ever smaller or disappeared as the years passed and all of the community home production projects—ranging from a handicraft store to the sale of goats milk and earthworms, to hydroponic gardens, to the Craft Guild—failed, victims of undercapitalization, mismanagement, or both. In 1953-54, Borsodi created the University of Melbourne. He proved his wide connections by building a visiting faculty that counted Charles Malik (former secretary general of the United Nations), Stuart Chase, Norman Cousins, Harry Elmer Barnes, Paul Tillich, Robert Maynard Hutchins, Lewis Mumford, and Louis Bromfield. But financing became a fiasco, only one full-time student enrolled, and the University soon degenerated into a lecture series (as historian Richard

Crepeau notes, "Borsodi was planning to have the students build the dormitories, but there were no students").[55]

Borsodi also drifted onto ever-more dangerous intellectual ground. In *Education and Living* (1949), his belief in a good society composed of three classes—the "quality minded" elite, the "quantity minded" administrators, and the "common people" who work—led him openly to advocate eugenics and euthanasia. Just as American eugenicists were abandoning the label in the wake of publicity on Nazi atrocities in Germany, Borsodi wrote:

> Normalization of the population of the community calls for eugenic breeding....Sterilization...also means the gradual elimination—by death, by what I call necrosis—of existing undersirable individuals and families....For those who cannot be taught [voluntary contraception]—the moronic and the psychotic—compulsory sterilization is called for....[Among] the growing proportion of the feeble-minded and other undesirable elements in the population requiring institutionalization, euthanasia is called for.[56]

In the mid-1950s, Borsodi's lectures in Melbourne Village began to involve discussions of "superior" and "inferior" races, and the perils of miscegenation.[57]

A majority of residents, moreover, were growing uncomfortable with the whole Borsodi influence. Early villagers tended to be disciples: curiously, they were usually unmarried women and childless couples. Crepeau reports that few of the married women who became members of the village even described themselves as housewives, despite Borsodi's open celebration of the task. Many were social workers. Some were activist Quakers. Later settlers, though, tended to be young newlyweds simply looking for a cheap place to build a home in an attractive locale. As early as 1951, the now reborn and relocated School of Living featured a debate on: "Should the Direction of the Community Be Shifted From the Original Idea of Homesteading to a Suburban Community?" Then, the answer was "no." By 1957, it had shifted to "yes," and Borsodi left for a lecture trip to India, never to return to Melbourne Village.[58]

So he began as prophet, and ended as crank, run off by the triumphant surburbanites. Combining profound insights into the nature of the family and the economy with a fierce hatred of revealed faith and an anti-democratic view of human society, Borsodi reinforced several of the more striking premises of the New Agrarianism, some for good and others for ill.

Notes

1. From: Ralph Borosodi, *Inflation Is Coming! A Practical Post-War Plan* (New York: Bayard Lane, Inc., 1945): 39-40.
2. From: William H. Issel, "Ralph Borsodi and the Agrarian Response to Modern America," *Agricultural History* 41 (April 1967): 156.
3. From: Richard C. Crepeau, *Melbourne Village: The First Twenty-Five Years* (1946-1971) (Orlando: University of Central Florida Press, 1988): 59-60.
4. From Ralph Borsodi, *Flight From the City* (New York: Harper and Brothers, 1933; 1935): 10.
5. Borsodi, *Flight From The City*, p. 15.
6. Borsodi, *The Distribution Age: A Study of the Economy of Modern Distribution* (New York: D. Appleton and Co., 1929): 153-54.
7. Borsodi, *The Distribution Age*, p. 310.
8. See: Ralph Borsodi, *Prosperity and Security: A Study in Realistic Economics* (New York and London: Harper and Brothers, 1938): 27-28, 30, 70, 97.
9. Borsodi, "Decentralization [Part II]," *Free America* 2 (February, 1938): 10.
10. Borsodi, *This Ugly Civilization*, pp. 14-15.
11. Borsodi, *Prosperity and Security*, p. 172.
12. Borsodi, *This Ugly Civilization* (New York: Simon and Schuster, 1928): 13-15.
13. Borsodi, "Decentralization [II]," p. 11.
14. Borsodi, *Prosperity and Security*, pp. 182-83.
15. Borsodi, "Decentralization [Part I]," *Free America* 2 (January 1938): 12.
16. Borsodi, *This Ugly Civilization*, pp. 195-197.
17. Borsodi, *Prosperity and Security*, p. 171.
18. Borsodi, "Family or Factory?" *Free America* 2 (November 1938): 3.
19. Borsodi, *Prosperity and Security*, p. 81.
20. Ibid., p. 153.
21. Borsodi, *Prosperity and Security*, p. 89. Sixty years later, a very sophisticated analysis of home production in the Australian economy produced exactly the same result: "home production" roughly equalled the official economy. See: Duncan Ironmonger, "The Domestic Economy: $340 Billion of G.H.P.," in B. Muehlenberg, ed., *The Family: There is No Other Way* (Melbourne: Australian Family Association, 1996): 132-146.
22. Borsodi, *This Ugly Civilization*, p. 417.
23. Ibid., pp. 416-417.
24. Ibid., p. 416.
25. Borsodi, *Education and Living* (New York: Devin-Adair Company, 1948): 550. Emphasis added.
26. Ralph Borsodi, "A Plan for Rural Life," in *Agriculture in Modern Life*, ed. O.E. Baker (New York: Harper & Bros., 1939): 189.
27. Ralph Borsodi, *The Time Has Come* (Suffern, NY: School of Living, 1942): 13.
28. Borsodi, *This Ugly Civilization*, p. 328.
29. See: John Chamberlain, "Borsodi and the Chesterbelloc," *New Republic* 52 (Jan. 1, 1940): 13-16.
30. Borsodi, *Flight from the City*, pp. 83-95.
31. Borsodi, "Decentralization (II)," p. 12.
32. Ibid.
33. Borsodi, *This Ugly Civilization*, pp. 285-86.
34. Borsodi, *Prosperity and Security*, p. 182.

35. Borsodi, *This Ugly Civilization*, pp. 282-83; and Borsodi, *Education and Living*, p. 540.
36. Borsodi, *Education and Living*, p. 436.
37. Ralph Borsodi, *The Time Has Come*, pp. 14-15.
38. Quoted in Borsodi, *Prosperity and Security*, p. 116; from Beard's *The Open Door*.
39. Ibid., p. 462.
40. Borsodi, *This Ugly Civilization*, p. 283.
41. Borsodi, *Education and Living*, p. ix.
42. From: George Weller, "America's First School of Living," *Free America* 2 (July 1938): 7-9.
43. Borsodi, *Education and Living*, pp. 411-15, 420-21, 638.
44. Borsodi, *Education and Living*, p. 435.
45. Borsodi, *This Ugly Civilization*, pp. 417, 420-427, 440-441.
46. Ibid., p. 429.
47. Ibid., p. 4.
48. Ibid., pp. 452-456.
49. Borsodi, *Education and Living*, p. 645.
50. Borsodi, *The Time Has Come*, p. 4.
51. Borsodi, *Education and Living*, p.437..
52. Borsodi, *Education and Living*, p. xiii.
53. Ibid., p. 288.
54. See: Ralph Borsodi, "Dayton, Ohio, Makes Social History," *Nation* (April 19, 1933): 448; Catharine Baur, "The Swiss Family Borsodi," *Nation* (Oct. 25, 1933): 489-491; Jacob Dorn, "Subsistence Homesteading in Dayton, Ohio, 1933-1935," *Ohio History* 78 (1969): 75-93; and Issel, "Ralph Borsodi, pp. 159-164.
55. Crepeau, *Melbourne Village*, p. 118.
56. Borsodi, *Education and Living*, p. 649.
57. Crepeau, *Melbourne Village*, p. 117.
58. Ibid., pp. 118-119.

4

The Jeffersonian Restoration of Louis Bromfield

The dehumanizing animus of the machine, the perversions of urban industrial life; and haunting religious themes animated the fiction of the Ohio agrarian writer, Louis Bromfield. These could be found with characteristic force in his first novel, *The Green Bay Tree*:

> The [furnace] structure bore a strange resemblance to the Tower of Babel. Swarthy workmen, swarming over the mass of concrete and steel, shouted to each other above the din of the Mills in barbaric tongues....

> "Yesterday," shouted William Harrison, in his thin voice, "there was a terrible accident yonder in the other yard. A workman fell into a vat of molten iron....They found nothing of him. He became a part of the iron. He is part of a steel girder by now."[1]

Winner of the Pulitzer Prize in 1926 for his third novel, *Early Autumn*, the author of over twenty best-selling fictional works, and by 1950 properly called "America's most famous farmer" residing on "America's best known farm," Bromfield is today "the forgotten author."[2] Both his successes and his ultimate failure cut to the heart of the New Agrarian dilemma. Growing up sometimes as townsman and sometimes as countryman, Bromfield wrestled for most of his life with the implications of America's rural crisis. That he was a philosophical agrarian and decentralist for the bulk of his literary career, there can be no doubt. As an agriculture student at Cornell, he met and developed a life long admiration for Liberty Hyde Bailey. In his "farm" book, *Pleasant Valley*, Bromfield summarized the case for agrarian fundamentalism: "This book is a personal testament written out of a lifetime by a man who believes that agriculture is the keystone of our economic structure, and that the wealth, welfare, prosperity, and even the future freedom of this nation are based upon the soil." His fiction also sparkled with vivid images of agrarian life, as in this passage from the novella, *Kenny*:

> As [Vincent] and the big black bull moved toward us, the geese, squawking, hissing, and flapping their wings, moved out of the way and I was aware of one of those swift and sudden moments of beauty and satisfaction which are a part of life on a farm. It was a moment which, curiously, went backward into time,...back indeed to the pastoral beginnings of man's civilization.[3]

He also understood how pride in rural independence translated into the details of farm living:

> The vegetable-garden was of the greatest importance. Out of it came not only all the vegetables for the summer, but for the winter as well, for Maria would have considered it a disgrace to have bought food of any sort. It had been part of the Colonel's dream that his farm should be a world of its own, independent and complete, and his daughter carried on his tradition. The Farm supported a great household that was always varying in size, and in winter the vegetables came from the fruit-house or from the glass jars neatly ticketed and placed in rows on shelves in the big cellar.[4]

Bromfield would abandon this faith in rural democracy and self-sufficiency only when he simultaneously ceased to write fiction and made his peace with machine and science.

Town and Country

Born in Mansfield, Ohio on December 27, 1896 as Lewis Brumfield,[5] his arrival was cast as something of a miracle. His mother, nee Annette Coulter (a family name that would, by coincidence, figure prominently in the fiction of Wendell Berry), had been told that she could bear no additional children and that her distended abdomen was the consequence of a tumor. The child's appearance convinced her that he would live an extraordinary life. A strong woman reared on a farm (although loathing the agricultural life), Annette or "Nettie" resolved early on that her son would pursue a literary career. She turned his whole education toward this end, immersing him in great fiction at a very early age.[6] His father, Charlie Brumfield, was a real estate agent, small-town politician, and rural romantic, usually just one step ahead of his creditors. Mansfield, itself, was in the midst of a transition from a farming center to heavy industry, subject as well to new waves of immigration from Eastern and Southern Europe. "The Town" in the throes of change would form the setting for many later volumes, including *The Green Bay Tree* and *A Good Woman*.

In 1914, Bromfield set off at his father's bidding to begin study of "scientific farming" at Cornell, by then established as America's leading agricultural school. While he stayed in Ithaca only one term, the outgoing freshman befriended the chairman of the English Department and managed at least one conversation with the already legendary, and recently retired, Liberty Hyde Bailey. The influence of the latter was "incalculable, but probably great,"[7] and Bromfield in his nonfiction would quote frequently and favorably from the sage's work, particularly *The Holy Earth*.[8]

Short on money, and with his parents resolved to return to the old Coulter Farm, Bromfield left Cornell in early 1915. For a year-and-a-half, he engaged in full-time farming. The venture was doomed at the outset, it appears: the land too worn out, the capital unavailable, prices too low, and the reliable neighbors too few. As Bromfield would later explain in his semi-autobiographical novel, *The Farm*: "Johnny [a.k.a. Bromfield] fought stubbornly, even after his father knew that the whole venture had been a hopeless impractical dream....But there were moments when he was seized by an insane recklessness and a desire to run away forever."[9] As he would tell it, the end came on an October day when, pulling up a team of horses in the barnyard, Bromfield heard a new sound, from miles away: "a dull, rhythmic, muffled sound, measured and monotonous." It came from the new rolling mills, "pounding out shells" to be sent to the war in France: "He felt a sudden sickness, and at the same time he knew that it was all over and that the Farm was finished. How could one any longer be a farmer with the sound of factories in your ears day and night forever?"[10]

In 1917, Bromfield enlisted in the U.S. Army Ambulance Service. He was attached to the French Army in the Section Sanitaire Americain as a driver and interpreter. Involved in seven major battles, Bromfield received the Croix de Guerre from the French government. On discharge, he spent time in Paris, then returned to New York, where for six years he served as a journalist, editor, and publicist. During this time, he met and married the New York socialite, Mary Appleton. His first book, *The Green Bay Tree*, appeared in 1924, followed by *Possession* a year later. Immediate critical and financial successes, the books' royalties allowed him to leave his administrative post at G.P. Putnam's Sons for an "extended vacation" in France. Bromfield stayed there for thirteen years, eventually leasing a *presbytere* in Senlis, sixty miles north of Paris, as his principal residence. Absorbed into the vibrant émigré literary circles of France, he developed an especially strong friendship with Gertrude Stein. However, he never saw himself as an expatriate. Instead, he believed that America had come of age, and was now duty bound to send its culture and experience to Europe.[11] By the early 1930s, Bromfield devoted much of his nonwriting time to his extensive garden at Senlis. He cultivated many friendships among the peasants and villagers as well and, to his great joy, received an honorary membership in the Workingmen-Gardeners Association of France and a medal from the French Ministry of Agriculture for introducing Hubbard squash and American corn to the region.[12]

The Early Fiction

Bromfield's first three books formed a trilogy, offering in their entirety a distinct interpretation of American history. Behind each story lay pioneer ancestors, strong of will and limb, who had settled a wilderness and forged an agrarian republic. But their children and, most especially, their grandchildren faced the more difficult challenges. As the elderly Julia Shane would explain in a famed passage from *The Green Bay Tree*:

> Life is hard for our children. It isn't as simple as it was for us. Their grandfathers were pioneers and the same blood runs in their veins, only they haven't a frontier any longer. They stand...these children of ours...with their backs toward this rough-hewn middle west and their faces set toward Europe and the East and they belong to neither. They are lost somewhere between.[13]

The most grievous challenge, in Bromfield's mind, came from industrialization, the war of the machine against human-scale community. In these early works, Bromfield identified the human enemy as the new middle class, symbolized by Rotary Clubs, chambers of commerce, and the Episcopalian Church. Opposing it was a strange alliance between the more vigorous descendents of the old settlers and the fiery leaders of "the dark people," those immigrants crowded into the new urban slums that circled the factories.

Fertility became an overarching theme. Bromfield contrasted the pitiable remnants "of a family whose founder had crossed the

Appalachians...to convert the wilderness into fertile farming land" with the superabundance of children found among the new immigrants.[14] In *Early Autumn*, the childless heroine, tempted by adultery, "wanted suddenly, fiercely to take part in all the great spectacle of eternal fertility, a mystery that was stronger than any of them or all of them together, a force which in the end would crush all their transient little prides and beliefs and traditions."[15] Bromfield also contrasted the voluptuous fertility and the "lush smell of damp growing things" with the products of factories: noxious gasses and poisoned ground.[16]

Female characters stood out in all of Bromfield's work, a probable legacy from his mother. With few exceptions, his men were weak or thinly drawn. But the women were robust, vital, iconoclastic, the true shapers of destiny. In *The Green Bay Tree*, the heroine was Lily Shane, the daughter of a Scotch farmer, whose beauty was that "of a peasant girl from which all coarseness had been eliminated, leaving only a radiant glow of health."[17] Hardly conventional (she bore an illegitimate child after a tryst with the governor of Ohio, a thinly fictionalized Warren G. Harding, and later became mistress to a French cavalry officer), she warred against the brutality of factory civilization, befriended the immigrant Ukrainian revolutionary Krylenko, and defended a key bridge in a World War I battle to save Paris from the murderous, machine-like Germans. In *Possession*, the heroine is Ellen Tolliver (very loosely based on Bromfield's older sister), who ruthlessly climbed from her Ohio origins to become a world-renowned concert pianist.[18] Olivia Pentland dominated the pages of *Early Autumn*, struggling between the powerful pull of fertility and the need to accommodate duty and responsibility to the past.

The same themes resurfaced, albeit more intensely, in his next volume, *A Good Woman*. Set in both East Africa and Ohio, it was largely a story of powerful women. Some, such as Lady Millicent in Africa and Emma Downes in Ohio, dominated the men in their lives for their own ends. At the volume's close, most of the characters were dead or ruined, with only Emma Downes left, marrying the local congressman, and soon a national leader "of a dozen committees and movements against whiskey and cigarettes, and for Sunday closing." Others, such as Aunt Mabelle, found their power in reproduction. According to the author, she was "born" to have children, with a baby's cry "stifled at once by opening the straining bombazine of her bosom and releasing the fountain of life."[19]

Indeed, fertility was again an overriding motif. Out in the Christian missions of Africa, Bromfield wrote, "[i]t was impossible to exist unchanged...among black people who lived with the simplicity of animals and held obscene festivals dedicated to unmentionable gods of fertility." This power of nature even swept over those characters who did not desire offspring: "It took not account of the fact that [Phillip] had never loved Naomi, or that neither of them had really wanted these children. *Nature* had wanted children, and it did not matter how they were created, so long as the act of creation occurred."[20]

A Good Woman also embraced a much more overt treatment of religion than his earlier books. On the one hand, the Protestant faith of the Ohio missionaries was cast as at war with nature and abundance, with Aunt Mabelle's artificially restricted fertility as consequence: "Married to another man she would undoubtedly have had ten or fifteen children." Bromfield concluded that Protestantism, in fact, was now dead to the world, an irrelevancy. One of the returning missionaries found perverse new truth in the factories: "The spectacle beneath him became alive with a tremendous sense of vitality and force that he had not found in all his mystical groping toward God." Others found God in the marching of the African virgins: "those black women pouring the water of the burning lake over the belly of an obscene idol—a God concerned with the whole growing spectacle of living."[21]

The co-mingling of strong women, natural fertility, and religious decadence surfaced most strongly in Bromfield's next book, *The Strange Case of Miss Annie Spragg* (1928). Late in his life, he would tell colleague Russell Lord that of the over twenty novels he had written, there were only two that he cared to re-read: *The Farm* and *Annie Spragg*.[22] The latter was a peculiar, tightly woven story, set off by two simultaneous events: the appearance of the Stigmata, or the marks of the Cross, on the body of Miss Annie Spragg, an elderly American émigré living in an Italian village; and the uncovering of an ancient Roman statue, one that had "a kind of quivering voluptuousness...a glorification of sensuality....No one could have remained entirely chaste after looking upon the statue."[23]

Religious figures populated the story, ranging from the duped to the cynical to the amusing to the corrupt. There was Father Fulco Baldessare, a simple Catholic priest who left the Church to become a reformer, "to purify Christianity...all over again," only to die at the hands of fascist thugs for preaching primitive Christian communism.

Or the charming Father d'Astier, whose mission for the church "was to convert the rich who married impoverished titles" and to bring to grace "any others of considerable wealth who felt a leaning toward Rome." Or the rich American widow, Henrietta Weatherby, the "experimenter of many faiths." Or the father of Annie Spragg, The Prophet, who had a revelation "that it was through his seed that the world would be redeemed and that all his children" were the authentic children of God: "It became a great honor for any woman to be chosen as the mother of God's children."[24] Bromfield wove their stories into a celebration of natural, exuberant life, triumphant over the corruptions of churches and theologies.

In several volumes which followed, Bromfield explored further the corruptions of the city, the salvific power of fertility, and the authority of Nature.[25] These themes fed into his most famous, most widely regarded, and most explicitly agrarian work of fiction, *The Farm*, published in 1933.

The Farm and After

Written at the same time as his retreat to the gardens of Senlis, *The Farm* reflects a weariness with the European literary scene and the continued enervating drift of the Continent. Bromfield turned instead to the American Midwest, to the saga of its frontier, and to his own family history as prototype of what had succeeded, and failed, in American life.

It is the semi-autobiographical story of the building of a family farm in Ohio's Midland County. It began in the early nineteenth-century as the project of "the Colonel," who left Maryland to settle in the Western Reserve. On arrival, he befriended Father Duchesne, bearer of the French Catholic civilization now in retreat. In those early days, the Colonel also met Silas Bentham, a trader from Massachusetts. The book evolved over the chapters into a contest between two visions for the new territory: the Colonel's Jeffersonian dream of a landscape of independent, self-sufficient farms; and Bentham's Hamiltonian quest for a commercial republic, a land of trade and industrial production.[26] The Colonel's daughter, Maria, married a hired man, Jamie Ferguson, who succeeded as master of the house, and who became grandfather to Johnny, Bromfield's fictional persona. In its prime, under the direction of Old Jamie and Maria, the Farm was a cornucopia. The breakfasts alone at Sunday gatherings were munificent: "sausages, waffles, and maple syrup from Jamie's own maple-grove, fresh strawberries or peaches if it were summer... hot fresh rolls, and sometimes chicken and mashed potatoes, home-dried corn, and an array of jams and preserves." All of this came from the Farm itself, and it marked but the beginning of "a day spent in high feasting," "a festival given over to plenty," one blessed by Old Jamie's prayers "to the Deity of plenty." Maria presided over the day as "a kind of priestess," watching happily as all her children and grandchildren consumed what she had grown and prepared.[27]

Yet the city, through its tentacles of trade, reached out and slowly strangled the Jeffersonian dream of Old Jamie. Price fluctuations and the entanglements of credit sucked away the material life of the farms. Riding in a buggy with his grandfather, circa 1905, Johnny "did not know...that not one of the farms along the way...was what it had been during [Old Jamie's] youth and middle age. Johnny never saw that some of the houses were in need of paint and that here and there a fence had been patched once too often. Nor did he notice that there were almost no young people and that as soon as the children grew up they disappeared." Nor could he see the mortgages, the falling prices for cattle and grain, and the rising costs of farm machinery and all the other things made and marketed by businessmen. Pressed ever tighter, the farmers cut corners, farmed less well, and drained the soil of its fertility. Independent yeoman became frail tenants. New immigrants appeared, "dark people," a "race apart," none of whom "could have fitted into the Colonel's dream of an agricultural democracy." Eventually, Old Jamie passed the farm on to his son and grandson, Johnny, who resolved to return. "They meant to show the County that it was still possible to live on the land and have a life that was good, comfortable and even rich." But they did not know that aside from "a little band of hard-working scientists [e.g., L.H. Bailey], harassed and handicapped by politicians," no one—least of all a government owned outright by the businessmen—had any concern for the well-being of farmers. In the end, "the peddler had won," leaving "a whole nation debauched by the mean instincts of the unscrupulous village shopkeeper," and Johnny knowing the bitterest of personal defeats.[28]

Bromfield so cast his own family history as a metaphor for the rise and fall of the Agrarian republic. He closed the book by recounting a plan to move the remains of his great-grandparents to the Town cemetery. But he found that there was nothing to move: "By now the

Colonel and the giddy Susan were a part of the earth, like the arrow-heads and the glacial boulders which long ago his great-grandchildren had scattered once more over the land from which they came."[29]

Bromfield's search for a way out of this end carried him, curiously, to India. Departing only weeks after finishing the manuscript for *The Farm*, the author found in the subcontinent a wondrous landscape of isolated villages and self-sufficient agriculture and a promising new adventure in nation-building, and he began work on another novel. Four and a half years in the writing, *The Rains Came* appeared in 1937. It was probably Bromfield's most carefully crafted work, with a strong plot, splendid characters, and a melodramatic yet believable resolution.[30] Familiar elements were present. Frequent passages wove in the theme of lush, exuberant fertility, both human and vegetable, across the subcontinent: "The palace belonged there, in India, with all its extravagance and disorder, as if it had been born in India herself out of an excess of vitality."[31] The reader also found the strong women favored by the author, in this case brought to a kind of perfection in the characters of the Maharani of Ranjipur and the Iowa-born teacher, Phoebe Smiley.

The juxtaposition of these two women was no accident, for the book was actually as much about America as India. Through the eyes of the untouchable leader, Jobnekar, Bromfield described "the simplicity and honesty and friendliness of Aunt Phoebe," traits still found "in the center of America," but "never" in the Eastern states. Yet Aunt Phoebe knew that even in the Midwest, these virtues were a vanishing thing, one of the reasons for her coming to India: "In her heart she couldn't bear to stay on there in Iowa watching the old life she had loved drooping and dying." The dissolute British-American hero, Tom Ransome, also was running away from an America with "no faith...save in the automobile factory and the stock market."[32]

The novel reached its climax when the great Ranchipur Dam, the product of Western technological skill, collapsed under the stress of a tropical rain. In this tragedy, though, Bromfield found new hope: "The dam had been in a way a kind of symbol—the symbol of Oriental faith in Occidental practical achievement and honesty, organization and superiority, a faith which like the dam had long since cracked and fallen."[33] "Builders" appeared—Major Safti, the fanatical Colonel Moti—who turned the crisis into an opportunity to start again, to create a new human community out of the ruins of the past.

While a less technically satisfying work, with weaker characters and an unlikely plot, Bromfield's 1941 novel, *Wild is the River,* carried the same themes. Set in New Orleans during the Civil War, the novel read the Jeffersonian-Hamiltonian contest into the very nature of the conflict. Slavery was not the issue, Bromfield insisted; it was a war between shopkeepers and farmers, "between the landowners of the South and the factory owners of the North...between two kinds of civilization." The Confederate officer, Hector MacTavish, hated the occupiers with "the contempt of the man who lives on his own land for the men who kept shop, a contempt as old as time." The Northern general, David Wicks, ruled "like a Hun chieftain over the civilized Louisiana city." Yankee "Liberators" seized a Plantation home, and held "a kind of witches ball...with field hands and mulatto girls and Union soldiers dancing without pattern or reason in a wild orgy of rum and music." The "horse-faced" Aunt Tam represented the "intellectual" side of the conquerors, always "too busy with ideas ever to touch and penetrate the beautiful simplicity of reality."[34]

Indeed, the physical setting for *Wild is the River* was as much India as Louisiana Bayou. "[H]eat and voluptuousness and fertility" were complemented by the natural sexuality of the Voodoo House, where "the octoroon girl made no move to put on any clothing but stood, naked and unconcerned near the fire drinking rum from a rusty tin cup with the air of a wild and beautiful animal."[35] The "smell of fertility" pervaded the very earth, the air, and the vast swamps.

Out of this surreal world, Captain MacTavish emerged as the Jeffersonian hero: "At heart he was a reformer, a builder, a colonizer, a creator. He wanted always to change things, to alter them for the better." Above all, he believed that a "young man should love his wife and breed children," for both the delights of sensuality and the need for "strong sons and daughters" to carry on the project started by "his own imagination and ambition." He gathered a rebellious Agnes Wicks, daughter of the general and his wife to be, her Yankee aunt, his mother and sisters, black Cesar and his family, and the Creole Chauvin Boisclair, to go west to a new place, "a wide green valley, all ours for the taking," to build a new home, "a whole village...a growing village."[36]

From *Pleasant Valley* to the New Agriculture

These renderings of renewal were the fictional product of Bromfield's own resolve to try the Jeffersonian experiment once more, his desire to find "a piece of land which I could love passionately, which I could spend the rest of my life in cultivating, cherishing and improving, which I might leave together, perhaps, with my own feeling for it, to my children who might in time leave it to their children."[37] Where the Colonel and Old Jamie, in a sense, had failed, Bromfield was moved to start fresh in building a "self sufficient" farm, a new "community," this time using "scientific methods" to avoid the errors and fate of "The Farm."

With war descending over Europe, Bromfield left Senlis in 1938 and brought his wife and three daughters back to America. He journeyed out to Ohio and, not far from the old Coulter homestead, purchased three contiguous farms. In honor of his epiphany in India, he named the combined homestead of over 700 acres Malabar Farm.

The course of his experiment would be described in a series of volumes, collectively dubbed the "farm books." The first of these was *Pleasant Valley*, published in 1945. It remains an immensely satisfying agrarian tract, one he readily labeled "romantic," the story of his vision in the early years. At the level of his own farm, Bromfield wanted to create a self-sufficient agricultural mecca, an association of families working in cooperation, a community that would lure others back to the land. He wrote that out of the "single crop" system, the "laxness" of farmers and their wives, and mechanization had grown an abuse at the core of "the sickness of our agriculture": "[t]he old economic independence of the farmer, his sense of security, that stability which a healthy agriculture gives to the economy of any nation has broken down." A sign of that breakdown "was the farmer's dependence upon things which he purchased rather than producing these same things off his own land."[38] Another sickness of American agriculture was the disappearance "of the family-sized farm" and its replacement by "great mechanized farms." At Malabar, he concluded, they would find "a way to operate a big farm without displacing families."[39]

On the national scale, he held that "a good deal more than half our population" must acquire the material independence born out of self-sufficiency in food production, if Americans were to know security as a nation.[40] This would require a massive counter-migration. But the stakes were high. Americans, in their "wild industrial development," had tended to forget "that agriculture is the base of our whole economy," the "cornerstone" of economic health. "It has always been so throughout history and it will continue to be so until there are no more men on this earth." Self-sufficient farms were the source of social and political progress for the nation, as well. Seldom, Bromfield said, did great leaders emerge from city slums or suburbs. They were almost always products of a farm.[41]

The most charming section of the book was Bromfield's careful delineation of "the Plan," the stages by which he and chief partner Max Drake would transform the old fields and run down buildings into a model agrarian community. A "Big House" would be built as well, in the "purest Jefferson Greek revival" style, reflecting "the simplicity and dignity" which characterized that great Agrarian.[42]

But while the house was built, the rest of the agrarian dream did not survive the decade. A very different mood animated the volume, *Malabar Farm*, published in 1948. With little embarrassment, the author admitted that his goals of "diversified farming" and "self sufficiency" had not been met. This was not a failure, he reasoned, but rather the product of "the changing pattern of modern economic life," where such goals were "uneconomic and even expensive." His original plan came from "a nostalgia born of memories of my grandfather's farm." He now realized that both "the pattern of the general farm" and "the pattern of self-sufficiency" had "outlived" their usefulness. Where the loss of these patterns had, three years before, been the very core of the American agricultural crisis, it was now to be welcomed. Bromfield cited mechanization, better distribution, the gains of specialization, the need for efficiency, rural electrification, health regulations, the advances of science, and increased markets and populations to explain his full embrace of an industrialized agriculture. Rather than the head of a family living on his own land and through his family's labor, the farmer of the future would be "a businessman, a specialist and something of a scientist."[43]

In further attempt at explanation, Bromfield cited the potato problem. He noted that under the plan, they had grown a supply of potatoes that sufficed for all residents on the farm, with a little left over. The acreage was small, and the work done by hand. However, the process "consumed considerable valuable man-hours which might profitably have been employed elsewhere." He discovered a neighbor down the road who raised potatoes commercially, "on a scale of thousands of bushels." Stumbling onto "the division of labor," apparently for the first time, Bromfield proudly reported that they could buy potatoes cheaper from their neighbor, while he in turn "came to us for meat and dairy products because that was our business."[44]

In place of self-reliance, self-sufficiency, and the new agrarianism, Bromfield embraced the New Agriculture. In *Malabar Farm*, he despaired over those farmers in his own county who had "reverted to subsistence levels," unmindful of his own encouragement of this act but a few years before. The imperative now was to reform and grow, or die. As he put it: "Those who do not choose to go along with the [New Agriculture] revolution are doomed. A good many have already been eliminated and the remainder will be liquidated, not by firing squads but by economic circumstances, within the next generation."[45]

In his last farm books, *Out of the Earth* (1950) and *From My Experience* (1955), Bromfield pressed his new critique of agrarianism still further. His ridicule of the old comment, "anyone can farm," became a guiding theme.[46] Farming was now for an elite, specialists combining science, technology, and reverence for the earth. Where *Pleasant Valley* had been a summons to all Americans to return to the soil, *Out of the Earth* was really for the new farmer-entrepreneurs and only secondarily for that larger group "who have a lively and even recreational interest in reading about...agriculture."[47]

Bromfield's alliance with the new organization, Friends of the Land, casts further light on this shift from Agrarian to Businessman-Scientist-Conservationist. Organized in the years 1939-1940, Friends of the Land focused on "defaced landscapes," "depleted water supplies," severe disruptions in hydrologic cycles, and "an all but catastrophic degradation of soil and man," usually summed up as the "erosion" problem. Russell Lord would later write that the organization "bore a remarkable resemblance to a proposal for a Society of the Holy Earth first advanced by Liberty Hyde Bailey" in 1917.[48]

Using the formula, "soil misuse makes people poor," Friends of the Land appeared at the outset to give equal weight to human habitation and agricultural health, with Conservation defined as "a working philosophy to reconcile the ways of Man and Nature."[49] As such, it was wholly compatible with decentralism and agrarianism. But it soon became clear that all the give in this reconciliation would come from Man. From the arguments that "we, too, are all one body" and that "we all live on, or from, the soil," the process became one primarily of getting people off the land and outside of farming. As a subsequent article in the journal, *Land and Water*, would emphasize, "Friends of the Land is *not* a decentralist organization." It categorically refused to "extol the esthetic values of country living." It resolutely opposed self-sufficient gardening, even by suburbanites, arguing that "much damage" had been done by magazine articles praising home grown produce. Instead, Friends of the Land emphasized how much hard work, skill, and experience were required; by implication, vegetable growing was best left in the hands of specialists.[50]

Bromfield hosted an early planning meeting for the organization at Malabar Farm; he was a close friend of Russell Lord, who drafted the Manifesto and edited the organization's journal, *The Land* (later *Land and Water*); he hosted the organization's first site visit in 1941; he served on its board of directors; and he gave hundreds of lectures on its behalf in the decade-and-a-half after 1941. These were the years when Bromfield also retreated from the decentralist goal of human resettlement on the land. Bromfield focused instead, with growing frequency, on the "secrets of life" contained within a cubic foot of soil, a quest he borrowed directly from Liberty Hyde Bailey. As he wrote in *Out of the Earth* (in an introduction to the chapter on "The New World in Agriculture" ridiculing the idea that "anybody can farm"): "...as yet we still do not know what a cubic foot of productive living soil really is....[T]here seems to be no one alive today who can put it all together." Even reducing the dimensions to one cubic inch would make no difference: "It would still contain billions of living organisms."[51]

Faced with personal economic pressures, some of his own making and some apparently beyond his understanding, Bromfield quietly abandoned the human and community aspects of agriculture, rooted in self-sufficiency, in preference for a kind of soil worship. It appears to be no coincidence that quotations from Bailey's *The Holy Earth*—wholly absent from *Pleasant Valley*—abound in *Malabar Farm* and *Out of the Earth*, for this in essence was the same troubled resolution that the Cornell professor reached sometime near 1930.

During his years at Malabar, Bromfield gained considerable notoriety. Brief stints in Hollywood (he wrote the screenplay for the epic *Brigham Young*, and worked on other projects) brought him a stable of motion picture friends. Humphrey Bogart and Lauren Bacall, for example, celebrated their marriage and "did chores" at Malabar Farm, to the delight of *Life* magazine photographers. Bromfield maintained a huge, often riotous household with, in his daughter Ellen's words, a "divergence of characters,...intrigue and chaos that sometimes reached the magnitude of Louis XV's court."[52] In politics, Bromfield moved from being a defender of the Soviet Union (in 1942, he favorably reviewed Joseph Davies' *Mission to Moscow* for the propaganda journal, *Soviet Russia Today*) and celebrant of the New Deal (a theme still evident in his 1942 novel, *Mrs. Parkington*) to a resolute libertarianism, opposed to all forms of farm subsidies and controls. As symbol of this move to the right, Ohio Senator Bob Taft, a Republican candidate for president in 1952, let it be known that Bromfield would be his choice as U.S. secretary of agriculture. By the early 1950s, nearly 20,000 pilgrims each year visited Malabar Farm, which had become the mecca, not of the Jeffersonian revival, but of the New Agriculture.

Yet this world quickly deteriorated. Within a brief few years, Bromfield saw his parents, his wife Mary, and his long time business manager George Hawkins die. His younger daughters left Malabar at the same time, for school, marriage, and—in the case of the youngest, Ellen—emigration to Brazil. By 1955, Bromfield had become something of a stubborn recluse. Financial pressures grew, as the capital demands of Malabar Farm continued to suck away his already diminished literary earnings and his own weakness in financial matters grew apparent.[53] Deteriorating health, attributed to a rare form of bone cancer, led to soaring hospital bills. Shortly before his death in March, 1956, Bromfield was even forced to sell off a treasured wooded portion of Malabar Farm.

New Agrarian Themes

Still, across all of Bromfield's work cut themes that reinforced the New Agrarian project. To begin with, he equaled, and perhaps surpassed, Ralph Borsodi in his spirited condemnation of urban living. One of his novels set in New York, *Twenty Four Hours* (1930), offered the conclusion that "the city was not civilized at all but only a kind of armed barbaric camp in which a savage warfare continued day and night."[54] *The Rains Came* contrasted the putative village exuberance of India with the urban sickness of the West, "the smoke and filth of factories," "the damp and blackness of mines," the "starvation and misery and strikes."[55] In *The Green Bay Tree*, an Imperial German officer described the cause of the war sweeping over Europe as the spread of urban-industrial civilization over the whole world "so that they might sell their cheap cotton and tin trays. They have created a monster which is destroying them."[56] The 1947 novella, *Kenny*, noted that "the cities were collapsing," because in urban areas "everybody is fighting everybody else just to live."[57]   The same messages prevailed in Bromfield's nonfiction. "Great cities inevitably produced populations which...can only be appeased by the 'bread and circuses' perilous to the security and welfare of any nation," he wrote in the 1946 book, *Cities are Abnormal*.[58] In *Pleasant Valley*, Bromfield condemned the urban kitchenette as "a slut's kitchen," and concluded: "the monstrous ugly cities...are in themselves violations of Nature which can only produce monstrosities....[Cities] are in themselves as perverse and murderous as Jack the Ripper."[59]

In contrast, farms were special places blessed by an abundance of healthy children, a view shared most notably with Carle Zimmerman. The natural end of fertility, Bromfield held, was large families. In *Wild is the River*, an old priest judged young Agnes, bound for a new farm in the West, concluding: "She was meant by God and nature to be a wife and the mother of many children."[60] In *Kenny*, the narrator talked of Vincent, rescued from the "filth and noise and despair" of the city, "who loved a wife who loved him, passionately, who kept right on having children because he liked them and because that was the natural thing to do."[61] Bromfield also held that the very presence of children on the farm transformed them: "All the children have changed a lot since they came [to Malabar]. Not only have they grown plump and gained color but they have lost the furtive, frightened look which they had acquired in the city."[62]

Bromfield shared with the whole New Agrarian cause a faith in salvation through science and the modern machine. True, the views expressed in his early fiction were quite different, with machines usually cast as malignant monsters. But as early as *The Farm*, Bromfield took encouragement from the faithful scientists and extension agents who worked to improve farming techniques. In *Pleasant Valley*, he insisted that the problem was slowness in innovation, that agriculture needed "farm machinery which is not twenty five years behind the development of the automobile and the radio."[63] In another essay from the same period, he argued that the "development of modern farm machinery" had made it more possible for small, part-time farmers to operate "profitably."[64] By *Malabar Farm*, Bromfield criticized old-fashioned general farms because they "can afford little mechanization"; indeed, he now allowed the available technology to dictate his farming plans. "We did not have enough acreage...in hay to support a baler, enough acreage in corn to support a cornpicker or enough acreage in small grain to support a combine," so he had simply dropped these crops.[65] By 1950, Bromfield argued that the principle problem in agriculture was lack of new machines. Even so, he refused to conclude that the once resented machine had won the contest over human community. In fact, he closed *Out of the Earth* with these words: "More than any other member of our society—indeed, perhaps alone in our society—the farmer has learned how to use machinery *to serve him* rather than *his serving* machinery. That is a very great secret indeed."[66]

Bromfield was also a foe of denominational Christianity, and the friend of an enlightened faith, views held in common with the Country Life campaigners. The frequency with which these themes appeared suggests that they were not passing or secondary aspects of his work, but near the core of his thought. In *The Green Bay Tree*, organized religion was cast as the handmaiden of the corporate exploiters.[67] In *The Rains Came,* the "chastity and barrenness of the Christian Church" stood in the way of progress; the only Christians of value were those, such as the Smileys, who had abandoned doctrine in favor of service.[68] In *The Farm*, Bromfield ridiculed the profusion of Christian sects in the countryside, where "[o]ne could get to heaven in a hundred different ways, ranging from celibacy...to standing on the head or rolling frantically on the ground and frothing at the mouth." Only the Unitarians and their cousins, the Congregationalists, were able to escape "the vulgar humbug...of the debased Christianity surrounding them." These folks "worked and built and begot families," and among them "intelligence burned with a clear blue flame."[69] In the conclusion to *From My Experience*, Bromfield lashed out at all the denominations, and their record of "evil, corruption, intolerance, and bigotry," from the Roman Catholic Church "down to the worst and most ignorant and insensible of the floor-rolling splinter sects." With varying degrees of explicitness, he went on to deny original sin, the Incarnation, the Atonement, and the divinity of Christ.[70] In another volume, the author juxtaposed a quotation from Liberty Hyde Bailey with the observation that the good farmer has "no yearnings for a silly heaven of pink clouds filled with angels' twanging harps."[71] In *Malabar Farm*, Bromfield asserted that the "best farmers" were in fact "not regular church-goers, usually because the church in their community was a dead or sometimes even evil thing."[72]

And yet Bromfield was a man of religious passion. His beliefs surfaced in *The Strange Case of Miss Annie Spragg*, where one character, a skeptic, "had a swift fleeting vision of humanity struggling to extricate itself from some colossal muddle," later defined as a "colossal struggle between all that was Christian and all that [was]... 'older than the church, older than Christianity itself'...."[73] The novella, *Kenny*, turned on the appearance at the farm of a boy with "an impish face" and ears "a little pointed at the tips," a lad who disappeared on the nights when the moon was full, who led the children and animals on parades "ancient and Bacchic," and who died on an European battlefield, only to be reborn through his own widow: a Greek God, the author implied.[74] Bromfield maintained that the farmer alone was in touch with these ancient mysteries. As he wrote in the conclusion to *Malabar Farm*:

> Your good farmer on good land is constantly aware, perhaps more than any other element of the population,...of an immense plan in which compensation, order and precision are all involved. It is a plan and a force with which he must live and he learns by necessity to understand and respect it....[The good farmer] has faith in the Great Plan [sic] with which he must live daily, as an infinitesimal part of the whole divine scheme. He knows that he must adjust himself to the immutable laws of that Plan.[75]

Within this larger understanding, Bromfield would at times equate Nature with God. In *A Good Woman*, the character Phillip rejected the "bogus God" of the Christians, embracing "a different sort of God," one concerned with "a kind of beauty and splendor," with "the whole glowing spectacle of living."[76] In *Kenny*, the true faith lay in "the remote and misty past when man was far nearer to Nature and its laws than he is today," when "none of us had any fear of that in us which lies so near to the very core of the earth and the pattern of the universe."[77] Bromfield asserted in *Pleasant Valley* that "the good earth and the true faith have never been removed from one another," being "as near today as they were ten thousand years ago."[78]

In his last book, *From My Experience*, Bromfield reported that he had been both Deist and animist in the past. While respecting the Ten Commandments and the Sermon on the Mount, he had no place in his mind for angels, harps, purgatories, hellfire, damnation, or sin. He now found comfort in Albert Schweitzer's concept of "Reverence for Life," with plants, animals, and humankind held in equal regard. This phrase, he said, had struck him like a mighty rocket bursting high in the darkness, because "it defined God for the first time, for if God is not Life, he is merely a vaporous figment of the imagination and the delusion of the weak."[79]

Bromfield shared other attributes of the New Agrarian Mind set out by Bailey, notably a deep ambivalence over the peasant style of farming. In *Pleasant Valley*, it is true, he gives recognition, and even praise, to the Amish and the Mennonites of Pennsylvania, "who lived closely among themselves, holding fast to their particular variety of religion, to their customs, even to the language." They remained on their ancestral ground and "made it richer and more valuable each year by farming well."[80] But this passage was unique, and overshadowed by a more common hostility. In the same book, for instance, he described German life as, "under any regime, abhorent," always leaving him "depressed and unhappy."[81] Germans and German-Americans were portrayed in all his fiction as either stolidly uncreative, or the incarnation of evil. His World War II novel, *Until the Day Break*, focused on the maniacal nature of the Germans. It was, in one critic's words, "one of the most outspoken condemnations of an entire people that has ever been produced by a prominent American writer."[82] In *The Farm*, Bromfield devoted considerable attention to the Schnitzes, German-American neighbors to young Johnny during his ill-fated return to the Farm. The author acknowledged their virtues, including the ability to survive and preserve their land. But they "were peasants," without imagination, politics, or appreciation for science. With Old Jamie, Johnny deplored the day when The Farm might pass to people like the Schnitzes, whose "dullness and limitations...were almost animal."[83]

Bromfield's personal resolution of the peasant problem could be found in the details of his plan for Malabar Farm. While gathering other farm families onto his land, the arrangement would not be strictly communal. Indeed, Bromfield consciously and oddly chose the collective farms of Soviet Russia as his model, with himself as "capitalist" taking the place of the "state." He would provide the others with a house, a garden plot, a few animals, and a salary, and he would have first claim on profits, with the others having a claim after he received his due.[84] But profits, apparently, were never shared.[85] Perhaps they did not exist. Or perhaps Bromfield was *too* Jeffersonian in character, residing in his big house, seeking "the old spacious comfortable life which farmers and landowners once lived," but an ambiance resting largely on the exertions of others.[86]

Later, Bromfield would also take to task those "romantics" who chose to live in the peasant-style, "willing to accept long hours, hard work and low profits," and believing that "the mental peace they get from such a life justifies these things." They added little to agricultural production, and he doubted that "they should be included in the category of a modern or even a sensible agriculture."[87]

Instead, Bromfield held to the Country Life belief that American farm life and farm people, as they were, had to be reconstructed. In *The Rains Came*, the author crafted the character, Colonel Moti, as part Kali the Destroyer, part Nietzschean superman. Moti despised the Brahmin priests and the religious superstitions that held India back. For decades, "he had cherished a suppressed desire to destroy an old world that a new one might be born." The collapse of the dam and the tragedy of the valley gave him his chance, "and he enjoyed it fiercely," setting out to build "a new people, a new kind of India."[88]

Bromfield's vision was almost as grand in the scope of needed social engineering. In the agricultural future, he said, "there will be no more floods to destroy the things that man has worked to create," "the abomination of great industrial cities" would be ended, and men and women "and above all, the children" would live in decentralized communities of "health and decency and human dignity." This "tremendous job...of reconstruction and restoration," he said, would be "infinitely more complicated than the job of subduing the wilderness by the first settlers."[89]

These views help explain Bromfield's effusive praise for the Tennessee Valley Authority, "an important kind of decentralization," where the plan allowed "both agriculture and industry" to exist side-by-side." Looking to a project worthy of Colonel Moti, Bromfield also threw his support behind a proposed "Missouri Valley Authority," a "whole new decentralized industrial-agricultural area with towns established where there is abundant hydroelectric power," a fresh landscape in a half-dozen states that would be "free from the evils...[of] vast industrial cities."[90]

Not only the farming landscape, but the farmers themselves must be changed. There were too many of them "who hate both their land and their livestock," "who produce very little more than they consume," "who hate the county agent and the soil conservation engineer." Indeed, these were "not farmers at all," but merely "shiftless" individuals,[91] composing about 60 percent of the farm population. They must either join the New Agriculture or get out. The agents for carrying out this human reconstruction would be those descendants of Bailey's beloved project, the Extension. For the good farmer "must not merely accept what the Department of Agriculture or the County agent tells him to do," but must also know "why the practice is good and how and why it works."[92] Simply put, the indoctrination must be complete.

Finally, Bromfield echoed the enthusiasm of the New Agrarians for the emerging American suburbs. It was time to do away with the great cities, he said, to see "the decentralization...of population and enterprise" into "rural areas and small urban developments." The author waxed enthusiastic over industrialist Henry Ford's interwar plan of "one foot in the soil," where factory workers would have a house and five acres along with their paying jobs.[93] This "process of decentralization" by means of "growing circles of small houses each with a small piece of land" was "one of the surest steps toward our economic security as a nation."[94]

The suburbs took on even greater importance as Bromfield jettisoned his argument for subsistence agriculture on farms. He insisted that a farmer employing the New Agriculture could not waste precious time in raising the vegetables, fruit, and animals for his own family's consumption. However, Bromfield held that the idea of "the farm as a family way of life" was still "an excellent pattern for the city office or industrial worker owning a few acres of land beyond the city limits."[95] For very different reasons, then, Bromfield wound up agreeing with Carle Zimmerman that the suburbs would be the necessary heir to the old rural virtues and to the family way of life.

The "New" Farm Family

Bromfield's willingness to sacrifice the independent farm family to a conservation-driven, machine-sustained form of soil worship still remains surprising. In passages from his later works, he would even describe the disruptive consequences, but could see them only as progress.

For example, *Malabar Farm* related the story of a farmer who, under the "general farming" system, often had his wife help him with the field work. However, he added, "I don't like my wife driving a tractor or working in a field." So he switched to the highly specialized and mechanized New Agriculture. "Now," he reported with satisfaction, "she never sets foot outside her house to work excepting in the flower garden or to hang out the washing."[96]

Unwittingly, Bromfield described this same loss of what Zimmerman called "co-living" in *Out of the Earth*. Here, the author celebrated the prototypical family of the New Agriculture. The farm wife is "spry and young and busy with her clubs and neighborhood activities." Indeed, Bromfield continued, she is "as young looking as her eighteen-year-old daughter who is a leader in the 4-H Club." The farmer-husband, for his part, "keeps city hours." Young and sturdy, he was able to "go with his boys...and attend their meetings."[97]

This is, in fact, not the depiction of a new family form. Rather, it is a description of a family unraveling, one pulled a hundred different ways, one no longer "co-living," working together, or even able to entertain itself. It is the prototypical non-functional or *dys*functional "companionate family." And it is, as well, symbol of the triumph of the new suburbs, and their peculiar social organization, over Bromfield's tattered Jeffersonian dream.

Notes

1. Louis Bromfield, *The Green Bay Tree* (New York: Grosset and Dunlop: 1924): 79-81.
2. This is the subtitle to historian Ivan Scott's excellent, unpublished manuscript "Bromfield: The Forgotten Author."
3. Louis Bromfield, *Kenny* (New York and London: Harper and Brothers, 1947): 17.
4. Louis Bromfield, *The Farm* (New York: Harper & Brothers, 1933): 88.
5. Fascinated by the French language in high school, Bromfield changed the spelling of his given name in those years to "Louis." Bromfield became his pen name in the early 1920s.
6. See: Morrison Brown, *Louis Bromfield and his Books* (London: Cassell & Company, 1956): 6-7.
7. Scott, "Bromfield," p. I-24.
8. For examples, see: Louis Bromfield, *Malabar Farm* (New York: Harper and Brothers, 1948): 63, 205, 295, 400; and Louis Bromfield, *Out of the Earth* (New York: Harper and Brothers, 1950): 8.
9. Bromfield, *The Farm*, p. 331.
10. Ibid., p. 343.
11. See: David D. Anderson, *Louis Bromfield* (New York: Twayne, 1964): 54.
12. Bromfield, *Pleasant Valley*, p. 8.
13. Bromfield, *The Green Bay Tree*, frontispiece.
14. Ibid., p. 64.
15. Bromfield, *Early Autumn*, p. 110.
16. Bromfield, *The Green Bay Tree*, p. 15.
17. Ibid., p. 50.
18. Louis Bromfield, *Possession* (New York: Frederick A. Stokes, 1925).
19. Louis Bromfield, *A Good Woman* (New York: Frederick A. Stokes, 1927): 105, 429-430.

20. Bromfield, *A Good Woman*, pp. 27, 264.
21. *Ibid.*, pp. 96, 273.
22. Russell Lord, "Tranquility Born of Satisfaction," *Land and Water* 17 (1956): 7.
23. Louis Bromfield, *The Strange Case of Miss Annie Spragg* (New York: Frederick A. Stokes, 1928): 18-19.
24. Ibid., pp. 17, 62, 77, 248.
25. See *Twenty-Four Hours* (New York: Frederick A. Stokes, 1930): 56, 93, 117, 398, 405, 459; also *Awake and Rehearse* (New York: Frederick A. Stokes, 1929); and *A Modern Hero* (New York: Frederick A. Stokes, 1932).
26. Scott traces Bromfield's view of the Jeffersonian-Hamiltonian divide to the work of the popular Indiana historian, Claude Bowers. From Scott, "Bromfield," p. IX-5.
27. Bromfield, *The Farm*, p. 93.
28. Ibid., pp. 140-141, 150-153, 298, 335.
29. Ibid., p. 346.
30. Anderson terms *The Rains Came* "Bromfield's most consistently executed novel." See Anderson, *Louis Bromfield*, p. 99.
31. Louis Bromfield, *The Rains Came* (New York: Harper & Brothers, 1937): 116.
32. Bromfield, *The Rains Came*, pp. 67-68, 103-104.
33. Ibid., p. 311.
34. Louis Bromfield, *Wild is the River* (New York and London: Harper and Brothers, 1941): 33, 89, 125, 154, 170.
35. Bromfield, *Wild is the River*, pp. 16, 74.
36. Ibid., pp. 183, 323-324.
37. Bromfield, *Pleasant Valley*, p. 8.
38. Ibid., p. 57.
39. Ibid., p. 60.
40. Ibid., p. 57.
41. Ibid., p. 51.
42. Ibid., pp. 60-61, 79.
43. Bromfield, *Malabar Farm*, pp. 44-46.
44. Ibid., pp. 48-49.
45. Ibid., pp. 258-259.
46. See Louis Bromfield, *Out of the Earth*, pp. 13, 47, 162.
47. Ibid., p. ix.
48. Russell Lord, *Forever the Land: A Country Chronicle and Anthology* (New York: Harper & Brothers, 1950): 39.
49. "Manifesto: Friends of the Land," *The Land* 1 (#1, 1940): 11-13.
50. "The Impact of Suburbanization Upon Rural Land Use," *Land and Water* 12 (#1, 1951): 12. Emphasis added.
51. Bromfield, *Out of the Earth*, p. 12.
52. Ellen Bromfield Geld, *The Heritage: A Daughter's Memoir of Louis Bromfield* (New York: Harper & Brothers, 1962): 175.
53. On these years see Geld, *The Heritage*, pp. 163-195.
54. Bromfield, *Twenty Four Hours*, p. 398.
55. Bromfield, *The Rains Came*, p. 98.
56. Bromfield, *The Green Bay Tree*, p. 301.
57. Bromfield, *Kenny*, pp. 31, 38.
58. Louis Bromfield, "To Clear the Dross," in *Cities Are Abnormal*, ed. Elmer T. Peterson (Norman: University of Oklahoma Press, 1946): 198.
59. Bromfield, *Pleasant Valley*, pp. 232-233.
60. Bromfield, *Wild is the River*, p. 322.

61. Bromfield, *Kenny*, p. 59.
62. Bromfield, *Malabar Farm*, p. 268; the same image, fictionalized this time, appears in *Kenny*, p. 62.
63. Bromfield, *Pleasant Valley*, p. 246.
64. Bromfield, "To Clear the Dross," pp. 195-196.
65. Bromfield, *Malabar Farm*, p. 47.
66. Bromfield, *Out of the Earth*, p. 300; also pp. 215ff.
67. Bromfield, *The Green Bay Tree*, p. 266.
68. Bromfield, *The Rains Came*, pp. 34, 472.
69. Bromfield, *The Farm*, pp. 60-61; also pp. 84-85.
70. Bromfield, *From My Experience*, pp. 342-343.
71. Bromfield, *Out of the Earth*, p. 8.
72. Bromfield, *Malabar Farm*, p. 404.
73. Bromfield, *The Strange Case of Miss Annie Spragg*, pp. 248, 310.
74. Bromfield, *Kenny*, pp. 12, 42, 72-73- 81.
75. Bromfield, *Malabar Farm*, p. 404.
76. Bromfield, *A Good Woman*, pp. 272-273.
77. Bromfield, *Kenny*, pp. 64-68.
78. Bromfield, *Pleasant Valley*, p. 296.
79. Bromfield, *From My Experience*, pp. 343-348.
80. Bromfield, *Pleasant Valley*, pp. 103-104.
81. Ibid., p. 4.
82. Anderson, *Louis Bromfield*, p. 128.
83. Bromfield, *The Farm*, pp. 318-325, 332, 342.
84. Bromfield, *Pleasant Valley*, p. 61.
85. Scott, "Bromfield," p. XXI-21.
86. Bromfield, *Pleasant Valley*, p. 66.
87. Bromfield, *Out of the Earth*, p. 162.
88. Bromfield, *The Rains Came*, pp. 548, 550.
89. Bromfield, *Pleasant Valley*, p. 300.
90. Bromfield, "To Clear the Dross," p. 197.
91. Bromfield, *Out of the Earth*, p. 88.
92. Bromfield, *Malabar Farm*, p. 54.
93. Bromfield, "The Clear the Dross," pp. 186-187, 194, 198.
94. Bromfield, *Pleasant Valley*, p. 123.
95. Bromfield, *Out of the Earth*, p. 162.
96. Bromfield, *Malabar Farm*, p. 51.
97. Bromfield, *Out of the Earth*, p. 299.

5

The New Agrarianism, Southern Style:
Lytle, Owsley, and Cauley

The best-known and the most analyzed of the twentieth-century Agrarians were the "Twelve Southerners" who authored *I'll Take My Stand* (1930) and the scholars who subsequently rallied behind their cause. Collectively known as the Southern, Tennessee, or Vanderbilt Agrarians (the latter after the university where the majority were affiliated in the 1920s), they sought to preserve an organic society of family and community, where man in nature could flourish. Arguing that the South, both historically and in their own time, was particularly hospitable to this vision, they urged the preservation there of an agrarian society, dominated by subsistence farms and rural traditions. Rootedness in place, the necessary bond between individual and kin, and the mutual reinforcement of experience and imagination were additional themes guiding their joint endeavor.[1]

Dozens of books and doctoral dissertations, and many hundreds of articles, have been written on the Southern Agrarians.[2] This chapter-length discussion of their work does not claim to summarize this great body of sometimes splendid scholarship. Rather it focuses on two special issues regarding the Southern Agrarians.

First, the tendency in analysis of this group and its members has been to move away from attention to their "agricultural" or "farming" side, and toward their literary intent. As Thomas Connelly laid the issue out in 1963, "the argument could be made that there was actually no real Agrarian school."[3] Instead, the work of the Twelve Southerners could be seen as part of "a world movement of criticism," rooted in classicism and neo-Scholasticism. For the group, agriculture was not much more than a "metaphor" for discussing philosophical issues such as man's relationship to nature. Accordingly, their calls for a return to subsistence farming were not to be taken too seriously.

This argument reached full flower in the introductions by Louis D. Rubin, Jr., to both the Harper Torchbook (1962) and LSU Press (1977) editions of *I'll Take My Stand*. The image of the Old South found in the book, Rubin argued, was one "that perhaps never existed." Rather, it was one that "should have existed." Seen this way, the import of *I'll Take My Stand* was "not" in its prescription for an agrarian South, "not" as a treatise on economics, "not" as a guide to political action, and "not" as "a sociological blueprint." Instead, it was "a calculated defense of religious humanism," "a commentary on the nature of man," and "a vision of what the good life can be." By his own admission, this view led Rubin to praise the non-farming essays of John Crowe Ransom, Donald Davidson, Allen Tate, Stark Young, and John Donald Wade, while almost ignoring the contributions of Andrew Nelson Lytle and Frank L. Owsley.[4] Without disputing Rubin's interpretation of the essays that he singles out for special merit, this chapter's analysis will give especial attention to those Southern Agrarians who clearly did take history, agrarianism, and farming seriously, and who argued for a broad return to the land: especially Lytle, Owsley, and the latecomer, Troy J. Cauley.

Second, this chapter will seek to delineate the degree to which the Southerners shared in New Agrarian themes. While the evidence suggests little direct, initial inspiration by figures such as Liberty Hyde Bailey or Carle Zimmerman, there are lines of parallel agreement on key themes and subsequent attempts at integration and cooperation. Moreover, and somewhat surprisingly, many of the distinguishing New Agrarian arguments can be found in the Southern Agrarians' work.

I'll Take My Stand, and After...

Critics of the Southern Agrarians, led by journalist H.L. Mencken, commonly mocked the group as "typewriter" or "literary" farmers. And on the surface, the co-authors appeared to have little real contact with the soil. The Twelve included five poets, two novelists, two historians, one English professor, a journalist, and one psychologist, professions not usually manure-oriented. Only one member of the group actually lived on a farm when *I'll Take My Stand* appeared in 1930.

Yet the truth is more complex. Half had grown up on, or had worked on, active farms, notably Owsley, Lytle, Tate, Davidson, Herman Nixon, and Lyle Lanier. They knew something about the realities of modern Southern agriculture. More significant, it seems, was the fact that the members of this group were reared and taught largely outside the mainstream American "common schooling" culture. Their education included "elements of classical and humanistic learning, a training in languages (Latin and Greek in several instances), education at home or by private tutors, private academies, and attendance at some southern university."[5] They were, in short, raised to be independent thinkers, within families that still saw the educational function as theirs.

The professional collaboration began at Vanderbilt where Ransom, Tate, Davidson, and Robert Penn Warren jointly edited a journal of poetry, the *Fugitive*, starting in 1922. Although the journal had no obvious agrarian content and while it ceased publication three years later, the project drew these writers into subsequent conversations and correspondence on the state of America. In the late 1920s, they brought into their circle young, bright students such as Lytle and colleagues from other academic departments such as Owsley. The Southerners grew increasingly disturbed by the country they observed. Davidson would emphasize the rampant commercialism of the 1920s, which had particular effect in the South, "where old and historic communities were crawling on their bellies to persuade some petty manufacturer of pants or socks to take up his tax-exempt residence in their midst."[6] They were distressed by the so-called "New Southists," such as Gerald W. Johnson, who dismissed the rural South as "a hook worm-infested, pellagra-smitten, poverty-stricken, demagogue-ridden 'shotgun civilization,'"[7] and spoke of the "glittering civilization" that would come in a thoroughly industrialized region.[8]

They drew no comfort, though, from the real situation in the Southern countryside. Between 1865 and 1930, most of the great plantations of the antebellum South had been broken up, with four out of five Southern farms now comprising less than 100 acres. Yet the welcome emergence of small farms had gone sour under more recent economic pressures. Nearly half of Southern farmers were tenants, who had lost their land, in Owsley's words, "through industrial exploitation, depression, and...high pressure salesmanship of radio, automobile, and farm machinery agents." Across the South, "[b]attered old cars, dangling radio aerials, rust-eaten tractors, and abandoned threshing machines" testified to "the tragedy of industrialism's attempt to industrialize the farmer and planter."[9] All the Agrarians would also point to the Scopes "Monkey Trial," over the teaching of evolution in the public schools, as a turning point. As Lytle later explained: "This religious attack on the Southern spirit seemed to have a double purpose: to denigrate us before the country and the world and to make us laughable as backward and ignorant."[10]

The response was *I'll Take My Stand*, published by Harper and Brothers in 1930. While the volume had no formal editor, Davidson was the catalyst for crafting the book. He guided the correspondence, negotiated the contract, and oversaw the copy editing.[11] The twelve essays covered history, art, education, philosophy, religion, race, and economics, and were not wholly consistent in argument or message. Nonetheless, all the contributors agreed to "A Statement of Principles," initially drafted by Ransom, and placed at the front of the book. As such, it stands as the definitive common denominator of the Southern Agrarian mind.

Significantly, the statement began with acknowledgement that they were not alone in their cause. Within the Union were "many other minority communities opposed to industrialism and wanting a much simpler economy." They asserted that "proper living" was a matter of will and intelligence, not local climate or geography. There was nothing uniquely "Southern" about their quest, and they "would be happy to be counted as members of a national agrarian movement."[12]

The statement's principle focus was on the nature of industrialism, which the authors defined as "the capitalization of the applied sciences." Choosing words carefully, they objected to its having become "extravagant and uncritical." The Twelve said that science's contribution to labor was "to render it easier by the help of a tool or a process"; this was appropriate when it assured "the laborer of his perfect economic security." But of late, the operative assumption behind "a labor-saving device or a machine" was that "labor is an evil." In industry, the new machines did not so much "emancipate" workers, as "evict" them. In agriculture, the machines steadily reduced the number of persons drawing sustenance from the soil.

The Southerners sought to protect labor as "one of the happy functions of human life," for too little labor and too much consumption led to "satiety and aimlessness." Religion, or "our submission to the general intention of a nature that is fairly inscrutable," could not flourish in industrial society. Nor could art, because it too depended "on a right attitude to nature." Industrial civilization also damaged the "amenities of life," including manners, family life, and romantic love.

The Twelve saw "modern advertising" and "its twin, personal salesmanship," as the "most significant development of our industrialism." They labeled it "the great effort of a false economy of life to approve itself."

In defining their alternative, the Southerners again chose their words carefully, using a revealing negative construct: "An agrarian society is *hardly one* that has no use at all for industries, for professional vocations, for scholars and artists, and for the life of cities." Viewed positively, the agrarian order simply placed agriculture as "the leading vocation, whether for wealth, for pleasure, or for prestige." It was a "form of labor" pursued "with intelligence and leisure," the "model" for other professions to emulate. Accordingly, the "culture of the soil" should claim "economic preference" and should "enlist the maximum number of workers."[13]

Beyond the specifics of this statement were additional shared arguments running through all the essays, without visible dissent. All contributors, directly or implicitly, emphasized the primacy of the family and the family economy. Ransom, as example, noted that industrialism was a force "of almost miraculous cunning but no intelligence." It had to be controlled, "or it will destroy the economy of the household."[14] Making essentially on the same point, Lanier saw how the "segmentation of both adult and child activities" in the corporate age left "little to the family beyond the details of finance and the primary sexual functions." In particular, the critical "moral and educational functions of the family" became increasingly entrusted to outside agencies "which simulate" the family, but "are entirely devoid of its content." Strong families were only to be found where "actual fathers, mothers, and children" lived and worked in one another's company.[15]

Regarding economics, the contributors actually offered original insights into the nature of the modern situation. Relative to the contest between industry and family, Tate noted that "the social structure depends on the economic structure, and economic conviction is the secular image of religion."[16] Lytle anticipated, by two generations, certain conclusions of modern micro-economics, in his comment that the core task of industrialism was "to convince the farmer that it is time, not space, which has value," his observation that "industrialism is multiplication" while "agrarianism is addition and subtraction," and his quip that "as soon as a farmer begins to keep books, he'll go broke shore as hell."[17] Lytle also offered a powerful and correct critique of modern accounting, noting that one could not honestly lift the "lower price" of store-bought shoes out of context: "the fifteen-hundred dollar tractor, the thousand dollar truck, the cost of transportation to and from town, all the cost of indirect taxation, every part of the money economy, enters into the price of shoes."[18] Nixon rooted his discussion of the Southern situation in a fair appraisal of interwar France and Denmark as nations that had an "even balance between rural and urban populations, between agriculture and industry, with agrarianmindedness predominate," despite long exposure to industry.[19] Davidson correctly summarized the Agrarian dissent from both the liberal and socialist dogmas of his day, as a belief "that life determines economics, or ought to do so, and that economics is no more than an instrument." Put another way, Davidson emphasized that the Agrarians stood for "a way of life that *will restore economics*" to its rightful focus on family and community well-being.[20]

Fletcher offered a short, but compelling history of education in America. He properly noted that the Founders of the United States, including even Thomas Jefferson, strongly opposed mass state education. They followed Goethe's maxim, "that everything that frees man's soul, but does not give him command over himself, is evil," and held that the purpose of education was to produce "balanced" persons, at home in the world yet also with strong spiritual and local roots. The Southern academies, dominant in the region before 1860, embodied this vision. In contrast, the public school system inaugurated by Horace Mann and widely copied in the North "ignored local and functional differences," producing persons "without roots," morals, or purpose. Indeed, as the final flower of the Horace Mann project, the modern high school was "nothing more than a mass-production factory."[21]

The burden of Southern history also weighed heavily on the Agrarians. Owsley summoned readers to learn the things for which the South stood that were "reasonable and sound." He insisted that the Civil War was not over the issue of slavery. The "fundamental and passionate ideal" for which the Old South stood, he said, "was the ideal of an agrarian society." The Southerners' love of the early Roman Republic, of Cincinnatus and the Gracchi, lay in this common love of the soil and respect for the yeomanry on the land. The true "irrepressible conflict" that reached crisis in 1860-61 was not between slavery and freedom, "but between the industrial and commercial civilization of the North and the agrarian civilization of the South." The northern industrialists and merchants had concluded that the South was "in the way; it impeded the progress of the machine"; it "had to be crushed out."[22] Even the contemporary race problem, Warren argued, was best left for Southern people to work out. While defending the practice of segregation, he emphasized how rural life softened its edges and provided "the most satisfactory relationship of the two races which can be found at present."[23] In his account of the writing of *I'll Take My Stand*, Davidson emphasized how this understanding of Southern history helped the Tennessee Agrarians conclude "that the Lost Cause might not be wholly lost after all," that the very "backwardness of the South" contained a "secret" that might make possible "its own reconstruction and possibly even the reconstruction of America."[24]

Finally, all of the Twelve shared a revulsion toward the aesthetics of urban-industrial life. Davidson emphasized how industrialization either destroyed the arts, or left them "diseased and disordered." The true artist was rooted in a location, or a place, where a balanced life was possible. He anticipated that artists would understand this, and would ally themselves "with programs of agrarian restoration," participating in a true "decentralization of the arts."[25] Lytle drew the image of the farmer who, "[i]n exchange for the bric-a-brac culture of progress" and the tawdry "products of the Power Age," would lose his land, sacrifice his independence, overproduce his money crop, and "send his daughters to town to clerk in ten-cent stores."[26] An agrarian society would restore appreciation for the creativity of handicrafts.

For a decade, the Tennessee Agrarians aggressively pushed their cause. Ransom and Davidson engaged in a series of public debates with "New Southists" in the early 1930s, before large but not always friendly audiences.[27] In 1933, the Manhattan-based Seward Collins founded the *American Review* and actively solicited the Southern Agrarians to join his "right-wing" melange of Humanists, neo-Scholastics, Chestertonians, Bellocians, and "the Action Française men." The Southerners enthusiastically agreed and, over the four years of the monthly's existence, contributed as a group over 100 articles and reviews, including important "action" essays by Ransom, Lytle, and Owsley.

Davidson reported that the *American Review* "gave us both understanding and hospitality of a sort we have never received, for example, from the *Virginia Quarterly Review*."[28] One historian of the
movement would label the *American Review* "a semi-official organ"
of the Vanderbilt group,[29] a viewed shared by Conkin.[30] The journal
folded after Collins, in a 1936 interview with a *New Republic* writer,
confessed to being a fascist and an admirer of Adolf Hitler. While the
Southern Agrarians as a group held fairly explicit antifascist views,
they still suffered some embarrassment from the episode. More importantly, they lost a valuable and—as it turned out—irreplaceable
outlet for the further refinement of their work.[31]

"Plain Folk" of the South, Present and Past

Of the Twelve, Andrew Lytle and Frank Owsley gave notable attention to the place of farm people and subsistence agriculture in the
joint project. They understood that the agrarian argument must have
two foundations: a showing that an "agrarian people" existed in the
South in their time; and proof that a "family farm" folk existed in the
antebellum past as well. Without these pillars, Southern Agrarianism
would be no more than a literary project, the "imaginary" effort mocked
by some of their critics. Owsley, the professional historian, took on
the second task. Lytle, under Owsley's guidance,[32] took on the first.

Most critics of Lytle's work, even someone as friendly as Virginia
Rock, have seen his description of the character of the yeoman farmer's
life in "The Hind Tit" as, at best, a "deliberate overstatement"; or
more likely, a fanciful creation.[33] The astonishing fact is how closely
Lytle's description parallels the "scientific observations" by Carle
Zimmerman of an Upland Southern family, as featured in the contem-
poraneous *Family and Society* (see chapter 2, pp. 44-45). In the antebellum days, Lytle reported, "the farming South, the yeoman South,
that great body of free men" took form. Found in the upland country,
the pine barrens, the hills, and the mountains, these people had little to
do with the early capitalists and their merchandise. "The plain people"
had been forced "into a state of self-sufficiency." After the war, some
came down from the hills, to occupy the abandoned plantations. Soon
at the beck-and-call of the money economy, many lost their independence, falling into tenantry, becoming "the poor white, the hook
wormed illiterate." Others, successful for a while, became "progres-

sive farmers," a fatal step, for it meant the effort "to industrialize" the life of their households.[34]

But others stayed in the hills, "kept their looms going and fed their stock home-grown feed," and still remained in 1930 as a human resource for the South, and the nation. Lytle gave a delightful account of their survival and adaptation, focused on the continued vigor of their home economy. In a typical "plain folk" home, "a quilting rack is drawn into the ceiling ready to be lowered to the laps of the womenfolk when the occasion demands." Activity centered on the kitchen, where the old, open-fire-place had been replaced by an iron range: "This much machinery has added to the order of the establishment's life without disrupting it." All the food was prepared here, as was "the canning and preserving necessary to sustain the family during the winter." Lye was now purchased in town, rather than made from ash, but the household still crafted its own soap and hominy, and the day of each family member was "filled with a mighty variety."[35]

Folk belief and superstitions remained (e.g., "sometimes witches get in the [butter] churn and throw a spell over it"). But Lytle insisted that these be viewed as "folk attempts to understand and predict natural phenomenon," and so be deemed useful and necessary to agrarian society.[36]

As would Bromfield in *The Farm*, Lytle delighted in describing the meals enjoyed by the rural yeomanry. "His table...is always bountiful," Lytle wrote. "The abundance of nature, its heaping dishes, its bulging-breasted fowls, deep-yellow butter and creamy milk, fat beans and juicy corn, and its potatoes flavored like pecans" filled the room with satisfaction, for the farmer did not yet look upon his produce "at so many cents a pound." Instead, each dish consumed by the family bore a special meaning, for they had as a body raised and created it.[37]

Lytle also emphasized the different sense of time held by the Southern hill people. If the fish were biting or the game in abundance, "the boys might knock off a day and go fishing, or hunting"; their father had not yet begun to keep a ledger, "so their time is their own." A nap followed the midday meal. The night featured one of the boys playing "ballets" on a guitar, tunes handed down from father to son, or a "play party," or a "Sacred Harp" gathering for the singing of hymns, or a square dance (with its "very fine balance...between group and individual action").[38]

Lytle also gave a reliable account of how this culture was threatened in his day. First came "the good roads," which made fortunes for asphalt, oil, automobile, bus, construction, and truck companies, and filled the pockets of politicians, but drove "like a flying wedge" through the countryside. The salesman arrived, and the farmer traded his mules or horses for a tractor, forgetting that, unlike livestock, the machine could not reproduce itself. The tractor also threw his boys out of work: "Thus begins the *home-breaking*. Time is money now, not property, and the boys can't hang around the place." Next came a truck, and perhaps a car, "three vehicles which must be fed from the oil companies" and three notes at the bank bearing interest. Then the farmer electrified, perhaps with a Delco generator. It gave light, but also pumped water, turned the churn, washed the clothes, heated the iron, and cooked the food. The result was destruction of the home economy:

> If his daughters had not already moved away, he would have to send them, for Delco has taken their place in the rural economy....The farmer's wife now becomes a drudge...she grows restive. She has changed from being a creator in a fixed culture to an assistant to machines.[39]

The farmer and his wife grew more careless of the garden. They reduced the number of farm animals, and purchased chemical fertilizers as a substitute. The country church faded, the square dances disappeared, and even the annual camp or revival meetings—long the central event of Southern rural life—lost their vitality. Meanwhile, the public schools finished the job, teaching the farmer's children "to despise the life he has led" and, now against hope, would like them to lead as well.[40]

Lytle saw the Agrarian cause as more than preserving a good way of life. If the family was to survive in health and vigor, rural reconstruction was the only alternative. Private property was important, "but only as a means of guaranteeing the security and self-perpetuation of the family."[41] The identification of a family with a farm also bore powerful religious significance, inducing "a respect for and concord with all of God's creation," to be found in no other way.[42] And the very existence of political society rested on a healthy agrarianism, "for only when families are fixed in their habits, sure of their property, hopeful for the security of their children, [and] jealous of liberties which they cherish, can the State keep the middle course between impotence and tyranny."[43] That nation which abused its farmers was, quite simply, "committing suicide."[44]

Accordingly, Lytle reasoned, there could be no compromise between antithetical ways of life. The great moral revolution behind
industrialism—from "the thing-to-be-used" to the "thing-to-be-sold"—
had to be reversed. America could still be saved, Lytle said, if one-
fourth to one-third of the population could be securely established on
"livelihood farms," devoted to home production or production for
use.[45] He called on Southerners, in particular, to "return to our looms,
our handcrafts, our reproducing stock. Throw out the radio and take
down the fiddle from the wall. Forsake the movies for the play-parties
and the square dances."[46]

In his contribution to *I'll Take My Stand*, Owsley emphasized that
the antebellum South was, in fact, "an agrarian civilization which had
strength and promise for a future greatness second to none." At its
core was a yeomanry, for whom farming was a way of life, rooted in
production for use, not a mere project for pecuniary gain: "The houses
were homes, where families lived sufficient and complete within themselves, working together and fighting together" and, when death came,
buried in family plots, "to await doomsday together."[47]

In so arguing, though, Owsley put himself at odds with the dominant historiography regarding the social structure of the Old South. From
Frederick Law Olmsted's *A Journey in the Back Country* (1863) to Alan
Nevins's popular mid-twentieth-century histories of the Civil War, the
prevailing view was that the Old South had three classes: the white
planters, black slaves, and poor whites. The latter group, counting six
million members, reputedly lived in squatter huts, ate sweet potatoes,
collards, and dirt, drank "rot gut" whiskey, and suffered from malaria, pellagra, and hookworm. In *Poor Whites of the South*, George Watson described "a
semi savage life, sinking deeper and more hopelessly into barbarism." J.E.
Cairne's *Slave Power* depicted "an idle and lawless rabble" who lived "in
a condition little removed from absolute barbarism."

Where Lytle described a Southern yeomanry still surviving in the
hills and mountains of the 1920s, Owsley set out to prove its existence
before 1860. With his wife Harriet Chappell Owsley, he examined
census reports, church records, wills, county court minutes, marriage
licenses, debt books, and reliable travelers accounts, to uncover what
he called "the Plain Folk of the Old South," a project not completed
until the 1940s. The Owsleys pointed to farmers, stockholders, and
their families who owned land, worked the fields, and had few if any
slaves. Holding between fifty and 500 acres, the Southern yeomanry

constituted a large rural middle class, with thoughts, traditions, and legends that were decidedly rural. Mostly descended from Scotch, English, and Scotch-Irish ancestors, they also were a genuine "folk," by which Owsley meant a people "bound together by ties of race, language, religion, custom, tradition, and history."[48]

Owsley emphasized the importance of home ties to this group, concluding that the "closely knit family with its ramified...kinship ties was a folk characteristic which the Southerners possessed to a degree second only to the Highland Scots of an earlier time."[49] Parents and grandparents exercised unusual authority over children and grandchildren, even after the latter were grown and married. Age, the Plain Folk assumed, brought wisdom. Co-living was the dominant feature of their lives, and parents enjoyed respect "because they demonstrated in their day-long work with their sons and daughters in field and house and in their play that skill and wisdom came from experience." Women's work was deeply integrated into the life of the farm: "Indeed, in stripping tobacco and picking cotton, the girls often excelled the men." The social life of the Plain Folk revolved around the rural churches, camp meetings, house-raisings for new settlers or the newly married, communal corn-shuckings and log-rollings where a "great deal of hard work was performed with little feeling of weariness," Sacred Harp sings, wedding parties, and square dances. Feasts were ubiquitous. At a "log rolling," for example,

> A sixty-gallon sugar boiler filled with rice, chicken, and fresh pork backbone—a sort of camp stew; a large pot of turnip greens and corn-meal dumplings, served with boiled ham sliced and laid on top; crackling or shortening bread; Irish potatoes; sweet potatoes; a variety of cakes; two-story biscuits.[50]

Owsley showed that these people resided on self-sufficient farms, practicing a diversified type of agriculture "where the money crops were subordinated to food crops, and where the labor was performed by the family or the family aided by a few slaves."[51] They were the cultural or "folk" ancestors of the highland Southerners of the twentieth century, and stood as models for the good and sufficient agrarian life.

Public Policy Agendas

Early critics of *I'll Take My Stand* commonly faulted the Twelve Southerners for their lack of specifics. Just how did they intend to create a land of contented subsistence farmers? Several of the Agrarians rose to the challenge. By 1935, they had crafted a series of very concrete ideas on how to change law and public policy in favor of the small farmer.

In 1933, John Crowe Ransom wrote "Happy Farmers" for the *American Review*. The author was clear on the nature of the desired form of agriculture, one found it on "millions of American farms" two or three generations before:

> ...to raise the great bulk of the foods for the family, including vegetables, fruits, poultry, dairy products, meats; to can, preserve, and cure for the winter (this involves the smoke-house); to do plain carpentering to the extent at least of repairs, to paint and whitewash, to do amateur landscape gardening, in order that the home may be pleasant and decent; to work mainly with literal horse-power, mule-power, man-power; to feed all the animals, as well as the persons, from the land; to fertilize the land by the periodic use of grass crops.[52]

Ransom reasoned that American commercial agriculture was "doomed," because its day in the sun was "beyond recall." When America had been a debtor nation, massive farm exports made sense, and balanced American imports. But by the 1930s, the United States had become the world's largest creditor nation. There were now new debtor nations, young lands with good soil and with cheap food to sell. Moreover, the international economic depression gave every sign of inaugurating a permanent constriction of trade. As a result, American agriculture was both "overcapitalized" and "overproductive." It made no sense to develop an exportable surplus in food that could no longer be exported. The destiny of American agriculture, Ransom concluded, was not to be a "simple food bowl." Rather, it was to support "an excellent order of citizens, who will be economic dualists," raising food first for their own abundant use and secondarily a modest surplus for the domestic market. These would be "farmers with more room, and more heart, than most of the farmers in the world; happy farmers."[53]

Toward that end, Ransom recommended that future borrowing by farmers be taxed, to discourage them from commercial production. Special state taxes, "high but not quite prohibitive," should be levied on tractors, heavy farm machines, and commercial fertilizers. Property taxes should be replaced by progressive income taxes. Farm subsidies should be skewed in favor of small producers. State agricultural schools and extension programs "should be reformed," to cease training in "money-making" techniques, focusing instead on "a proper farm economy," called "the art of making a family decently and pleas-antly at home on the farm." Finally, Ransom urged that all future government land and homestead grants contain "one radical provi-sion" in the condition of the gift: the homesteader must take training in agrarian farming, followed by regular inspections to make sure he is making "a direct living," rather than merely "an income," subject to loss of the property.[54]

Spirits at Vanderbilt were lifted in early 1935 with the appearance of the book, *Agrarianism: A Program for Farmers*, by a "new sup-porter," Troy J. Cauley, professor of Economics at Georgia Tech Uni-versity. Donald Davidson could hardly contain his glee that "a profes-sional economist," someone who actually knew "all the mystic signs, signals, passwords, and catchwords" of that arcane trade, someone actually free of suspicion of "having written poetry or biography or literary criticism," had come down on their side. Himself skeptical of the work of Ralph Borsodi (which he dismissed as "agrarianism for commuters"),[55] Davidson praised the Cauley volume as the first "to come forth with anything like a well ordered analysis and defense of the economics of agrarianism."[56] Defining that term as "an economic and social system under which the chief method of making a living is that of tilling the soil, with a consequent rather wide dispersion of population, and a relatively meagreness of commercial intercourse," Cauley had no reluctance to label the South uniquely fitted for such an economy. In the region, plants grew easily and early. There were many "free goods" in the countryside, including: abundant timber for building a cheap house; wild berries commonly regarded as free prop-erty; peaches, persimmons, and walnuts; and squirrels, opossums, and wild hogs in abundance. Custom permitted "cheap clothing," the teth-ering of a cow along a road, the maintenance of a garden by almost every country house, and pleasure in the eating of sweet potatoes, peanuts, and roasting ears of corn. It was possible in the South to work spasmodically, and still gain sufficient food from hunting, fish-ing, and berrying. The main problem lay in the restricted nature of land ownership in the region: too many tenants; too many absentee landlords.[57]

Cauley described, without adequately systematizing, the compo-nents of an "agrarian economics." The home would always have "meal in the meal-barrel, meat in the smoke-house, sorghum in the jug, fruits and vegetables in the cellar,...cows and chickens out around the barn," and probably "a spinning wheel and a hand loom in the chimney corner."[58] Where the industrial economy relied on "increasing the quantity of goods and services" to meet the problem of scarcity, the agrarian economy devoted relatively little attention to increasing goods. Rather, it tackled scarcity "by reducing the number and variety of material wants." For example, where advertising in the urban-industrial sector rested on the message, "more and faster, more and faster," this orientation had "no place" in an agrarian community. Citing another difference, Cauley described rival ways of caring for the very young and the very old, "major burdens" common to the human race. In industrial societies, such dependents were nonproductive and became objects of great expense. The typical urban family was, at best, only "a spending unit"; and "if there be children the bulk of the expenditure is usually for them." In contrast, the agrarian economy "greatly reduced" these nonproductive periods. The nature of farm work—spasmodic, diverse, and seasonal—was well adapted to "the capacities and temperaments of growing children" and usually found roles for the elderly as well. Where prestige in the city involved "conspicuous consumption," country folk found other ways to secure status, such as physical contests involving wrestling and running. In short, the "low material standards" of rural life were not a liability, but rather the mark of a society operating on radically different economic principles.[59]

Turning to public policy, Cauley indicted the unremitting efforts by the Federal government to increase agricultural production: the Extension service, experiment stations, university research, road building, open immigration, and high tariffs were all at fault. The only possible result had been rising production, mounting capital costs for farmers, and falling prices for every unit produced. Cauley also condemned a tax system that relied primary on property taxes. Farm property was real, and almost never escaped full assessment. Industrial property, in contrast, was more ephemeral, and usually undervalued.[60]

In response, the author proposed a program focused heavily on tax reform. To begin with, he urged that property taxes be levied on a progressive basis: higher valuations would pay a higher percentage of tax. Still higher property tax levies would fall on corporate or absentee owners. Cauley also urged adoption of a tax-exempt minimum of $5,000, which would take most subsistence-level farmers off the tax rolls. Coupled with a sharp increase in inheritance taxes, the elimination of all protective tariffs, and a heavy swing in favor of a progressive income and sales taxes, and the results would be a sharp drop in agricultural land prices and the elimination of "the investment value of farm land." Viewed positively, his goals were that people "come to desire the ownership of property as against the receipt of money income," and a massive shift from large to small owners, and from corporate and absentee tenure toward family and local control.

On related matters, Cauley urged generous, subsidized government loans to small farmers for up to 80 percent of the value of land and improvements. He endorsed the subsistence homestead program as a positive contribution to "the general redistribution of farm property."[61] In an article for the *American Review*, Cauley argued that all forms of farm credit should be made dependent on the adoption of a diversified agriculture. At a far more radical level, he joined Ralph Borsodi in urging the abolition—over a period of time—of the corporation as a legal form of business organization. "There is fundamentally no reason," Cauley explained, "why a group of persons by combining their financial resources should acquire special privileges...as against those possessed by individuals." With corporations eventually abolished, he expected the abandonment of mass-production methods, the return to handicrafts manufactured in towns and cities, and the disappearance of "the socially most undesirable advertising and high-pressure-salesmanship techniques."[62]

A still more radical agenda came from Frank Owsley, in his 1935 essay, "The Pillars of Agrarianism." Arguing that the first priority should be the rehabilitation of the population still living on the soil, white and black, Owsley called for a massive redistribution of land. The national and state governments should buy all the farm land owned by insurance companies and absentee landlords and part of that held by remaining large planters. The governments should then give to every qualifying landless tenant eighty acres of land. They should also build him "a substantial hewn log house and barn," fence off twenty acres of pasture, provide him two mules and two cows, and advance him $300 for the first year. All this would be as outright gifts, subject to the condition that the land never be sold or mortgaged. If abandoned, the property would revert to the government. State constitutional amendments should also be adopted making it illegal to mortgage any land, except with approval by a court of equity.

To encourage "the rehabilitation of the soil," Owsley called for mobilizing the country extension agents into "a kind of court" on erosion questions. Undrained and unterraced lands would be *"prima facie* evidence that the homesteader is not a responsible person," with his land subject to expropriation.

To achieve an agrarian order, state regulations must also insure that subsistence farming was "the first objective of every man who controls a farm or plantation." The land must first support the people who live on it, and then the livestock. Only after subsistence was gained would the money crops come into play.

Owsley also returned to the tariff question. Protective tariffs had been the greatest factor in destroying the foreign markets on which the South depended. If the South could not win free trade, then it must receive a quid pro quo: "a subsidy on every bale of cotton and pound of tobacco," determined by the difference between world and domestic prices.

Finally, Owsley demanded "a new Constitutional deal," essentially a total reconstruction of American governance. Arguing that the United States "was less a nation than an empire made up of a congeries of regions," the author urged creation of new *regional* governments that would assume the powers of the states, plus additional autonomy. They would probably number New England, the Middle East, the Middle West, the Rocky Mountains, the Pacific States, and—of course—the South. These regional governments would have equal representation in the federal legislature, in the election of the president and cabinet, and in the selection of the Supreme Court. In a way coming full circle, Owsley also urged that the regional governments have control of the tariff.[63]

He concluded that once founded on these principles, an agrarian society could grow without further state intervention. "The old communities, the old churches, the old songs would arise from their moribund slumbers." Literature, music, and art could "emerge into the sunlight" from the dark holes to which "industrial insensitiveness" condemned them. And "[l]eisure, good manners, and the good way of life might again become ours."[64]

A Curious Convergence

Were the Southern Agrarians actually partisans of the New Agrarian Mind? Did they share in the same novel attitudes born in the quintessentially Yankee mind of Liberty Hyde Bailey? While the direct influence is problematic (although Davidson did emphasize their

awareness of "malcontents even in the North who were asking embar-
rassing questions"),[65] the accent surely different, and the writing defi-
nitely of higher stylistic caliber, the answer to both questions appears
to be yes.

To begin with, the Southerners were fervent believers in the engineering of a whole new economic order. Owsley's advocacy for an
unprecedented land redistribution, the transformation of property ownership into "a modified form of feudal tenure where, in theory,
the...state has a paramount interest in the land," and the complete
reconstruction of the American nation and Constitution were, taken
altogether, staggering in their scope.[66] Add to this Cauley's statement
that "Democracy, both political and economic, is impossible once the
principle of the corporation is established," and his call for abolishing
all joint-stock corporations, and you have a political program almost
unprecedented in ambition.

Moreover, the needed social engineering would include a thorough
remaking of the existing farming population, another New Agrarian
idea. Despite Lytle's words of praise for the Highland Southerners,
the Tennessee Agrarians as a group had no more respect for existing
farmers than did Bailey, Borsodi, or Bromfield. Ransom decried the
"apostasy of American farmers from primary subsistence farming,"
terming it "the greatest disaster our country has yet suffered." These
farmers now were "economically ruined" and "spiritually desperate,"
and in urgent need of reconstruction.[67] Owsley concluded that many
white tenant farmers of his time were "beyond redemption," to be
permanently consigned to weak minds, bad food, and disease. He
called on county and state pubic health departments "to take the steps
necessary to salvage the children of such families"—presumably by
taking them away from their parents—so that the offspring of "po'white
trash" might become good farmers and citizens in the future.[68] Lanier
termed the agrarian project one that demanded "far-sighted 'social engineering,'" including the remaking of the rural population, the huge task
of creating "a synthesis" of rural family and community bonds with "the
energy and inventiveness that has been diverted into industrialism."[69]

While their diagnosis was somewhat different, the Southern Agrarians also tended to view rural Christianity and rural churches as problems needing correction. They were advocates for Christian humanism. They were motivated to their project, in part, by the negative
publicity surrounding the Scopes trial. And they distrusted scientism.

All the same, the Tennessee Agrarians had few good words for the dominant religious expressions of the Southern folk: Baptist, Presbyterian, Methodist, and Church of Christ.

Some of their criticisms did focus on the inroads being made by modernist philosophy. As Lytle urged near the end of "The Hind Tit": "turn away from the liberal capons which fill the pulpits as preachers. Seek a priesthood that may manifest the will and intelligence to renounce science and search out the Word in the authorities."[70] Ransom's book, *God Without Thunder*, urged modern man to resist "the usurpation of the Godhead by the soft modern version of the Christ."[71] And there is evidence of occasional, guarded defense of Southern fundamentalism, particularly by Davidson and Allen Tate.[72]

But the more common view within the group was that there was something wrong at the very core of "the Southern religion." In his prominent contribution to *I'll Take My Stand*, Tate praised the Medieval Catholic Church for its use of science, reason, and nature to defend Christian dogma. This effort, centered on Thomas Aquinas, "performed a tremendous feat of spiritual unity, and *the only kind of unity* that the Western mind is capable of." In contrast, America in general, and the American South in particular, were founded by merchants and traders, "theoretically Protestant." Jamestown, for example, was "a capitalistic enterprise" guided by persons "who were already convinced adherents of large-scale exploitation of nature." The American South evolved into "a feudal society without a feudal religion." Its faith was "inarticulate" because it tried to reach its destiny through Protestantism, "a non-agrarian and trading religion," indeed, "*hardly a religion at all*, but a result of secular ambition." Tate even suggested that the South had lost the Civil War *because* of its grounding on a frail Protestant "half religion."[73]

While certainly holding to the importance of religion, direct or implicit criticism over the Southern attachment to Anabaptism and fundamentalism appeared with some frequency among the Agrarians. In *I'll Take My Stand*, Stark Young despaired over "the vast growth of the denominations formerly associated with the most bigoted and ignorant classes" and "the preacher-ridden towns."[74] Cauley and Owsley also turned up their noses at certain base realities of the Southern faith.[75] Ransom discounted religious institutions and expressions that lacked ritual and sacrifice. At the same time, he jettisoned most orthodox Christian beliefs, embracing in their place an extreme naturalism.[76] Even Lytle would later indict the "strict construction of the Bible with its literal fallacy," as a common trait of Southern Protestantism.[77] In short, the Southern Agrarians leaned as a group toward the New Agrarian view that rural revival depended in part on a fresh religious dispensation.[78]

Even on the issue of technology (and despite a dissent by Lytle), some of the Southern Agrarians saw innovation or the application of science to production as a positive good, even as *necessary* to their project. Actually inching close to the arguments of Borsodi, Davidson emphasized that the group did not mean to condemn all forms of industry and machinery, only the extreme of "giant industrialism." As he wrote, "[u]ndoubtedly the South is a part of modern economy. Who could deny that?" The real need was to encourage "modified handicrafts with machine tools."[79] Ransom was adamant that the South "must be industrialized," within the limits of moderation,[80] a view reiterated by Young[81] and Nixon.[82] Cauley became almost euphoric over the promise of certain mechanical devices. For example, believing it "greatly to be desired that there be a much farther reduction in the rural birth rate," he argued that "we now possess the knowledge and the mechanical appliances necessary to act."[83] Henry Blue Kline, in *I'll Take My Stand*, praised the prototypical Southerner who understood that "he would do better to make intelligent use of the fruits of material progress," to engage in a "critical and selective use of mechanical and mechanized facilities." Specifically, "[m]otor cars, talking pictures, the radio, [and] labor-saving devices" had "amazingly great potentialities for the extension and enrichment of the leisure one might devote to humane pursuits."[84] Lanier denied that their goal was the scrapping of industrial technology. To the contrary, he actually urged the "further mechanization of industrial production," arguing that this would mean the use of fewer workers in industry, persons who could then be returned to agriculture.[85]

In the same vein, the Southern Agrarians generally held to the view that history was moving toward a decentralist order. The cities and urban capitalism had failed. Indeed, Owsley reported that "[i]t seems quite clear to the Agrarians that technological unemployment is destined to increase with rapid acceleration," a development that fed into the hands of an agrarian reorganization.[86] Cauley saw American history at a turning point, where the turmoil and confusions of "the pioneering period" and the effort to fit agriculture into the money economy were giving way. The new order would allow for a more sedate, small-scale, decentralized life.[87]

Even on the question of the desirability of a peasant style of life, the Southern Agrarians were at best schizophrenic. On the one hand, their common project of building an agrarian society composed of subsistence farms could be seen as endorsing a peasant-like society. Indeed, Owsley explicitly called for a new form of "feudal" tenure over the land, while Tate urged the adoption of a religious faith in the South that would be fit for a "feudal" order.[88] Lytle's vision of the good society was one without mortgages, with horses, without much money or roads, and with the security born of living in close proximity with neighbors;[89] in short, a peasant community. On the other hand, this would be a peasantry without its native fundamentalist faith, one under the prying eye of welfare (relative to their children) and Extension (relative to their produce) officials, one in the throes of extensive social engineering.

Dispersion

The 1940s saw the dispersal of the Vanderbilt Agrarians, and an end to the aggressive phase of their project. John Crowe Ransom left Vanderbilt for Kenyon College and the *Kenyon Review*, where he soon renounced his agrarian work. Others left for locations spread from New York to Iowa to California. By 1943, only Owsley and Davidson remained in Tennessee.

Andrew Lytle, perhaps the most "pure" of the Agrarians and the only one to survive into the last decade of the twentieth century, took no solace from the rise of the American suburbs. For Bailey, Zimmerman, and Bromfield, they represented the unexpected answer to their decentralist quest. For Lytle, the "ordered slums of suburbia" were "made for the confusion of the spirit."[90]

In 1980, on the Fiftieth anniversary of *I'll Take My Stand*, Lytle noted that the family and the neighborhood had made up the world in which the Twelve had grown up. But "[t]ravel through the countryside today and you will find it empty." "[T]he Agrarians failed," he concluded, certainly in their inability to affect "the amoeba-like growth of the machine and its technology."[91] No one at the time could believe that the world they had known, and still knew, stood at the precipice. This was why the communities threatened with destruction at best only sympathized with the Southern Agrarian cause, and had failed to act.[92]

Yet the analysis offered here points to intrinsic flaws in their joint project, ones common to the new Agrarian Mind and ones that undercut the probability of influence or success: an extraordinarily ambitious political-economic agenda; a certain hostility toward the very folk they sought to defend; damaging criticism of the Christian faith actually found in rural America; a residual faith in technology; a misplaced belief in the prevailing course of history; and a schizophrenic attitude toward the peasant life. In truth, Lytle—along with Davidson—were probably the Southern Agrarians least affected by these views: but they were a minority.

In his commentary on "The Southern Religion" Allen Tate observed that "the scientific mind always plays havoc with the spiritual life when it is not powerfully enlisted in its cause; it [science] cannot be permitted to operate alone." Ironically, it would be the rural radical Protestants, adherents of the "half religion" derided by Tate, who would alone find a workable, community-based solution to the very real problem that he posed.

Notes

1. A solid short analysis of this group is found in: Virginia Rock, "The Twelve Southerners, Biographical Essays," in *I'll Take My Stand: The South and the Agrarian Tradition* (Baton Rouge and London: Louisiana State University Press, 1977 [1930]): 361-410.
2. A good list of the more significant published works from the 1980s alone is found in: Michael Jordan, "A Myopic Study," *Chatahoochee Review* 9 (Summer 1989): 34-35; a review of Paul Conkin, *The Southern Agrarians* (Knoxville: University of Tennessee Press, 1988).
3. Thomas Lawrence Connelly, "The Vanderbilt Agrarians: Time and Place in Southern Tradition," *Tennessee Historical Quarterly* 22 (March 1963): 23.
4. Louis D. Rubin, Jr., "Introduction," in *I'll Take My Stand*, pp. xiii-xiv, xxviii, xxxi-xxxii, xxxv.
   Donald Davidson, it should be noted, objected to this line of interpretation. In an August 12, 1962 letter to Allen Tate, he wrote: "I still don't like the notion found both in Louis Rubin's writings and—less specifically—in hers [Virginia Rock's]—that all of our agonizing, brooding, studying, discussing, philosophizing, writing about what we had seen, known, experienced, fought-through, lived through, was but a 'metaphor'...." (Allen Tate Papers, Princeton University); I am grateful to Michael Jordan for bringing this letter to my attention.
5. Rock, "The Twelve Southerners," p. 363. Emphasis added.
6. Donald Davidson, "I'll Take My Stand: A History," *American Review* 5 (Summer 1935): 304; hereafter, referred to as "History."

7. Gerald W. Johnson, "No More Excuses: A Southerner to Southerners," *Harper's Magazine* 162 (Feb. 1931): 333-334.
8. Davidson, "History," p. 302.
9. Frank Lawrence Owsley, "The Pillars of Agrarianism [1935]," in Harriet Chappell Owsley, ed., *The South: Old and New Frontiers. Selected Essays of Frank Lawrence Owsley* (Athens: University of Georgia Press, 1969): 181.
10. Andrew Nelson Lytle, "They Took Their Stand: The Agrarian View After Fifty Years [1979]," in M.E. Bradford, ed., *From Eden to Babylon: The Social and Political Essays of Andrew Nelson Lytle* (Washington, DC: Regnery Gateway, 1990): 222.
11. Rock, "The Twelve Southerners," p. 372.
12. "A Statement of Principles," in *I'll Take My Stand*, p. xxxix.
13. "Statement," pp. xxxix-xlvii.
14. John Crowe Ransom, "Reconstructed but Unregenerate," in *I'll Take My Stand*, pp. 15-16.
15. Lyle H. Lanier, "A Critique of the Philosophy of Progress," pp. 146-147.
16. Allen Tate, "Remarks on the Southern Religion," *I'll Take My Stand*, p. 168.
17. Andrew Nelson Lytle, "The Hind Tit," *I'll Take My Stand*, pp. 211, 216, 241.
18. Lytle, "The Hind Tit," p. 245.
19. Herman Clarence Nixon, "Whither Southern Economy?" *I'll Take My Stand*, p. 178.
20. Davidson, "History," pp. 310, 320.
21. John Gould Fletcher, "Education Past and Present," *I'll Take My Stand*, pp. 95, 99, 104-105, 110-111, 118.
22. Frank Lawrence Owsley, "The Irrepressible Conflict," *I'll Take My Stand*, pp. 67, 69-70, 74, 91.
23. Robert Penn Warren, "The Briar Patch," *I'll Take My Stand*, p. 262.
24. Davidson, "History," p. 308.
25. Donald Davidson, "A Mirror for Artists," *I'll Take My Stand*, pp. 29, 51, 57, 60.
26. Lytle, "The Hind Tit," p. 205.
27. Rock, "The Twelve Southerners," p. 365; and Michael Jordan, "Donald Davidson's 'Agrarian' Creed of Memory." Doctoral dissertation, University of Georgia, 1989: pp. 95-96.
28. Davidson, "History," p. 317.
29. Idus A. Newby, "The Southern Agrarians: A View from Thirty Years," *Agricultural History* 37 (July 1963): 145.
30. Conkin, *The Southern Agrarians*.
31. The role of Herbert Agar, the appearance of *Who Owns America?* in 1936, and the relationship of the Southern Agrarians to the journal, *Free America*, will be discussed in chapter 6.
32. As Lytle would report, the Scopes Trial "...set me to studying American and Southern history, about which I knew little to nothing. I kept at it for seven years, with Frank Owsley to guide me." In: Lytle, "They Took Their Stand," pp. 222-223.
33. Rock, "The Twelve Southerners," p. 383.
34. Lytle, "The Hind Tit," pp. 208, 213-17.
35. Ibid., pp. 219-220, 223.
36. Ibid., pp. 222-224.
37. Ibid., p. 227.
38. Ibid., pp. 225-232.
39. Ibid., pp. 235-237.

40. Ibid., pp. 237-242.
41. Andrew Nelson Lytle, "The Backwoods Progression [1933]," in *From Here to Babylon*, p. 81.
42. From Andrew Nelson Lytle, "Semi-Centennial: An Agrarian Afterward [1981]," in *From Eden to Babylon*, p. 187.
43. Andrew Nelson Lytle, "The Small Farm Secures the State [1936]," in *From Eden to Babylon*, p. 44.
44. Andrew Nelson Lytle, "John Taylor of Caroline [1934]," in *From Eden to Babylon*, p. 48.
45. Lytle, *From Eden to Babylon*, pp. 43-44, 80, 87.
46. Lytle, "The Hind Tit," p. 244.
47. Owsley, "The Irrepressible Conflict," pp. 71-72.
48. Frank Lawrence Owsley, *Plain Folk of the Old South* (Baton Rouge: Louisiana State University Press, 1949): vii-ix, 7, 10, 16-17.
49. Owsley, *Plain Folk*, p. 94.
50. Ibid., p. 110; also; pp. 95-96, 104-108, 111-115, 125-130.
51. Ibid., p. 135.
52. John Crowe Ransom, "Happy Farmers," *American Review* I (October 1933): 529.
53. Ibid., p. 531; also pp. 514-521.
54. Ibid., pp. 533-535.
55. Donald Davidson, "Agrarianism for Commuters," *American Review* I (May 1933: 238-242).
56. See Donald Davidson, "The First Agrarian Economist," *American Review* 5 (April 1935): 106.
57. Troy J. Cauley, *Agrarianism: A Program for Farmers* (Chapel Hill: University of North Carolina Press, 1935): 3, 104-108.
58. See: T. J. Cauley, "The Integration of Agrarian and Exchange Economies," *American Review* 5 (Oct. 1935): 585.
59. Cauley, *Agrarianism*, pp. 111-117.
60. Ibid., pp. 176-185.
61. Ibid., pp. 188-208.
62. Cauley, "The Integration of Agrarian and Exchange Economies," pp. 593, 598-599.
63. Owsley, "The Pillars of Agrarianism," pp. 180-187.
64. Ibid., p. 189.
65. Davidson, "History," p. 106.
66. Owsley, "Pillars of Agrarianism," pp. 182, 184, 186.
67. Ransom, "Happy Farmers," p. 530.
68. Owsley, "The Pillars of Agrarianism," p. 181.
69. Lanier, "A Critique of the Philosophy of Progress," pp. 152-154.
70. Lytle, "The Hind Tit," p. 244.
71. From John Crowe Ransome, *God Without Thunder: An Unorthodox Defense of Orthodoxy* (New York: Harcourt, Brace, 1930): 327-328.
72. See Jordan, "Donald Davidson's 'Agrarian' Creed of Memory," pp. 63-65.
73. Tate, "Remarks on the Southern Religion," pp. 164-168; emphasis added.
74. Stark Young, "Not in Memoriam, But in Defense," *I'll Take My Stand*, pp. 340-341.
75. Cauley, *Agrarianism*, p. 159; Owsley, *Plain Folk*, p. 98.
76. See Kiernan Quinlan, *John Crowe Ransom's Secular Faith* (Baton Rouge: Louisiana State University Press, 1989): 84-106.

77. Lytle, "They Took Their Stand," p. 222.
78. In later years, several of the Twelve would confess that they gave too little attention to religion in their campaign. See "The Agrarians Today: Five Questions," *Shenandoah 3* (Summer 1952): 20, 29; and "Discussion: The Agrarian-Industrial Metaphor," in William C. Havard and Walter Sullivan, editors, *A Band of Prophets: The Vanderbilt Agrarians After Fifty Years* (Baton Rouge: Louisiana State University Press, 1982): 176.
79. Davidson, "History," pp. 313, 318-319.
80. Ransom, "Reconstructed But Unregenerate," p. 22.
81. Young, "Not in Memoriam, But in Defense," p. 355.
82. Nixon, "Whitter Southern Economy?" p. 176.
83. Cauley, *Agrarianism*, p. 156.
84. Henry Blue Kline, "William Remington: A Study in Individualism," *I'll Take My Stand*, pp. 320, 325.
85. Lanier, "A Critique of the Philosophy of Progress," pp. 151-152.
86. Owsley, "The Pillars of Agrarianism," p. 183.
87. Cauley, *Agrarianism*, pp. 165-167.
88. Owsley, "The Pillars of Agrarianism," p. 184; and Tate, "Remarks on the Southern Religion," p. 164.
89. Lytle, "They Took Their Stand," pp. 226-227.
90. Quoted in Rock, "The Twelve Southerners," p. 387.
91. Lytle, "They Took Their Stand," p. 229.
92. A sympathetic analysis of the Southern Agrarians 'in exile' is found in: Richard M. Weaver, *The Southern Essays*, eds. George M. Curtis III and James J. Thompson, Jr. (Indianapolis: The Liberty Press, 1987): 29-49.

6

The American Distributists and the Quest for Fusion: Herbert Agar

•

Distributism was the name applied to the political and economic program of two prominent English writers: Hilaire Belloc and G.K. Chesterton. Prior to 1933, their advocacy for "the property state" had relatively minor impact in the United States. That changed with the appearance of the *American Review*, "one of the chief purposes" of which was to make better known their work.[1] As noted earlier, editor Seward Collins also successfully drew the Southern Agrarians into the magazine's circle in a conscious act of ideological fusion.

But the Distributist-Agrarian alliance stumbled over the shortcomings of the *Review* and the journal died in 1936. The task of translating Distributism into an American idiom then fell to the popular American historian, Herbert Agar. For the balance of the decade, he crusaded for the ideas, reconfigured, of Belloc and Chesterton. Moreover, he sought to build a grand coalition of New Agrarians, one embracing not only the Distributists and the Tennessee Agrarians but also the Borsodians, Catholic and Protestant rural movements, and the Country Life campaign. His initial success was made all the more bitter by his intellectual abandonment, even betrayal, of the cause shortly after the turn of the decade.

The Chesterbelloc[2]

The first six issues of the *American Review* in 1933 serialized Belloc's *The Restoration of Property*, the finest and most detailed exposition of the Distributist program. Combining the egalitarian

125

Jacobinism of the French Revolution with traditional Roman Catholicism, Belloc maintained that political democracy required economic democracy; and the latter, in turn, required the widest possible ownership of productive property. "The family is ideally free," he wrote, "when it fully controls all the means necessary for the production of such wealth as it should consume for normal living."[3] Modern men, living under industrial conditions, became "wage-slaves" who thought only of income. "Free men," in contrast, "think of income as the product of property, and the typical form of property, which is also the foundational form, is property in land."[4]

Openly seeking "to re-erect a peasantry in a society where the idea of a peasantry has almost disappeared" could not succeed by letting economic processes flow freely. Rather, Belloc held that there must be "a deliberate reversal of economic tendencies," through government subsidy and protection. A "free peasantry" would only be gained through acts of massive social and economic engineering.[5]

In his effort to rally the "radicals of the Right" or "the revolutionary conservatives" of America behind the same project, editor Collins gave attention to both the major themes and the nuances of English Distributist thought. He welcomed contributions to his journal not only from Belloc, but also from Chesterton, including a revealing "Mild Remonstrance" by the latter over an article in the review that had ridiculed the Roman Catholic opposition to birth control.[6] Collins gave regular praise and attention to the "Guild Movement," including "a plan to incorporate nationally into the industrial fabric of the United States a modernization of the old Guild system," a project backed by such prominent figures as Frank A. Vanderlip of New York and Senator Gerald Nye of North Dakota.[7] He sought to refine Distributist theory, through reviews and essays such as Hilary Pepler's "The Distributist," where the author:

> Hence the effect of Distributism is only to be seen in the lives and actions of those who believe in the same truth. It has taken some men 'back to the land,' others to municipal and political work aiming to direct the laws of state and locality in consonance with this justice, others to home work for themselves rather than factory work for another, others to the study of the Popes and the Gospels –but all to a realization that—to quote one of your own poets—*They enslave their children's children who make compromise with sin.*[8]

Collins also sought to show how quintessentially American events and movements fit into Distributist themes, typified by a portrait of

Mormonism in Utah as replaying "the ancient dream of agrarian man that all men, avowedly and prayerfully suckling the earth as the mother, may live very near one to the other in body and in soul, one great brotherhood."[9] He gave particular attention to encouraging a uniquely American distributist culture, ranging from publication of essays on America by T.S. Eliot,[10] to the encouragement of an American art rooted in Western civilization,[11] to guarded praise for the Iowa "folk novelist" Ruth Suckow.[12]

The Southern Agrarians produced some of their finest essays for the *Review*, including Donald Davidson's splendid analysis of the continuing power of American regionalism, "Still Rebels, Still Yankees."[13] The magazine's implicit alliance affected Southern Agrarian ideas in other ways, as well. Distributist economic analysis and policy schemes, several decades in the making, helped to fill the empty corners of the Southern Agrarian argument, giving a welcome specificity to their work. And the *Review's* base in New York added to the impression that a national audience had been found for the New Agrarian cause.

All the same, there remained something slightly alien, or "non-American," about the *American Review*. This was due, in part, to the "medievalism" that percolated through the journal, a deference to the archaic themes and language of "guildsmen" like A.J. Penty. Despite their oft-repeated rejection of fascism, some of the Southerners began to mix their distinct accent in the dangerous currents of Europe's contemporary radical right. In his otherwise able critique of Lewis Mumford, for example, John Gould Fletcher proceeded to endorse a curious economic agenda. "We must build again," he wrote, "within the framework of the twentieth-century mechanical state, the medieval state of the guildsmen. In other words, we must tend toward the corporate state of European Fascism."[14] In this respect, the demise of the *American Review* over the very question of fascist sympathies probably came none too soon.

Land of the Free

The task of fitting Distributism into an American context then fell to Herbert Agar. Born 1897 in New Rochelle, New York, the son of a prominent corporate attorney, Agar attended the Newman Preparatory Academy, and received degrees from Columbia (A.B.) and Princeton

(M.A., Ph.D.) Universities. For five years, he taught at the exclusive Hun School in Princeton, NJ, and collaborated on several books with another young teacher, Eleanor Carroll Chilton, the daughter of a U.S. Senator from West Virginia. They co-authored a volume of poetry, *Fire and Sleet and Candlelight*, to which Agar contributed twenty-two torrid sonnets on frustrated love, and a lengthy tome on the nature and "necessity" of poetry, entitled *The Garment of Praise*.[15]

The problem was that there already was a Mrs. Agar: Adeline, daughter of a distinguished Princeton geology professor, whom Agar had married in 1918 and who was home with their two young children. The complications of this triangle contributed to Agar's departure for England in 1928, where he took a junior editorial post at *G.K.'s Weekly*, the journal owned and edited by G.K. Chesterton. Here, Agar drank deeply from the well of Distributist ideas. In 1930, he became London correspondent for the *Louisville* (Ky.) *Courier-Journal* and the *Louisville Times*, and the following year took the additional post of literary editor for the *English Review*. He remained in London until 1934 when, with a recent divorce, a new wife, and a fresh Pulitzer Prize for his first solo book, he returned to The United States.

Agar's award-winning volume, *The People's Choice*, was a popular political history of the United States, focusing on the lives and character of each of the presidents, from Washington through Harding. A major theme of the volume was the creation of an agrarian republic in the late eighteenth century and its apogee during the presidency of Andrew Jackson. Then came the growth of industrial capitalist power, and the destruction of the agrarian dream. Agar's conclusion regarding Abraham Lincoln aptly captured his purpose:

> There is no telling whether [Lincoln] would have made [war] if he had realized that the South was fighting for an agrarian society against the threat of a businessman's oligarchy. Lincoln would have hated that oligarchy almost as much as did Jefferson Davis, and if he had grasped the main issue, Lincoln might have felt that his real fight lay elsewhere.[16]

Agar directly entered the campaign for a native Distributive order through a 1934 article for the *American Review*, entitled "The Task for Conservatism." Seward Collins, in a commentary on the first year of his journal, would cite this article as the most representative essay that he had published.[17] In using the label, "conservative," Agar admitted that it had been thoroughly "discredited," twisted by the apostles of plutocracy into the defense of "gamblers and promoters." He wrote: "According to this view, Mark Hanna was a conservative."[18] He sought to save the term by appealing to "another, and an older, America," a time when there was virtue and a moral plan for the nation.

Central to this plan, Agar insisted, was "[t]he widest possible distribution of property." To some, notably Jefferson, "this meant agrarianism," or self-sufficient farming. To others, such as John Adams, "this meant an interdependent community" of farmers and modest merchants, with government maintaining the balance. All the founders held that "a wide diffusion of property...made for enterprise, for family responsibility, and in general for institutions that fit man's nature and that give a chance for a desirable life."[19]

But America had lost its way, Agar said, becoming "the victim of economic determinism." The natural wealth of the nation in conjunction with the industrial revolution had intensified "the normal human temptation to sacrifice ideals for money," lifting "the rewards for a successful raid on society to dangerous heights." The culture of diffused property had simply not struck deep enough roots before the attack by "the barbarism based on monopoly." Moreover, Agar said, the dominant American faith—Protestant Christianity—was at that time already in decline and incapable of restraining the commercial "buccaneers." Finally, the political franchise was expanded at the very moment that "the temptation to plunder was growing irresistible," opening up the system to a form of mob rule, guided by the plutocrats. The latter destroyed "an intrenched landed interest" during the Civil War, and so had their way for fifty years. By 1914, the American capitalists no longer needed an agricultural surplus for export, and they planned the coup de grace for the independent farmer. Indeed, the "Coolidge prosperity" masked the wholesale destruction of private property in rural areas.[20]

Could the situation be reversed? Agar thought it possible that trends had gone too far in the wrong direction: "If Americans have come to believe that a wage is the same thing as freedom; if they prefer such a wage, with its appearance of security, to the obvious danger and responsibilities of ownership, then they cannot be saved from the servitude which awaits them."[21] Yet he concluded that a "redistribution of property" could still be accomplished; this was "the root of a real conservative policy for the United States." The ownership of land, machine-shop, small store, or a share of "some necessarily huge machine" needed to become the normal thing, to set the moral tone for society. This would make "for stability in family and community life, for responsibility, for enterprise" and for all the other virtues which "have long been taken to cover abuses of an unclean monopoly." Along with Belloc, Agar agreed that this goal was *not* in line with existing economic trends: "It must be produced artificially and then guarded by favorable legislation." But there was little choice: "Either we restore property, or we restore slavery," through a communism that waited at the end of monopoly capitalism's work.[22]

Where "The Task for Conservatism" ably translated English Distributist ideas into American history and language, Agar's next book, *Land of the Free,* would powerfully summarize the New Agrarian argument. In light of his radically altered views only a half-decade later, it is notable that Agar here consciously turned his back on Europe. Eight months of travel through America had convinced him that: "It is our job to save a corner of the world from the despotisms that encroach on Europe." The best traits in American life were not those copied from the old continent, "but the traits we have freely adapted, or else originated—the traits which are our own."[23]

Agar proceeded to praise the American countryside and its provincial towns and small cities, and to condemn—in the harshest terms— "world-cities" such as New York, Chicago, and London. "The giant world city, with its cosmopolitanism, its scepticism, its falling birthrate, its lack of morals, its imitative and decadent art," was the sure sign of an end of a civilization, of the decline of a people. In such "world-cities," man "is stricken with sterility," finding himself "too bored or too unzestful even to breed normally." Where the birth of a new culture was marked by "a new affirmation of life," the end featured "a hospitality to death," where man "lies down tired in the midst of his marvels," his numbers dwindled, and his cities soon "half-empty."[24]

The decadence of Europe could be found in Chicago and New York, where ideas, interests, and habits of life pushed toward ruin. But where these cities were "colonial and rootless" and doomed, America still had a living "native" culture. As in ages past, out of a group of farming settlements, a new culture had been born. Adapting a term from Oswald Spengler, Agar celebrated the "culture-man," a creator or builder who knew there were "plenty of things in the world worth fighting for" and who had a rootedness in a place or in the land.

"Culture men" could still be found in many parts of America: the villages and farms of New England, rural Pennsylvania ("especially the country west of Philadelphia round about Lancaster and York"), and the deep South. But the creative soul of America now lay in the great Mississippi Valley. As he wrote:

> [T]here are signs of the conversion of the intellectual class in the Mississippi Valley to the idea that if America is to have a culture of her own the intellectuals had better stay at home and take part in that culture instead of streaming to New York and becoming good little copies of an alien Civilization. This conversion is one of the most important events in American history.[25]

Agar praised regional cities such as Nashville and Indianapolis, which had held on to their native-born writers and thinkers. He specifically cited the Vanderbilt Agrarians for rejecting the fraud of the "Coolidge prosperity" and for staying immersed in the deeper and richer culture of the South: "As a result of their secession from the world-city, there are now four or five country towns where the local life is richer, where American Culture is closer to defining itself." For a "culture man" to leave Nashville or Indianapolis for New York would be "to tear up strong roots and plant puny ones," to give up spiritual intensity for "the mass of tenants and bed-occupiers in the sea of houses." A real Culture, rooted in the great agrarian mid-section of the country, was now taking form. If it could only avoid contamination from New York and Europe, a grand destiny awaited America, the opportunity to create a "third way out," avoiding both communism and decadence, and building a true property-owning free society.[26]

This celebration of an *agri*-cultural America was accompanied by the usual New Agrarian themes. Turning to religion, for example, Agar maintained that Protestantism was again the problem. It tended to endorse the concentration of ownership, to confuse the duties of religion with the call of business, and to support easy credit (Protestant fundamentalism was not even worthy of note). In contrast, Catholicism tended to favor "small property" and "hard money." By implication, Agar held that a lasting American agrarian culture would necessitate abandonment of Protestantism, and a turn to Catholicism: views very close to those of Allen Tate. As Agar put it, "a nation without a strong religious basis is not disciplined enough to know freedom."[27]

Concerning technology, Agar threw himself enthusiastically into the argumentative arms of Borsodi. In calling for the "quick decentralization" of industries such as textiles, he pointedly referred to the "startling presentation of the facts and figures...by Ralph Borsodi." Quoting extensively from *The Distribution Age*, Agar concluded that "[m]ost people agree that the excesses of modern advertising are socially evil" and that in many lines of production "we can revive small property...without interfering with economic efficiency." Indeed, at the close of the book, Agar rested his whole case on the assumption that technology would be the friend of agrarianism reborn:

> But now we have the age of electricity and the internal combustion engine—both of which are well suited to small and scattered industrial plants. The Power Revolution of the past twenty-five years has come to the aid of small property.[28]

Agar also turned the Agrarian cause into an argument for massive social engineering. Those who had "confidence in America" must now take radical steps to fulfill the nation's destiny, "and in taking them we must use all the dangerous modern methods of propaganda." These should be turned to tasks ranging from convincing citizens to save "the institutions of real private property," to curbing credit finance, securing hard money ("the friend of small property"), and redistributing property on a massive scale (Agar borrowed extensively here from Owsley's "Pillars of Agrarianism"). A model would be "the Scandinavian countries," where the people had stared down the urban capitalists and had created a viable social order resting on small property and rural survival.[29]

In all this, the existing farmers would have to be remade as well. The future required pure agrarianism, where "the farmer first makes himself, his family, and his beasts, as self-supporting as possible" and only then "sells a surplus." But America now had an agricultural sector that was "over-capitalized and over-productive." Accepting Ransom's argument that America was finished as a food-exporting country ("Happy Farmers"), Agar saw "ninety million acres of redundant land." The "agrarian farmer" simply could not get a fair return on his surplus as long as he had to compete with "half-ruined commercial farmers," in the sale of goods to the nonagricultural population. In the short run, "bounties" could help sustain the *agrarian* farmer. But in the long run, it would be necessary for farm policy "to eliminate the purely commercial farmer by means of differential taxation."[30]

By this time, Agar had developed direct friendship with several of the Tennessee Agrarians. Full of energy, and with a gift for pulling ideas and groups together, he set out to solidify further the Agrarian-Distributist alliance. Together with Allen Tate, he compiled and edited a collection of essays, entitled *Who Owns America? A New Declaration of Independence*. Eight of the Twelve Southerners participated (Davidson, Lanier, Lytle, Owsley, Ransom, Tate, Wade, and Warren), along with Cauley and literary critic Cleanth Brooks. From the *American Review* circle, Agar pulled in Father Rawe, David Cushman Coyle, Henry Clay Evans, Jr., and Hilaire Belloc. Agar's friends, Willis and Mary Shattuck Fisher, also joined in the effort.

As an agrarian tract, *Who Owns America?* was less satisfying than either *I'll Take My Stand* or *Land of the Free*. The writing was less spirited; the integration of Distributist and Agrarian themes sometimes forced (as example, compare Lytle's "The Hind Tit" from 1930 with the subsequent "The Small Farm Secures the State"). Moreover, new ideologies drifted into the text, ones only prefigured in earlier Agrarian argumentation, including secular social democracy and liberal feminism.[31]

In his introduction, Agar gave a summary of the American Dream. To him, it meant that the large majority were free, meaning they were no one's dependent or "toady"; it meant that they could count on a "reasonable permanence," both of residence and occupation, "which makes a stable family possible"; and it meant the chance to do creative work, to bear responsibility, and to live in an atmosphere of social equality. The chief enemy of this dream, Agar said, was monopoly capitalism. This system claimed to offer freedom, but it was freedom of a different sort. It meant that a workman should be "free" from a home, for such attachment made him less mobile. Capitalist freedom meant, above all, a "freedom" from the presence of children. In fact, the liberty of the pro-business "Liberty League" left the citizen "landless and toolless, vagrant as the red Indian." The current volume, Agar said, drew together Protestants, agnostics, and Catholics, Southerners and Northerners, men of the city and of the country. "Our common ground," he wrote, "is a belief that monopoly capitalism is evil and self-destructive, and that it is possible, while preserving private ownership, to build a true democracy in which men would be better off both morally and physically."[32]

In a characteristic essay, a young Jesuit priest at Creighton University, John C. Rawe, attacked the joint stock corporate charter, a system which now sought to extend its domain into the countryside. The capitalists saw thirty million persons who should become "efficient wage slaves" and millions of acres that "should be factories." "To this the Agrarians object," Rawe declared. "They will offer every opposition to the extension of the joint-stock factory system from industry to agriculture." The Agrarians demanded that laws prohibit the ownership of farm land by corporations. The government should also teach farmers "how to use their own products for family subsistence," how to operate efficiently their farms as family units, how to diversify and rotate crops to replenish the soil, and "how to employ and care for efficient machinery built for use on the small farm." Claiming the support of the American heritage, Rawe called for "a new Declaration of Independence," involving the return to Jefferson's conception of "widespread ownership and co-operation under a general freehold tenure of property."[33]

In "A Plea to the Protestant Churches," Cleanth Brooks delivered the characteristic New Agrarian slaps at fundamentalism. He understood why liberal Protestants had "naturally found the cruder aspects of Fundamentalism repugnant." While calling the present numerical state of fundamentalism "impressive," he felt it would soon wither away. Its hold was "chiefly in rural areas" (an odd criticism to make given the overarching goal) and was tied to an aging generation of leaders. When they passed on, Brooks said, fundamentalism would "not be able to survive the present intellectual climate." The main thrust of his article was an attempt to convince liberal Protestants to abandon a left-wing social reform agenda, in favor of the agrarian-distributist platform.[34]

Agar's own essay for the compendium was a denial that "bigness" and corporate consolidation were historically or economically determined. It was only necessary to turn to Sweden, he said, "to blow this so-called economic law sky high." Twenty years earlier, Agar reported, the Swedes had decided that they would be free men and women. As citizens, "they would own and control the basic utilities"; as producers, "they would own the means of production"; and as consumers, they would organize "cooperative societies." Agar gave particular attention to the work of *Koopertiva förbundet* in beating the margarine and flour monopolies to the ground. The "Swedish experiment" also showed that the optimum size for industrial plants was "the smallest size which can use the most modern, labor-saving machinery." In Sweden, you found "[d]ecentralized factories producing for local use," using technologically superior machines. The Swedes were also re-educating their small-holding farmers for their role in the new order of things. Carefully avoiding mention of the role of the Swedish Social Democratic Labor Party in all these changes, Agar concluded that "the Swedish people have shown that the property State can be made real in the modern world."[35]

Sweden, and its Social Democratic neighbors Denmark and Norway, received still more praise in Agar's next book, *Pursuit of Happiness: The Story of American Democracy*. Ostensibly a history of the Democratic Party in the United States, from Jefferson to the Great Depression, the book was in part a defense of democratic socialism, under the guise of New Agrarian rhetoric. Modern Sweden, Agar insisted, contradicted the theories of Henry George: "[the Swedes] have used their advancing technology for the benefit of their people as a whole, so they [know] progress without destitution." Sweden showed "that a system of widely distributed property" could work.[36] More conventional New Agrarian themes also appeared. Agar said that serious democracy required "immense sacrifice" and "immense self-discipline." At its core must lay a comprehensive system of free public schools in order to give democracy "a fair chance to justify itself." Jefferson himself understood that technology was the friend of decentralization. Agar quoted the sage of Monticello: "We have reduced the large and expensive machinery for most things to the compass of a private family, and any family of any size is now getting machines on a small scale for their household purposes." But Agar insisted that while anticipating Borsodian economics by a century, Jefferson had made a serious blunder in acquiescing to majoritarian rule (a mistake not repeated by Borsodi). For Agar, democracy meant rule by an elite, one property-owning and one properly educated.[37]

Free America

A bolder step to rally the New Agrarian movement behind Agar's leadership came with the founding of the journal, *Free America*, in 1936/1937. Its origins lay in New York City, where the appearance of *Who Owns America?* had stimulated formation of a small group of distributists, including Chard Powers Smith, Katherine Gauss Jackson, and Chauncey Stillman. Calling themselves the "Independent Americans," they met at first in Smith's apartment. They soon drew Agar into their circle, along with Catholic, Protestant, and Jewish "rural life" sympathizers, Ralph Borsodi and School of Living enthusiasts, and the Tennessee Agrarians.

Two formal meetings convened in 1936, one in Nashville and the other in Princeton, New Jersey, to form a unified organization built around a statement of common principles. At Nashville, they agreed that the "end of man is the development of his individual and social nature," and that in a "just society power is distributed among everyone." Freedom and security required "the wide distribution of active ownership of land and productive property." Population should also be "decentralized," while agriculture "should be given its rightful recognition as the prime factor in a secure culture." The group also agreed that "civil rights" and social protection would be best secured "by a decentralist or distributist economy." They further held that the "efficiency of smaller local production units" derived from "the latest developments of science."[38] On this basis, they assented to the creation of a new journal, to be called *New America*, as a vehicle for the galvanizing movement.

Renamed *Free America*, the inaugural issue appeared in January 1937. The editors were Agar, Borsodi, Bertram B. Fowler, Jackson, Smith, and Stillman. The last, a recent Catholic convert, was from an old Eastern family and heir to a fortune built on Texas oil and New York banks. Stillman bankrolled the *Free America* project and donated space in his home at 119 East 19th Street for use as the magazine's editorial and business office.

Conspicuous for their absence were any of the original Twelve Southerners. Nonetheless, in his front page article for the first issue, also entitled "Free America," Agar turned to them as the inspiration for the journal. During "the high unpleasant noon of Coolidge prosperity" and "[a]s if directed from without," this "band of friends," these New Agrarians, began the ferment: "For example, Mr. Allen Tate and Mr. John Crowe Ransom were suddenly moved to write to one another on the same day, raising the same questions of political philosophy and suggesting some of the same tentative answers. Neither of them had faced these questions before." At about the same time, Agar himself had traveled to England and came to know the English Distributists, "democrats whose ardor came straight from the French Revolution" and "whose thought was rooted in the spiritual affirmation of democracy which underlies the Christian faith." These two schools of thought found a common enemy in "Plutocracy" and a common political program in the quest for "a wide distribution of productive property." Agar emphasized "the interesting fact" that the Southerners had "made [this] Affirmation before they had read a word of their British predecessors."[39]

The lead editorials for the first issue defined Distributism as "the meeting ground for those who are equally opposed to finance-capitalism, communism and fascism," with "the fundamental principle of *distributism*" being "decentralization." The editors recognized "a fundamental community of aim in the Borsodi Homestead Movement, the Southern Agrarians and their allied Distributist Groups throughout the country, the Consumer Cooperative Movement, the Catholic Rural Life Conference, certain of the Protestant rural life organizations, and the Single Tax Movement." The purpose of *Free America* was no less than the crafting of a common ideology and social and political program. As the editors put it:

> *Free America* aims to act as a forum wherein the identity of aim between many current movements may be discussed and crystallized, and apparent inconsistencies between some of them reconciled, to the end of building up a body of doctrine acceptable to all, and, based upon this, a program of action.

Already, the Southern Agrarians in their work to relieve tenant farmers and "the Single Taxers" in their quest for stable land tenure, showed the way for "distributist political action." The Catholic and (some) Protestant groups, together with the Borsodi Homestead movement, had begun "distributist educational action." The Consumer Co-ops stood for "distributist economic action" while the Southern Agrarian "Discussion Groups" sparked the quest for "a common and inclusive" doctrine.[40]

The early issues, even years, of *Free America* did convey a real energy, occasionally bordering on giddiness, born in part out of writers and activists coming to discover new friends in unexpected places. The February 1937 issue, for example, welcomed Hilaire Belloc to America for lectures at Fordham University. "As befits our different traditions," the editors wrote, "we have rephrased the English doctrine in adopting it...and have disputed among ourselves in our own idiom." Yet the primer that "first opened the eyes of most of us" was Belloc's *The Servile State*, originally published in 1913. Under the title, "Catholic

Agrarian Notes," urban social activist Dorothy Day wrote about the small farm that her movement had purchased in eastern Pennsylvania. They raised vegetables, fed a cow, and "did a good bit of canning," while also caring there for "invalids and children...the halt, the lame and the blind whom we do not wish to pass on to the state." Her community was "turning the thoughts of those who have been driven from the land back to it," showing the unemployed "that there is another way open to them which will enable them not only to earn a livelihood for themselves but for the wives and children which our industrial civilization would tend to deprive them of."[41]

The quest for unity in doctrine dominated the early issues. The editors, for example, endorsed labor unions when tied to a plan of "economic liberation" of workers. This meant the principle of small industry; the placement of "farmers and industrial workers alike" on subsistence homesteads; the use of consumer cooperatives; and the nationalization of those few necessary large industries. The problem of the machine loomed large as well, and drew frequent, consistent comment. In response to critics who accused them of turning back the clock (as though laboring under a sign in Old English, "Ye Dyftrybutyft Moovemente"), the editors "advocated a wider use of machinery than communists or technocrats ever dreamed of."[42] Several months later, Agar wrote that "the machine today is giving promise of a subtlety and an adaptability which suggest that man may soon be able to use it to implement whatever form of life he chooses."[43] The editors declared themselves "reactionary" only to the extent that they believed in the wide *re*distribution of real property, "with the addition, of course, of the latest mechanical and electrical aids."[44]

The March, 1937 "editorials" sought to clarify the "moral and spiritual" foundation of their cause. The editors wrote that "each of *the three roots*" of the "modern phase" of the American campaign—"the Catholic Agrarian Movement, the Borsodi Homestead Movement, and the Southern Agrarian Movement"—represented "a revolt against materialism" and "a reassertion of the belief that spiritual motivation was ultimately stronger in man than economic motivation" (a conclusion that required politely ignoring Borsodi's *This Ugly Civilization*). While reminding readers again that "research and the newer mechanics" showed that "the distributist argument...now walks clothed in economic and mechanical arguments," the editors restated their core spiritual axioms: "the moral proposition that the purpose of humanity" is to realize "the free and responsible individual human being"; "the economic proposition" that this goal was best achieved by effective ownership of the means of production; and "the political proposition" that the individual could maintain this moral freedom and economic security only if he also had a share in determining the policies of his government. "If you prefer, you can think of distributist doctrine as a tripod resting alike on all three of these propositions."[45]

In subsequent issues, the magazine took more open and specific stances on public policy. For example, it endorsed a proposal by Senator Borah of Idaho to prohibit the extension of Fourteenth Amendment protections to the "artificial persons" known as corporations. The editors also urged that the pending Bankhead-Jones "housing bill" be amended to give preference to "suburban building" over urban construction; to require that all new dwellings "include a tract of tillable land, preferably an acre or more," and that "suburban and sub-rural [sic] life" be recognized as "more secure economically and healthier physically and morally" than urban living.[46]

Frequent meetings also marked the early years. In an April, 1937 article, Michael Williams described a gathering "of the friends and advisors of this young journal," and his excitement as "some of the oldest and most indomitable forces of history" flowed together into a single cause, the restoration of a property state:

> Here were men whose line of attachment goes back to the Great Tradition by way of the most vital forces of Israel, when those forces were rooted in the soil of the earth, patient mother of man's physical life, and were nourished by religion. There were men for whom The Great Tradition is hallowed and made continuously vital and re-creative by reason of...Christianity: both Catholic and Protestant. And those forces in turn are linked with many of the fundamental values of Greece and Rome, and with the newer, cruder, energizing forces brought by wild tribes out of the North.[47]

More conventional coalition building included events such as Herbert Agar's keynote address to the Fifteenth Annual Convention of the National Catholic Rural Life Conference, where the "views and articles" of *Free America* were "frequently referred to, as were the accomplishments of Ralph Borsodi."[48]

The editors of *Free America* also sought to pull still other American agrarians into their project. Their first feature under the label, "These Men, This Land," was a tribute to Liberty Hyde Bailey. "The issues before the American eye a quarter century ago, when [he] quitted public life, were similar to those shimmering in the tangled tapestry we face today," the article stated. In Bailey's time, the question was "democracy and the land." In the author's time, it was "democracy and decentralization." Bailey "gave the country life movement in America its first big advance," employing every means possible, "from handshaking farmers to writing poetry" to crafting "his finest and most spiritualized" volume, *The Holy Earth.* The major difference was that *Free America* faced a situation that was "more acute," but one still calling for a rededication to Bailey's cause.[49]

Louis Bromfield directly joined the magazine's circle. Following interviews on his efforts to "establish a maximum of self-sufficiency" and to "reconcile man and nature" through repair of the soil,[50] the Ohio Jeffersonian wrote on occasion for *Free America.* In one review, Bromfield condemned industrialism as the source of "a vicious and Hellish puzzle," including the "concentration of wealth in the hands of a few" and the "dispossession of the earth for the many." Still in his pure agrarian phase, he concluded: "A piece of land for every family is the soundest of all bulwarks; indeed it is the ultimate one."[51]

Eventually, the Southern Agrarians overcame their reluctance to join wholeheartedly in *Free America.* Allen Tate first appeared on the masthead as an "Editor" in October, 1939. The next month he took the title of "Literary Editor." Over the following half year, book reviews by Davidson, Owsley, Ransom, and Tate filled the back pages of *Free America,* to the virtual exclusion of non-Tennessee Agrarians. Such reviews also extended, for the first time, beyond policy-oriented volumes to fiction and literary criticism.

As *Free America* matured, efforts to define a common body of doctrine continued to appear, albeit with less frequency. Herbert Agar, as example, drew on both R.H. Tawney's *The Acquisitive Society* (1920) and Peter Drucker's *The End of Economic Man* (1939) to define "the right to private property." There was no contradiction, Agar insisted, between encouraging a multiplication of peasant farmers and small masters of independent shops while also abolishing private ownership in industries with absentee owners. The right to private property existed only "so far as property helps to keep men free, to give them dignity and self-earned security."[52] Thomas Haile sought to define agrarianism as a nonreactionary cause: "It does not seek to recover the form of the past but to preserve and revitalize the ideals of such a past, to express those ideals in forms conditioned by technological and scientific advances." Agrarianism was "an effort to dominate the machine" and to secure a "higher" standard of living without sacrificing spiritual and cultural values.[53] In December, 1939, John P. Chamberlain defined the "Principles of Decentralization" as resting on the contention that, for many product lines, "a small-scale system of production for local markets is more efficient in reducing costs than mass production." This article symbolized a new shift in editorial policy: the more American term "decentralism," almost completely displaced the vaguely European-sounding word, "distributism," in *Free America*'s pages.[54]

The journal offered frequent pieces on the nature of subsistence farming in America. One writer explained that such efforts failed when the land was heavily mortgaged or when the family failed to diversify sufficiently. A true "subsistence" farm required three or four cows, 100 chickens, five hogs, a truck garden, a team of horses, and sufficient land for fodder.[55] Another author described with enthusiasm the resettlement of war refugees on American land: "Like grafted trees, these sons of European peasants are re-rooting on Eastern back-country farms....[T]heir children and women work in the fields."[56] The magazine took boosterish heart from census reports in 1939 showing that the growth of American cities had ceased, or reversed, while the birth rate was still high in the countryside. U.S. Department of Agriculture economist O.E. Baker wrote that these pockets of high fertility could be found among "the poor but independent people of the southern Appalachians, the croppers and tenants of the Cotton Belt, the hill folk that live along the Ohio River and its tributaries, the religious sects that have settled in many counties of the Dakotas and Kansas, the Mormons of Utah and Idaho, and other small, often self-sufficing farmers who have been more or less isolated by their locations or by their religious convictions from the influences of modern urban civilization."[57]

This welcome attention to the plain folk surviving, even growing, within separatist religious sects was rare, however. More attention focused on the secular creation of "productive homes" in "semi-rural" regions. In the new "humanistic, organic and regional" suburbs, one could foresee the application of "biodynamic principles" to family living. A "far higher science and technology" would be bonded there to "different social and domestic habits." The bio-dynamic home would have "space for hobbies and other productive activities." There would be studios, workshops, loom-rooms, laboratories, and an "increasing perfection of small power tools and instruments."[58]

The magazine's promotion of the productive home did stimulate an impressive Architectural Contest. *Free America* asked entering architects to design "the owner-occupied home of the free man," where "living and producing a livelihood are welded into an harmonious whole." Designs submitted must treat "the family as [the] primary economic and social unit," and craft the home to encompass gardening, animal husbandry, and handcrafts. As Ralph Borsodi explained in a commentary on the contest: "The kitchen-garden, the chicken house and the barn, not to mention the manure pile and the compost heap, are things which architects have hitherto sought to ignore." However, "they are inescapable facts if America is not to be completely urbanized." Over 500 entries were received, with most of them working out the problem "within a distinctly modern style of architecture." *Free America* named winners for each of the five distinct American regions—Northeast, Midwest, South, Southwest, and Pacific Northwest—and chose fifty-five for inclusion in the book, *The Productive Home*, co-edited by Borsodi and *New York Times* garden editor F.F. Rockwell, and to be published by McGraw-Hill.[59]

Other magazine features sought to build the sense of a spreading coalition and consciousness, moving into ever new fields. One writer reviewed the new movie, "The City," calling it "America's first decentralist film," through its depiction of the super-metropolis as "an unfit place for human existence" and its message that "families ought to move away to the country."[60] Architect Baker Brownell claimed to find a "new agrarian art" in the "dancing" of the people, in the music of nonprofessionals, in the "little theatres," and in the "splendid brilliance" of American poets such as Sandburg, Frost, and Jeffers.[61] The magazine also gave monthly attention to new signs of "decentralist" or "agrarian" organization, both locally[62] and internationally.[63]

"London Calling"

Yet the effort to build a grand "agrarian-distributist-decentralist" coalition came to an abrupt halt in mid-1940. The cause was the German invasion of the Low Counties and France, and the subsequent Battle of Britain. Simply put, Herbert Agar's lingering attachments to England combined with Ralph Borsodi's sentimental internationalism to lead *Free America* to mount a rousing advocacy for American intervention into the war. Tossed away was Agar's contempt for the "world city," his weariness with the "dying" civilization of Europe, and his advocacy for the "culture-men" out in the American provinces. Instead, he clearly cast the issue as "whether we are to permit total war, total nationalism, and total industrialism to triumph not only in Europe but over the whole Earth." In a stunning reversal of views, he declared that there was "no such thing as an independent national interest....no such things as sovereign nations." Science and machinery, the new agrarianism's friends, had "finally destroyed the basis for the old nationalism." Moreover, he cast Nazism as "total industrialism" on the march. He acknowledged that both sides of the war were industrialized, and still held to the view that industrialism was "obsolete" and "disastrously overextended." But in the free nations, "industrialism is really in the process of dissolution." In Germany, by way of contrast, industrialism "concentrated and centralized" its control over the state. In short, Agar cast the war as one between a "deindustrializing" West and a "super-industrializing" Germany. America was forced to fight "to retain the right to re-make America into what we believe she should be."[64]

Agar soon distinguished himself as a leading proponent of American intervention. "By invitation of the British government," he flew over to London on a British bomber, to see the war effort first hand. His impressions were broadcast on the BBC Shortwave service and printed in *Free America* under the title, "London Calling." Agar lashed out at American isolationists such as "Senator Wheeler in far-off Montana," who "dream about wicked imperialists fighting 'the same old war.'" Agar denied that Britain's war was for defense of Empire. Instead, he implied, it was a kind of distributist war. The Britons were fighting "for a chance for decent men and women to live their lives without cruelty....They wanted to be left alone, to tend their gardens and look after their businesses...." This was a "people's war," where defeat would mean "death for millions of *plain* men who dare to resist." The "people of Britain, *the plain people*," finally saw the facts. Indeed, Agar insisted that "[w]ar today is almost a sign of health," for it meant that the "revolution" of total industrialism was "somewhere still being resisted." American isolationists were preparing for the "physical" and "moral" destruction of their country: If Britain fell to Hitler, they would condemn American children "to a diminished life."[65]

In a speech to a St. Louis rally, "Fun to be Free," held three days after the Japanese attack on Pearl Harbor, Agar abandoned even the pretence of distributist rhetoric. The war, he said, was to preserve a common civilization and, above all, American "high technology":

A world which could watch with indifferent eyes what Hitler did to the Jews and to the Poles is a world which is in danger of losing all—not only its soul but its high technology as well, its radios and airplanes and plumbing—because technology is a by-product of civilization.

Indeed, instead of being the bearer of hyper-industrialism, Germany now stood—in Agar's view—as the bearer of a dreaded new agrarianism:

[The German Barbarian's] "new order" will be the oldest order of all. Man will return again to the primitive beginnings of life: to suffering *and breeding and tilling the soil.* Our *high technology* will go the way of all things that are not sufficiently served by the spirit.[66]

High fertility and farming were now the marks of a terribly diminished life; high technology, in contrast, was the raison d'être of existence.

In mid-1942, Navel Reserve Lieutenant-Commander Herbert Agar was called to active duty. He would go on to serve as naval attaché to the Court of St. James. Other names on the *Free America* masthead also soon bore an asterix, denoting fulltime military service. With a good share of its editorial staff away, *Free America* became a quarterly.

The turn by *Free America* to the interventionist cause did not occur without opposition. Allen Tate cut his formal ties to the journal at this time, and the Southern Agrarians disappeared from its pages. In his last contribution, Donald Davidson warned that war could only feed the Roosevelt's administration's "highly industrialized, centralized, and socialistic order." He added: "I should have thought agrarians and decentralists would oppose our entry into the conflict when such, no matter what results might be achieved in Europe, would probably be ruinous to their hopes for a healthy reconstruction in America."[67]

In retrospect, it would probably have been wise to put *Free America* on the shelf, for the duration. Even those convinced of the need for intervention should have admitted the incongruity of seeking "agrarian decentralism" in a period of total mobilization for total war. Instead, the "decentralists" still left at *Free America* tried to find positive "straws" in a gale of centralization. These efforts primarily testified to the frailty of "decentralism," when standing alone, as a meaningful intellectual construct. For instance, Lewis Mumford, newly energized, said the aim of wartime social planning "must be to establish every new industry, every new highway, every new housing development with the new regional pattern of decentralized communities." Both "military danger" and "social opportunity" pointed to the necessary growth of the suburbs. Peter Van Dresser saw industrial decentralization as the best defense against *blitzkreig* and aerial bombing, a view that became a regular drumbeat. "Decentralize the War Effort-Now!," urged Richard Neuberger, by spreading government agencies around the country and writing "propaganda" on a region-specific basis. Bertram Fowler urged a massive new federal program to build up stockpiles of food, which could be called "production for use on a global scale." Stringfellow Barr argued for creation of a "world republic," saying that "[d]ecentralists and agrarians ought most surely to be in the ranks of those who have discovered the TNT concealed in national sovereignity." Another writer suggested that faithful ally China was on the verge of a great "decentralized" industrial revolution. Still others saw the looming demobilization of over twelve million servicemen as a splendid opportunity to promote "primary dependence on the land and only partial dependence on industry."[68]

In a 1943 magazine symposium, a more sober contributor concluded that *"Distributism seems to be a casualty of the war....*For the war, thus far at least, is less a fight for freedom than a war in which freedom, on all sides, becomes less and less significant."[69] While this second judgment might be disputed, it is significant that the farewell article in the last issue of *Free America*, dated in early 1947, emphasized the highlighted line.[70] Agar, Borsodi, and Stillman remained as editors to the end, but their vision of a great fusion of movements behind the New Agrarianism was already over. By 1945, *Free America* seemed almost schizophrenic in approach, some contributors veering toward the "Swedish model" of social democracy,[71] and others—such as the last Managing Editor John P. Chamberlain—toward an antistatist libertarianism and a "fusionist" conservatism.[72] By then, authentic agrarian and distributist ideals had been lost in the shuffle; the suburbs, the machines, and War—hot and Cold—remained.

Notes

1. Seward Collins, "Editorial Notes," *American Review* 2 (Nov. 1933): 122.
2. George Bernard Shaw gave this name to the Distributist "monster" which he at one time "rushed out to slay."
3. Hilaire Belloc, "The Restoration of Property, I" *American Review 1 (April 1933): 2.*
4. Hilaire Belloc, "The Restoration of Property, VI. The Essential Principles," *American Review* 2 (Nov. 1933): 46.
5. Hilaire Belloc, "The Restoration of Property. II. The Handicap Against Restoration," *American Review* 1 (May 1933): 204-205.
6. G.K. Chesterton, "A Mild Remonstrance," *American Review* 5 (Sept. 1935): 451-458. Also G.K. Chesterton, "Sex and Property," *American Review* 2 (Jan. 1934): 277-281.
7. "Small Industries and Handcrafts," *American Review* 2 (Mar. 1934): 508-511.
8. Hilary Pepler, "The Distributist," *American Review* 4 (Dec. 1934): 207.
9. R.L. Burgess, "This Is the Place! The Mormons and the Land," *American Review* 4 (Feb. 1935): 420.
10. T.S. Eliot, "Tradition and Orthodoxy," *American Review* 2 (March 1934): 513-528.
11. E.P. Richardson, "American Art and Western Culture," *American Review* 2 (Mar. 1934): 595-607.
12. Joseph E. Baker, "Regionalism in the Middle West," *American Review* 4 (Mar. 1935): 603-614.
13. Donald Davidson, "Still Rebels, Still Yankees," *American Review* 2 (Nov. 1933): 58-72; 2 (Dec. 1933): 175-188.
14. John Gould Fletcher, "Dewey's Latest Disciple [Review of Lewis Mumford's *Technics and Civilization*]," *American Review* 3 (June 1934): 397.
15. Eleanor Carroll Chilton, Herbert Agar, and Willis Fisher, *Fire and Sleet and Candlelight* (New York: John Day Co., 1928); and Eleanor Carroll Chilton and Herbert Agar, *The Garment of Praise: The Necessity of Poetry* (Garden City, NY: Doubleday, Doran & Co., 1929.
16. See Herbert Agar, *The People's Choice* (Boston and New York: Houghton Mifflin, 1933): 185. In his enthusiastic review of the book for the *American Review*, Allen Tate said that this quotation "should be engraved in stone, for the perpetual enlightenment of those Americans who have assimilated Lincoln into the myth of capitalist origins in this country." See: Allen Tate, "Where Are the People?" *American Review* 2 (Dec. 1933): 236.
17. Seward Collins, "Editorial Notes: The American Review's First Year," *American Review* 3 (April 1934): 119.
18. Herbert Agar, "The Task for Conservatism," *American Review* 3 (April 1934): 2.
19. Agar, "The Task for Conservatism," p. 5.
20. Ibid., pp. 6-8.
21. Ibid., pp. 13-14.
22. Ibid., pp. *15-16.*
23. Herbert Agar, *Land of the Free* (Boston: Houghton Mifflin, 1935): vii, 3.
24. Ibid., pp. 16, 18, 22.
25. Ibid., p. 131; also pp. 14, 25, 128-30.
26. Ibid., pp. 132-134, 257.
27. Ibid., pp. 266-269, 286.
28. Ibid., p. 287, also pp. 280-284.

29. Ibid., pp. 262-265, 286.
30. Ibid., pp. 274-278.
31. Regarding the latter, see the confused and anxious conclusion to the essay by Mary Shattuck Fisher, "The Emancipated Woman," in Herbert Agar and Allen Tate, editors, *Who Owns America? A New Declaration of Independence* (Boston and New York: Houghton Mifflin Company, 1936): 320-321.
32. Herbert Agar, "Introduction," in Agar and Tate, editors, *Who Owns America?*, pp. viii-x.
33. John C. Rawe, "Agriculture and the Property State," in Agar and Tate, *Who Owns America?*, pp. 36-51.
34. Cleanth Brooks, "A Plea to the Protestant Churches," in Agar and Tate, *Who Owns America?*, pp. 323-324.
35. Herbert Agar, "But Can It Be Done?" in Agar and Tate, *Who Owns America?*, pp. 95-108.
36. See: Herbert Agar, *Pursuit of Happiness: The Story of American Democracy* (Cambridge, MA: Houghton-Mifflin Company, 1938): 5, 362.
37. Agar, *Pursuit of Happiness*, pp. 26-27, 35, 50, 54.
38. From an account found in: J.P. Chamberlain, "Looking Backward: Ten Years of *Free America*," *Free America* 9 (Winter, 1946-1947): 3-4.
39. Herbert Agar, "Free America," in *Free America* 1 (Jan. 1937): 1-2.
40. "Editorials," *Free America* 1 (Jan. 1934): 3-4.
41. "Editorials" and "Catholic Agrarian Notes," *Free America* 1 (Feb. 1937): 3-4.
42. "Editorials," *Free America* 1 (Jan. 1937): 3-5.
43. Herbert Agar, "The Marxian Myth: A Reply to Mr. Corey," *Free America* 1 (Mar. 1937): 12.
44. "Editorials," *Free America* 1 (Aug. 1937): 3.
45. "Editorials," *Free America* 1 (Mar. 1937): 3.
46. "Editorials," *Free America* 1 (Apr. 1937): 3-4.
47. Michael Williams, "The Great Tradition," *Free America* 1 (Apr. 1937): 9-10.
48. "Catholic Agrarian Notes," *Free America* 1 (Dec. 1937): 11.
49. Cornell Cassandra, "These Men, This Land," *Free America* 4 (Oct. 1940): 8-12.
50. Ken Woodman, "Farming for the Future: An Interview with Louis Bromfield," *Free America* 5 (Dec. 1941): 4; and Victor Weybright, "Friends of the Land," *Free America* 5 (Nov. 1941): 13.
51. Louis Bromfield, "Review of *Ill Fares the Land* by Carey McWilliams," in *Free America* 6 (May 1942): 18-19.
52. Herbert Agar, "The Right to Private Property," *Free America* 3 (June 1939): 4-8.
53. Thomas H. Haile, "On the Nature of Agrarianism," *Free America* 3 (Oct. 1939): 12-15.
54. John P. Chamberlain, "Principles of Decentralization," *Free America* 3 (Dec. 1939): 3-6.
55. H.A. Highstone, "Why Subsistence Farming Fails," *Free America* 4 (May 1940): 3-6.
56. Waldo C. Wright, "America's Peasant Farmers," *Free America* 10 (Winter, 1946-1947): 7-8.
57. O.E. Baker, "Population Trends: The Rural People Survive," *Free America* 3 (Aug. 1939): 3-6.
58. See: Peter van Dresser, "The Productive Home," *Free America* 3 (Feb. 1939): 3-5, 13.
59. "Prize Winning Designs in the Productive Home Architectural Competition," *Free America* 3 (May 1939): Special Supplement; and "Editorials," *Free America* 3 (May 1939): 2. For unknown reasons, the book apparently never appeared.

60. George Weller, *"The City*: America's First Decentralist Film," *Free America* 3 (Aug. 1939): 18.
61. Baker Brownell, "The New Agrarian Art," *Free America* 3 (Dec. 1939): 13-15.
62. For example, "Minnesota Decentralists," *Free America* 6 (Jan. 1942): 22.
63. For example, P.B. Stoyan, "Quiet Miracles: The Balkan Peasant Cooperatives," in *Free America* 4 (Oct. 1940): 3-6; and Elizabeth McG. Graham, "Scandinavian Small Holdings," *Free America* 4 (Feb. 1940): 3-6.
64. "Editorial," *Free America* 4 (July 1940): 2, 10-11.
65. Herbert Agar, "London Calling," *Free America* 5 (Sept. 1941): 11-12. Emphasis added.
66. Herbert Agar, *A Message to America* (St. Louis, MO: Fight for Freedom Committee to Defend America, 1941); from The Pamphlet Collection, Wisconsin Historical Society, Madison, Wisconsin. Emphasis added.
67. In "Decentralization: The Outlook for 1941. A Symposium of Opinion," *Free America* 5 (Jan. 1941): 11-12.
68. "Decentralization: The Outlook for 1941," p. 14; Richard Neuberger, "Decentralize the War Effort-Now!" *Free America* 6 (June 1942): 3-6; Bertram B. Fowler, "Food for Victory," *Free America* 6 (March 1942): 3-5; Stringfellow Barr, "The Choice: World Republic or National Tyranny," *Free America* 10 (Spring 1946): 3-4, 15-16; Bertram Fowler, "China's Decentralist Revolution," *Free America* 5 (Feb. 1941): 3-6; Elizabeth Graham, "Land Settlement for Veterans," *Free America* 8 (Winter 1943): 6-7; and "Editorial," *Free America* 5 (June 1941): 2, 17.
69. "The Future of Distributism: A Symposium of Opinion," *Free America* 7 (Spring 1943): 10.
70. Chamberlain, "Looking Backward," p. 12.
71. G. Howard Smith, "Sweden: Decentralized Way of Life," *Free America* 9 (Spring 1945): 13-16.
72. See John Chamberlain, "Planning versus Progress," *Free America* 9 (Spring 1945): 15-16.

7

God, Land, Community, and
Father Luigi Ligutti

The churches of America, commonly viewed as part of the problem by the line of New Agrarians, actually joined the County Life cause with fervor during the 1930s. While the Federal Council of Churches rallied the mainline Protestant denominations to an advocacy for rural life under the Town and Country banner, the more dramatic and influential conversion took place on the Roman Catholic side. Within a religious body that was overwhelmingly urban on U.S. soil, the Reverend Edwin O'Hara led the formation of a special rural life conference, and his own writings came to reflect an almost pure Agrarianism. However, the Catholic initiative reached fruition only later, under the guidance of Luigi Ligutti, an Italian-born parish priest whose work in rural Iowa become a model for the nation and world. With some irony, it would be the Roman Catholic Church that would, almost alone, carry an undiluted New Agrarianism through the 1940s and 1950s. In the process, Father Ligutti also worked through several of the common New Agrarian themes to develop richer and more satisfying resolutions.

A Rural Church?

In the early 1920s, fewer than one out of five (19.4 percent) Roman Catholics in the United States lived in rural areas. This compared to a national average of 44 percent, while certain large Protestant denominations reached much higher (e.g., 62 percent for Southern Baptists and 54 percent for Southern Methodists). Proclaiming Catholicism to be "rural in philosophy" albeit "urban in composition," Father Edwin V. O'Hara organized the National Catholic Rural Life Conference (NCRLC) in 1923 to "rebalance" the Catholic equation. The organization's specific purposes were: to provide care for underprivileged Catholics living on the land, to retain on the land those Catholics who were already there, to settle still more Catholics in rural areas, and to convert non-Catholics in the countryside. O'Hara emphasized that "the burning concern" of the Catholic Church with farming arose "from the altogether unique relationship which exists universally between the agricultural occupation and the central institution of Christian, nay, of all civilization; namely, the family." For centuries, the Church held "a special kinship" with cultivators of the soil, one that had often exasperated its enemies. But the reason was not hard to find: "The farm is the natural habitat of the family." Where industrial society encouraged divorce, desertion, temporary unions, and "companionate marriage," a farming society showed "strength, permanence, and unity of the marriage bond." Marriages were stronger due to the "very nature of the farm," which required "the home-maker as a partner in the whole enterprise." Moreover, the authority of parents was more pronounced here, and country children were more likely to become "deeply indoctrinated with the religious and moral ideals of their parents" than were city children. Indeed, the farm house was still a true school, providing "the only extended apprenticeship left in America, an apprenticeship where the parents are the teachers."[1]

Equally important was the issue of population. O'Hara summoned statistics to show that "the farm family is the most important source of population growth" and that the "children are overwhelmingly in the country." The NCRLC published a long paper by O.E. Baker, senior agricultural economist with the USDA (and himself a Protestant), which carefully documented the rural-urban fertility difference. The author emphasized the lessons of history: social stability and progress required a strong, functional family organized for cooperative economic ends. As he wrote, "A civilization to be permanent must be based primarily on agriculture, or on some other culture in which the family is an economic unit." Rural youth must be made to see "the earth as the mother of mankind" and "above them, like a cloud of witnesses, the farmers and farm women of the past," their ancestors and heroes. The young "must achieve a sense of the continuity of life." They must see in front of them "the opportunity to build not an urban but a new rural civilization," to which, Baker hoped, "the Christian churches, in all its [sic] branches, could lead them."[2]

The early NCRLC also held that agrarianism was the real alternative to communism and its strange ally, sterility. As Father W. Howard Bishop wrote, capitalism, which had its chief strength in big cities, had been "responsible for the rise of two great social heresies, birth control, its friend, and Communism, its enemy." He added, "Both friend and enemy are working towards [capitalism's] destruction," the former by creating a shriveling population with diminished demand and the latter through direct assault. "The Country," however, offered "a natural resistance" to these heresies. The push toward sterility was overcome by "the demand for children on the farms, where chores are to be done" and where the cost of raising the young was comparatively low. Communism, meanwhile, faced "the stern individualism of the farmer," his sheer inability to adapt to a regimented order. Relative to all "home destroying influences," agricultural society rested on the circumstance that on farms, home life and farm enterprise were inseparable; work and residence unified in the working home.[3]

The Granger Experiment

Yet by the mid-1930s, the NCRLC still remained on the margins of the American Church, with little to show for its effort and without full-time leadership. It was Father Luigi Ligutti who would move the New Agrarianism to near the center of Catholic attention. David Bovee, the most thorough historian of the NCRLC, has concluded that "no other person in the Conference's history has come close to being the personal embodiment of the movement that Ligutti was."[4] For twenty-five years, he served as a remarkably effective Agrarian apostle to American Roman Catholics, leaving an enduring legacy.

Ligutti was born 1895 on a small farm in the Ludine region of Italy. "My mother's family," he later reported, had "cultivated the same valley and hillside fields for over 1000 years." During his youth, the family owned twenty acres, and each day "we went out of the village to work our separate fields....We sang and prayed on our way to work....We exchanged work....We bowed our head[s] at Angelus Time." However, after the death of his father in 1911, Ligutti reluctantly agreed to leave Italy with his mother, to join two brothers and a sister already in America. At age seventeen, he arrived in Des Moines,

Iowa. Shortly thereafter, he enrolled at St. Ambrose College in Davenport. He spent his summers working as a gardener.[5]

During this time, he resolved to become a priest. "Two things attracted me in the Church," Ligutti wrote. "Its ancient and solemn Ritual liturgy and its social teachings." He pointed especially to *Rerum Novarum*, the extraordinary 1891 encyclical of Pope Leo XIII which analyzed the ills of industrial society and offered a distinctively Christian response. Graduating from St. Ambrose in 1914, he spent the next six years at the Catholic University of America, the Teachers College at Columbia University, Des Moines Catholic University, and the University of Chicago. Through his Latin and Greek studies, he read the ancient works of Hesiod, Homer, Vergil, and Cicero, and "discovered a wealth of rural philosophy and inspiration in them."[6]

Ordained in 1920, Ligutti was assigned by the bishop of Des Moines to a small rural parish in western Iowa. "It was hard," he recollected later. "[M]y dear mother was with me. I hunted—I fished—I gardened—I went out to help farmers....I learned to know and appreciate rural people." Despite a lingering depression in agricultural prices and the early inroads of the new machines, Ligutti also recognized at this time that "The rural home is the natural habitat of the Christian family." The family found unity "thru [sic] living where there is space - light-air & *common work* for the whole family."[7] In 1926, he moved to Assumption Parish in Granger, a village of 300 souls roughly twenty miles northwest of Des Moines.

It would be incorrect to see Ligutti as a young radical priest, setting out at once to change the world. Rather, his quest was spiritual, toward purity, and his early politics fairly conservative. He would later report that he was "a consistent Iowa Republican in the primaries," including 1932 when he "did not vote for F.D.[R].," viewing campaign slogans about a "New Deal" and "the forgotten men" as "bunk."[8] Yet he began reading more broadly at this time, including works by Belloc and Chesterton. He would specifically cite the influence on him of Ralph Borsodi's *Flight from the City* and Herbert Agar's *Home of the Free*. He took to calling himself an "Agrarian Distributist" and during 1936 was drawn into the New York circle of "Independent Americans," quietly guided by Chauncey Stillman, a young Catholic convert from an old and wealthy American family.[9]

Active in the NCRLC from its inception, Ligutti emerged in the early 1930s as an up-and-coming leader. At the organization's 1932 conference, he gave a speech where he termed the farm an "ideal place to raise children," one furnishing "ideal home surroundings for mutual love and help."[10] More important, though, was the urgent need to relieve economic and social distress in his own parish. Since the turn of the century, bituminous coal mines had operated in the Granger area, mainly supplying coal for winter heating in central Iowa. By the early 1930s, five remained in operation, seasonally employing 1,600 men. About 200 of the latter were Ligutti's parishioners, mainly Slavs recently arrived from Croatia and Carniola and Italians from Modena. These families lived in mining camps, beset by "overcrowded homes—child delinquency and truancy—boot legging and drunkenness—sex offenses—forced marriages." Moreover, in these camps children were "no economic asset, hence birth control." During the summer months, the mines largely shut down, and the families often turned to emergency relief.

By 1932, Ligutti had developed a plan to improve their circumstances, and he actively sought private financial backing to set it in motion. He proposed to transplant the Catholic homes, including the small houses themselves, from the mining camps to the area around Granger Church and School. Through loans or gifts, he would acquire several hundred acres of land, and settle each family on about ten acres, which "would easily bring a sufficient return to pay for the living expenses of a family of six." These settlers would be allowed to buy their house and land through small payments over a number of years. Serendipitously, he noted that "[t]hese miners have early European training for farming on a small scale....Small varied orchards, vineyards, vegetables for home use—two cows—half a dozen hogs, a hundred chickens, some goats or sheep, ducks or geese." The slow pace of the mines during the warmer months also gave the fathers ample opportunity to work a small holding. More importantly, "[c]hildren on a small farm are an economic asset. [You] [s]eldom find birth control among Italian gardeners."[11]

Yet in those dark days, private support or bank loans could not be found. Instead, Ligutti would gain the opportunity to turn his plan into reality through the Subsistence Homestead Program, implemented as part of the New Deal in 1933.

In their official history of this experiment for the USDA, Russell Lord and Paul H. Johnstone emphasized the role of various "back-to-the-land" movements in stimulating the scheme. Since the 1890s,

Johnstone wrote, "the suburbanward movement of the population" had been motivated by the desire for a home on a piece of land: "Clean air, a wholesome atmosphere in which to rear children, the chance for a large lawn and flowers...a place in which to reduce out-of-pockets living costs by...a subsistence garden."[12] The early 1930s brought forth more active promoters, ranging from Bernarr McFadden, publisher of the *Graphic* and *Liberty* magazines, to the American Friends Service Committee. However, he said, the philosophical grounding for the subsistence homestead campaign lay primarily among the Agrarians. Johnstone's history specifically cited the Southern Agrarians ("a distinct school having a more-or-less coherent philosophy and program"), "distributist decentralists like Ralph Borsodi," the circle that eventually brought out *Free America*, and the Protestant and Catholic rural life campaigns. Notably, Franklin D. Roosevelt first expressed his interest in rural resettlement for displaced industrial workers at the 1931 Country Life Conference in Ithaca, New York, which Liberty Hyde Bailey had chaired as his last "rural activist" duty.[13]

While extensively debated in 1932, the Subsistence Homestead program became a reality only the next year, as Section 208 of the National Industrial Recovery Act. Building on the unstated assumption that industrial stagnation would be permanent, Section 208 sought to correct "the overbalance of population in industrial centers" by moving people into the country. M.L. Wilson, an agrarian enthusiast from Atlantic, Iowa, won appointment as first director of the Division of Subsistence Homesteads. He believed that part-time farming would "create a sturdy rather than a servile citizenry" and that this project "could be laying the basis for a new type of civilization in America."[14]

Inspired by the 1931 papal encyclical, *Quadragesimo Anno*, which affirmed the positive role that state policy could play in social reconstruction, and by soaring levels of farm tenancy in Iowa (60 percent by 1933), Father Ligutti was first in line with his Plan for Granger. He held that "the restoration of a balance between rural and urban populations" was more than a palliative measure; it was "a radical remedy...reaching to the very *causa causans* of our social ills."[15] "Practically singlehanded," the official history explained, Ligutti "gathered the necessary data, obtained the endorsement of state legislators and agricultural and labor leaders, submitted the applications to Washington, and won a favorable verdict."[16] In setting up a local corporation to manage the homestead, Ligutti wisely chose a lay board, relegating himself to the job of consultant. (When challenged about the board's composition in Washington by a skeptic—"and I suppose they are all Roman Catholics"—Ligutti replied, "Yes, they are all devout thirty-third degree Masons!").[17] However, he did chair the committee that chose the original group of fifty homesteaders. Factors of selection included the size of the family and its needs, the qualities of industry, sobriety, frugality, and stability, and the desire for home ownership. In the end, the group included sixteen Italian and sixteen Croat families; overall, two-thirds of the homesteaders were Catholics.

The new homes, either Dutch Colonial or "Williamsburg" in style and each on a plot of about four acres, were occupied in December, 1935, and Ligutti remained very much part of the project. He attended the frequent homesteader meetings, which included: discussion groups for the men on Tuesday evenings, rotating from home to home, and featuring speakers on horticultural topics from nearby Iowa State College; similar meetings for women on budgeting, home accounts, sewing, and nutrition; and the Homesteader dramatic club, glee club, and fifty-piece WPA band. Ligutti taught many of the children at Assumption High School, where he developed a curriculum designed to support subsistence farming. When "a garden tract showed evidence of neglect or disuse," Father Ligutti delivered "a vigorous reminder of the duties of a homesteader." For the Catholics in the group, he also served as confessor and spiritual guide. In the public's mind, Granger properly became "Father Ligutti's project." Despite seizing direct administrative control of the project in mid-1934 (much to Ligutti's despair), the federal government's role was mostly "incidental."[18]

Did Granger succeed? From the perspective of late 1940, when Ligutti departed from the settlement, the answer was undoubtedly "yes." Relative to the goal of food-production-for-use, Granger was probably the most successful of the nearly 200 federal projects undertaken under the broad "Homesteading" banner. Every Granger home featured a large, well-kept garden and chickens; most had a cow and a few pigs as well. Cooperatively owned canning equipment aided in food preservation, and produced a surplus for sale to curious visitors from Des Moines, and beyond. In December, 1937, when the Granger Homesteaders celebrated the second anniversary of their project with a dinner at Assumption Parish Hall, the menu was a feast fit for Louis Bromfield's "Old Jamie":

Tomato Juice Cocktail
Salted Peanuts
Dill Pickles—petite onions—celery-beets
Vegetable Potage
Wheaten buns—strawberry jam—butter
Cabbage Salad
Ham o'Granger—Chicken a la Homestead
Mashed potatoes—gravy
String beans—Peas—Asparagus
Pumpkin Pie
Home-made ice cream—Angel Food Cake
Honey
Coffee

Except for the coffee, all had been raised on the Homesteads: "Peanuts at Oyers, ham at McMullen's, Wheat at Joe Bondi's, honey in Father's backyard—and the rest—well, all over." The candlesticks had been turned by the boys in Father Gorman's "Farm-Shop," the candles had been molded from the wax of Granger bees, and the pieces of fancy work and woven material displayed had all come from the girls in Assumption High School's Arts and Crafts Department. Indeed, the school could even claim a new "Borsodi fly-shuttle loom, gift of Chauncey Stillman," and soon expected to turn out "the finest material fit for a pastor."[19]

The project succeeded in other ways, as well. Between 1935 and 1939, cash income from the coal mines steadily declined; but the value of increase and retained home production in food and fibers more than compensated for this. An August "project fair" allowed homesteaders to exhibit their gardening, sewing, and animal husbandry skills, along with entertainment provided by the children in old ethnic costumes. Blessed by a heavily immigrant population used to peasant ways, by a mining schedule almost perfectly suited to the maintenance of large gardens, and by Father Ligutti's indefatigable energy, Granger worked.

But it is also true that portents of trouble could be seen by the early 1940s, as well. Some of the younger adults, American-born and without direct knowledge of European ways, were "more attracted by the good times in Des Moines" than by meetings devoted to gardening. Delays in the transfer of real ownership developed, as the actual costs of a mortgage still proved to be beyond the capacity of many Grangers. Finally, there was no mechanism in place to integrate the next generation into the scheme. The sons of homesteaders left for Des Moines or Chicago. As a troubled window on the future, a 1941 report noted that "the situation has been eased, during recent months, by the fact that 13 young men have gone from the project, 5 to the Army and 8 to shipyards and airplane factories."[20]

The Philosopher Priest

Ligutti began to develop his own gloss on Agrarianism in the mid-1930s. He was resolute in grounding his arguments in an applied sociology, indeed insisting that his purpose was to translate the findings of the science of rural society into action. As he told the inaugural convention of the American Catholic Sociological Association: "I believe it is within the scope of sociological science to gain knowledge in its field, to examine it, to interpret it, and...to seek to achieve certain results, thus translating the knowledge into action in accordance with a definite philosophy."[21] Befitting this view, he drew frequently in his lectures and writings from the work of Pitirim Sorokin and Carle Zimmerman.[22]

As would be expected, Ligutti held at the core of his philosophy the purpose of restoring Christ to "His true and proper place in human society." From Catholic social teaching, he also drew the conclusion that agrarian distributism and the cooperative had important parts to play in "rebuilding the social order and reestablishing the Christian life." The concept of "natural law" found in the Catholic tradition further allowed Ligutti to distinguish between the natural right of property—"to have, use, and dispose in accordance with moral law"—and the unnatural right, involving exploitation.[23]

Ligutti became famous for his quip, "No man who owns a cow can be a Communist." In his "Letter to a Contented Cow," he sought to explain the ennobling and liberating qualities of private property. The cow was in fact the secret solution to a myriad of "social and economic problems." Addressing "My dear Betsie," he explained: "You are first of all, the property of the goodly man who lives by the side of the road...They prize you highly. The Smith family is a little bit better socially and economically...because they hold a legal title to you." They "work for you and they love you because you are productive property." Wanting milk for their children, cream for their coffee, and butter for their bread, only "you" can change the corn, oats, or hay into milk, cream, and butter. "You give the little Smiths work, too, and you know that that's a real blessing for them." In doing their chores, the children "train themselves to work." Moreover, "you return to the soil over 95 percent of what you take from it in the form of fertilizer." The writer admitted to falling in love: "Dear Betsie, I have a confession to make: You're my socio-economic sweetheart."[24]

Ligutti gained the opportunity for a more systematic presentation of his views when WHO, the 50,000 watt radio station in Des Moines ("the Voice of Iowa"), invited him to make weekly lectures during the last three months of 1937 on the philosophy and objectives of the Agrarian Distributists. "[A]lso called the Independent Americans," he explained in the first talk, the group had its "main literary proponents" in Belloc and Chesterton and in the work of the Twelve Southerners at Vanderbilt. The movement was "headed by Herbert Agar," and his book, *The Land of the Free*, "may be considered as the Bible of the movement because it gives the history and philosophy and views the possible future for the cause." It was through Ralph Borsodi, his wife ("a native of Red Oak, Iowa"), and their School of Living that the Agrarian philosophy was "carried into action." Other leaders included Chauncey Stillman of New York, while "the official publication of the Independent Americans" was a monthly called *Free America*.[25] As Ligutti said at the close of the series, Agrarian Distributism was a movement "barely beginning in the United States but having the vigor, strength and resiliency of youth coupled with the enthusiasm arising from the vision of a better day."[26]

Given these sources of inspiration, one would expect that the major themes of New Agrarianism would percolate through these and subsequent lectures; and they did, although often with a revealing twist or innovation on Ligutti's part, reflecting a more fundamental grounding to his work. For example, he held with the New Agrarians that political liberty was not possible except "where there is widespread ownership of productive property." Self-reliance—"the sense[s] of superiority and independence that [come] from directly cooperating with nature in producing food, clothing, and shelter"— had vital political consequences. This implied in turn that a "satisfactory" economic system be, to the greatest possible extent, "a home making agriculture and not a commercial industry." At present, the race for profits, the flow of people from country to city, and the rule of the machine had caused deterioration in the countryside. Yet unlike many earlier Agrarians, Ligutti refused to be drawn into any scheme of state coercion, or large scale social engineering. He insisted that no government or private agency could undo the harm that had been done. The state should not guide or fund the needed land reforms. The calling into existence of a group of people requiring the support of the state was "harmful and dangerous to the individual's personality, to the family, to society and to the ideals of democracy."[27] Referring indirectly to the nature of human sin, he concluded that "a change in the philosophy and practice of the individual and the family is the only real effective remedy."[28]

While avoiding the more coercive forms of social engineering, Ligutti did share the New Agrarian desire to remake the farming population. The farmer who produced largely for an international market "presents and will always present the real problem." These farmers caused tenancy; they had depopulated the countryside; they had "closed our rural churches and schools"; they had ruined the small trading centers. In his time, "[t]he government is paying for their groceries because they are too busy raising food for the Board of Trade and the Railroads."[29] The urgent need was for "A Green Revolution,"[30] albeit a voluntary one. His advice to Iowa's commercial farmers was to raise "an abundance and variety of food stuff—all that your family will need for a whole year (a little extra for the parson). Spend plenty of time in caring for your garden and in the direct production of home needs." Farmers, he said, should also butcher their own meat, and make their own butter and cheese. They should raise their own fuel for fieldwork, notably oats and hay. They should also make sure that a tractor both saved work and made money, for "[i]t seldom does." Finally, they should downsize: "a 40-acre or even a 20-acre farm would be amply sufficient in Iowa to furnish a real, good high standard of living."[31] The "Green Revolution" would also involve the creation of subsistence homesteads for those on relief, and the "one-foot-in-industry, one-foot-on-the-soil" plan for those with other jobs, as modeled at Granger.

In his October 23, 1937 "agrarian" lecture, Ligutti focused on the "most powerful of all positive arguments" for the agrarian vision: the welfare of the family. "It is the farm home that furnishes the most natural habitat for the family," he declared. "There alone under our present industrial concentration and specialization we find the father and mother as King and Queen of the home, there we find the children as economic assets and not liabilities." The family's position as an economic unity extended into social and recreational functions as well. "The farm family has even more religious unity," for the whole family came to church as a group and, if not "citified," the farm family "still prays together."[32] The farm family produced the future members of society and the church; it was "the stronghold of natural and supernatural virtues, of Christianity and citizenship."[33] To the young people, he declared: "Be a farmer if you're a boy! Be a farm home mother if you're a girl." To existing commercial farmers who claimed they had no work for their children, Ligutti replied "you think in terms of corn, oats, of tractor and combine, marketing your products and buying your needs. You have forgotten your children for the sake of bringing yourself bankruptcy both financial and human."[34]

Unlike most New Agrarians, he happily embraced the "peasant" label. Regarding the charge of "peasantry," Ligutti was unruffled. "What do you mean by peasantry?" he asked. "We agrarians want more families living on the land and we counsel the family living on the land to make the raising of its own needs the first purpose of its farming activities…and *then*…corn and hogs." What was objectionable about these aims? Did the opponents prefer "more industrial slaves in the cities?" Ligutti concluded that if "farming for a living first" must be called peasantry, than "let us have it in place of the heartbreaking renting and mortgage of the big farms." For so understood, peasantry actually meant "liberty" and "independence."[35]

Regarding the issue of population, Ligutti placed primary emphasis on the needs of the Church and the salvation of souls, avoiding implications of racial struggle or national superiority. After tracing in detail the course and consequences of declining fertility, he concluded that "we are becoming a decadent nation." Drawing a distinction from his secular "fellow travelers." Ligutti wrote: "The Agrarians contend that the movement to the cities has caused these effects to come to pass. We Catholic Agrarians know perfectly well that the Catholic Church must have her people on the land if her future is to be, what she hopes it to be."[36] He asked his fellow believers: "Suppose a dictator, a Stalin or a Hitler by the name of Joe Doakes or Bill Brown, were to seize power in the United States." And further suppose that he ordered the closing of Catholic schools at the rate of over fifty a year. What indignation! What cries for vengeance! But that was just what was happening in the United States during the 1930s, albeit "the result of impersonal social forces" rather than dictators and without any outcry,

but with every bit as much of damage.[37] He looked with some admiration to the "hillbillies" in the Southern Highlands, whose fertility was
four times that of Catholic city dwellers, and three times that of Mid-
western commercial farm owners.[38] Borrowing a theme from Carle
Zimmerman, Ligutti asserted that "it is the children of the Okies, the
children of the Grapes of Wrath...who will populate tomorrow's
America."[39] The Catholic Church needed families; it needed children.
Only "the countryside will give them to us."[40]

In one related area, Ligutti was, without qualification, in the New
Agrarian camp: his opposition to the city. His views could be summed
up in the title of one of his articles: "Cities Kill."[41] Industrial civilization and urban life were the very antitheses of the church, Ligutti said.
The Church must continue to care for urban people, but they were in a
sense foredoomed. Movement of people from farm to city saw "the
feeling of family solidarity" replaced by "the spirit of *a car in place of
a baby* tradition." Speaking at a Communion breakfast in the East,
Ligutii asked the audience to pray for Long Island, calling it "the
concentrated graveyard of Catholicity." In Illinois, he noted that "to
keep Chicago alive," babies had to be imported from the countryside.
"Where is Chicago's virility?" he asked. As urban ideas spread into
the country, there came utter failure. They were intended to give economic advantages to farmers, but instead brought "loss of ownership
and wage slavery." Urban ideals sought to give pleasure, but instead
"produced suffering."[42]

Regarding the machine, Ligutti admired and used Borsodi's arguments. But he refused to be locked into the narrow criteria of efficiency. As he explained in his December 4, 1937 lecture: "The Agrarians are not blind to the fact that modern invention and industrialism
have changed the world almost overnight." They held that inventions
could be great blessings and industrialism "made to serve man," provided that both were "kept within bounds" and treated as "a real gift
of God."[43] Agrarian farming did not exclude machinery or commerce,
but it made them "secondary not in extent but in intent."[44] In a more
striking turn of argument, Ligutti also tried to change the way that
people understood the machine. He suggested that they study "the real
God-made" machines on the land. "I do not speak of tractors or com-
bines," he said. "I speak of a kernel of corn or of the tiny flower
seed....It grows, you care for it, you cooperate with God in the ever
new process of Creation for as a farmer you are a coworker of God."

Viewed in this way, the soil became a complex and wonderful thing, a natural wonder calling for stewardship and respect. Yet in so "mechanizing" the soil, Ligutti also avoided descent into the soil worship that mesmerized Agrarians such as Bailey and Bromfield. And he kept protection of the soil and the preservation of human community *on* the soil in balance.[45]

As a Catholic priest, Father Ligutti might have been expected to join in the pummeling given by most New Agrarians to the rural sects and fundamentalisms, mostly Protestant in nature. But he did not. Instead, he sometimes emphasized that the problem with Rural America was the very decline of Protestantism. The countryside, in fact, was "pagan," marked by too many abandoned churches.[46] At other times, he gave clear recognition to the positive good of fundamentalism in rural areas. Speaking to the American Country Life Association, he delivered an almost direct rebuke to the sectarian phobias of Liberty Hyde Bailey:

> Historically the various churches in the U.S. have been responsible for the building of rural communities. The Mormons in the West, the Mennonites in the Middle West, the Amanas in Iowa, the Lutherans in Minnesota and the Dakotas, Fr. Pierz in Stearns County, Minn[esota], Fr. Kundek in Jasper, Indiana, Fr. Tracy in Nebraska.

Under the influence of these churches and sects, "the desert blossomed like a rose, the mountains became human beehives, the valleys echoed with chimes and song."[47]

Yet, more commonly, Ligutti pulled away from the positive examples of the successful "sectlike" Catholic communities that he sometimes cited, not to mention the Granger experience itself and the whole Catholic monastic tradition. Instead, Ligutti stayed loyal to the Church in the world. As he explained in his October 30, 1937 WHO lecture: "No Church can hold its members and care for them if the surrounding world has a philosophy of life diametrically opposed to her own."[48] For Catholic Agrarians, this meant there could be no broad retreat into sectlike behavior, no withdrawal from the world into small, familial communities. Rather, the Church must seek to capture the larger culture, or it must fade, even die, in the attempt.

Rural Roads

By the late 1930s, Ligutti's fame was spreading. Pilgrims came to Granger by the hundreds to see this small, functioning, government-funded, informally Christian utopia. A Catholic "Back-to-the Land Movement" began to pick up steam, including new periodicals claiming that "Fr. Ligutti's Granger Homestead [is] Proof That 'It Can Be Done.'"[49]

In 1939-1940, Ligutti teamed up with "a brilliant young" Jesuit at Omaha's Creighton University, John C. Rawe, to produce his only full length book: *Rural Roads to Security.* Rawe carried to the collaboration a more direct and harsher critique of the joint-stock corporation as an inappropriate and family-disrupting grant of privilege. He also brought a practical interest in agriculture, and he would later guide an experimental farm in Maryland.[50]

Parts of *Rural Roads* clearly were adaptations and expansions of Ligutti's Agrarian lectures for WHO. The authors gave special acknowledgement to Herbert Agar, Ralph Borsodi, and the other editors of *Free America,* for their inspiration. Ligutti and Rawe described an America where "rootless land drifts away by wind and water" while "rootless people herd themselves by the millions in industrial slums." They also saw "a nation of secure and free, landowning people" transformed into "a nation of servile dependents" ruled by "a mechanistic plutocracy, inefficient and exploiting." They sought to define the steps needed "to rebuild our land, our homes, our democracy, our culture, and our religion."[51]

Ligutti and Rawe saw America in a "third struggle" for liberty, the first being against the British crown in the Revolution and the second against slavery in the Civil War. The current campaign was against "the Liberalistic system which Europe had fostered," spawned by the Reformation, which paved the way for a materialistic philosophy. Offering a short, but insightful economic history of the United States, they noted that as late as 1850, the bulk of American goods were still home-produced. But over the following half-century, "deluded Americans flocked to the factory as though it were the gate to prosperity." As women entered industry, they drove down the wages of men and "the idea of a family wage for the head of the family" slipped to that of "a mere individual wage" given to women and children. "Labor declined rapidly," losing the ownership of productive tools and homes, as well. Home occupations rapidly disappear. Family life dissolved through the absence of one or both parent; children were left without care, while childless homes proliferated.[52]

Agriculture changed as well, as Western lands closed off and industrial organization spread to the countryside, with similar consequences:

"Mammoth-scale industry, commercialized farms, human lives ground by marvelous machines, efficiency substituted for liberty, money codes dispensing justice, with God and His Spirit forgotten—these...are life-less bones."[53]

The vital goal of the Third American Struggle must be to restore "family-unit operation and fee-simple, family-basis ownership of land based on religious principles and spiritually motivated." Family resto-ration required the return of "some natural economic functions" to the family, specifically "family-centered production, family-centered ac-tivity where the child can soon become an economic asset." This was why every new housing program in America should be "a homestead program."[54] Under "the Homestead way," the father and his family "living on a few acres of their own land with a culture that is agrarian and a religion that is Christian," would serve as the "last bulwark against an extreme enslaving centralization," the "last bulwark in an urban civilization which is losing its property and freedom and failing to reproduce itself."[55]

Rural Roads gave significantly greater attention to Borsodi's argu-ments about the positive gains from a technology freed from mo-nopoly corporate control. This shift from Ligutti's earlier, more cau-tious statements was probably due to the influence of Rawe. The authors dismissed high-rise public housing as "birth control homes." They should be replaced by "productive homes on small acreages" linked to large cities by "multi-lane highways, one-hundred feet wide," and a welcomed doubling in the number of motor cars. Full-time farmers should also make "a most complete application" of all modern tech-nologies. Electricity, "with its efficient operation of many family-unit machines," would make home food processing both "profitable" and "pleasant." Referring repeatedly to Ralph Borsodi, the authors praised new technology as a vital factor in their quest for renewal.[56]

This embrace of modern technology was so complete that the au-thors openly derided the "old type" of farm, without electricity and with horses and buggies. As they wrote,

> Most emphatically, we are not advocating a return to the old type of farm....We can still remember—and with a feeling which even now, years after, amounts almost to repugnance—the old water buckets with their family dipper; the dim, smoky oil lamps with their encircling halo of nasty little bugs; the dread that always came with the darkness, the feeling of utter isolation, the almost palpable stillness. And then, the long rides at night, in the old buggy, often in pouring rains...with nothing to light our way but a tiny carbide light.

Such a farm life had little to attract. But "this was the farm of yester-day," gone forever.[57] The new "landward movement" would bear a technological richness to dazzle even the city man.

The most satisfying sections of the book described the Granger experiment, and were undoubtedly penned by Ligutti. Looking back from the perspective of 1940, the book emphasized the promise found in that Iowa settlement: "Direction of the people to the land; keeping the people on the land; encouraging the people to hold to the land, to work the land, to love the land is practical as well as poetical. There is both poetry and sound economics in such a community as Granger."[58] *Rural Roads* gave a fine summary of the work of Assumption High School to prepare its pupils for a home in the country: "This school strives to imprint deeply in the minds and hearts of children the phi-losophy of agrarianism." For the boys, it held up "farming-for-a-living (subsistence)" or "homemaking agriculture" as the ideal. Courses included animal husbandry, vegetable production, landscaping, fruit growing, bee culture, woodwork, metal work, soldering and forging, plumbing, the care of ignition systems, leatherwork, and wiring. The girls were taught that "a home on the land means children and a working husband." They studied "how to conduct a home in the country" and "the arts and crafts," with courses including clothing construction, care and repair, weaving, rug making, planning and pre-paring food, home care of the sick, and home management. The boys made looms in the farm shop; the girls used them to produce rugs and patterned pieces, some of which "have won prizes" at the Iowa State Fair. Where most high school education aimed at "the white collar job and the swivel-chair position," Assumption High School sought "the economic, social, and spiritual enrichment of rural life."[59]

Agrarianism in War and Peace

Nineteen Forty saw Monsignor Ligutti (a title granted in 1938) leave the Granger parish for national, and eventually international work. For several years prior, he had been drawn directly into the affairs of the School of Living, at the instigation of Chauncey Stillman. The latter had taken on a financial interest in the Suffern, New York, project. By 1940, however, "unsatisfactory management" had made clear that it would soon "go under," and Ligutti aided Stillman in putting Borsodi's school to rest.[60]

At the same time, Ligutti accepted election as the full-time executive secretary of the NCRLC. While able to move the commission's offices from St. Paul to Des Moines, the new job meant leaving his pastoral duties in Granger. This post also required extensive fundraising to accommodate plans for growth, and a grueling travel schedule. By the mid-1940s, Ligutti would spend only about fifty days each year in the home office. He devoted much of his time to promotion and public speaking, giving over 200 lectures and addresses in 1948 alone. He transformed the *Catholic Rural Life Bulletin* into the periodical *Land and Home* (1942-1947), followed by the *Christian Farmer* (1947-1951), which in 1948 counted 15,000 subscribers. Annual NCRLC conventions drew large numbers, counting 30,000 participants in 1948 (at LaCrosse, Wisconsin) and 20,000 the next year (at Columbus, Ohio). The only disturbing note was the relatively low attendance by actual farmers; the bulk of conferees were priests, teachers, and rural activists.[61]

Ligutti gave especial attention to the Catholic liturgy, seeking to give it a more rural flavor or tone. Speaking at a Liturgical Week conference in Chicago, he assumed the persona of a devout Catholic farmer, and restated his religious view of the soil:

I am a farmer. I am at Mass. My family kneels beside me....

My grandparents settled here almost 100 years ago. Their name is on one of the parish church windows. I hope my children's children will be [here] at Mass generations from now....

How can I, a farmer, grow in appreciative of my noble calling?...It is not merely clods of inert soil I work with, but millions of God's invisible creatures. It is not just a wheat shoot or a kernel I behold, but God's rain, sunshine, blue sky, captured therein and held prisoner so that on the altar [Christ] himself may become a prisoner of love.[62]

He called for pastoral instruction in rural parishes to make "the farmer folk conscious of their closeness to the sacrifice," the "full translation of the Ritual in understandable English," development of a prayer book for the farm family, special retreats for farm men and women, and the portrayal of saints "of and from the soil" in the windows and paintings of rural churches.[63] He also celebrated the appearance of new documents from the Vatican archives, detailing the traditional or historic Catholic view of agriculture as "the first and most important of all arts" and "the first and true riches of states."[64]

New issues also came forward during the 1940s. While Ligutti did not share the Southern Agrarian interpretation of the Civil War, he did agree with Donald Davidson on the emerging war in Europe: the United States should stay out. As he explained to one critic in January, 1941, America did not enjoy liberty because England or any other nation "gave it to us...or preserved if for us." Rather, Ligutti held that American liberty and freedom could only be preserved if "the United States continue in the traditions of George Washington and Jefferson."[65] Later that month, in a letter to Iowa Senator Clyde Herring, he urged opposition to any legislation that directly or indirectly involved the United States in the European war. He elaborated: "If we are to maintain [the American way], we must continue and develop the works for social and economic reconstruction within our beloved land and we must not go out in battle array to save periodically our democracy."[66]

Once America was in the conflict, Ligutii struggled to preserve the possibility for Agrarian Distributist action during and after the war. As Congress set out to divert funds from the Farm Security Administration—the most recent bureaucratic "home" of the Homestead program—to the war effort, Ligutti urged that it continue its work: "We feel that the family and countryside should be protected, continued, and developed; we feel that ownership of productive property—especially in the form of land for the family... is most important for a democracy."[67] He also urged a broadened view of national defense. The "greatest friends" of totalitarianism were "the advocates, the defenders and the ones who practice concentration of wealth." The proper view of farming by men of the soil formed "[a]nother line of defense," for one-crop farming was "a prison" that had turned the once-beautiful South "into a pitiful, wretched state of misery." A "better rural-urban balance" in population was also necessary to American defense.[68]

Ligutti tackled as well the growing public acceptability of birth control. He acknowledged that poverty and misery existed in the United States, but emphasized that their cause was neither a lack of resources nor too many people. "Far from it!" In the city of Des Moines alone, the average family had one-and-a-quarter children, the same as Brooklyn or Manhattan. Cities had long been, and continued to be, "the graveyards of the family," and sources of the long-term destabilization of the economy.[69]

Another important new initiative was to give ecumenical religious expression to the New Agrarianism. Working closely with Rev. Dr. Benson Landis of the Federal Council of Churches, Ligutti crafted the 1946 document, "Man's Relation to the Land." Unlike earlier ecumenical efforts in 1940 and 1941, which had focused primarily on urban industrial dislocations, this declaration was "much more comprehensive" and stood as "the first joint statement on land policy in religious terms." Signed by a prominent group counting twenty-eight Catholics, thirty-five Protestants, and twelve Jews, the statement was a nearly pure expression of New Agrarianism.[70]

Since "God created the world," the statement began, "all humans" possessed "a direct natural right" of access to needed resources. "God's intention in creation" was to allow man to live in dignity, to develop his personality, and "to establish and maintain a family." Since the land was "God's greatest material gift to mankind," it must be seen as "a very special kind of property," carrying social responsibilities of just and fair use. "Since the family is the primary institution," the prelates continued, "access to land and stewardship of land must be planned with the family unit in view." They emphasized the "special adaptability of the farm home for nurturing strong and wholesome family life" as the reason for their "universal interest" in agriculture: "The farm is the native habitat of the family." This meant that use of the land could not be restricted to a favored few. Indeed, "the worker on the land and his family" possessed "the first right to fruits of their toil"; the claims of the absentee owner and the state came second. Society also held responsibility for ensuring the education of land stewards in proper and efficient land use.

On the basis of these principles, the ecumenical group insisted: "that education for land stewardship and the productive home" be the central features of rural education; that the "family-type" owner-operator farm be "a major objective of legislation and planning"; that tax reforms improve security of tenure and land-use and discourage large land holdings "as undemocratic and anti-social"; that "a living family wage" be paid to workers where industrial farming existed; and that the "one foot on soil and one foot in the city" type of living, or subsistence homesteads, be encouraged as "greatly advantageous to the family."[71] Simply put, the New Agrarianism had "got" religion, under terms largely developed by Ligutti.

During these years, the monsignor also launched a massive campaign, "Christ to the Country—The Country to Christ." According to

Ligutti, when Christ said, "my father is a husband man," he pointedly meant "a yeoman...a tiller of the soil...a free man...the family type of farmer." "Christ to the Country" meant "a share in educational opportunities—a chance to develop God given gifts amidst the rural surroundings—songs and feast days—harvest dances arising from the very work of the people—a Christian rural culture—enlightened, tasty, neither abjectly superstitious, nor sophisticated and meaningless." This meant "a Christian way of looking at the soil," binding a family to a parcel of land over the generations and a duty by the farmer "to enrich the soil he tills and to hand it down to future generations as a *thank offering* to God, the Giver."[72]

"Christ to the Country" involved an evangelism plan of 200 years duration (a timeline perhaps possible only in an organization as old as Roman Catholicism). During the first one hundred years, "we must strengthen our rural parishes," where every church with a pastor *built* a school, and where every parish without a pastor gained a resident priest. During the second one-hundred years, one-half of all urban Catholics should move "where they can have space, light, air, and the ownership of some productive property." The Church would continue to work "as zealously" as it could for those left in cities, "but let us not forget that in doing so we are caring remotely for a cemetery."[73]

The latter 1940s witnessed, for the first time, the widespread complaint that there were "too many farmers." The older generations of agricultural economists and extension agents who had studied—literally or figuratively—at the knee of Liberty Hyde Bailey, were giving way to a new breed. The word, "agri-business," reared its head for the first time, and the family farmer now found himself at times an object of scorn. Ligutti, though, remained faithful to Agrarian goals. In a 1948 radio address, he denied that there were "too many farmers." Rather, there were not "enough farmers in America today—if farming is defined as a noble Christian profession and the farm home as the natural and best place for a family to live." He called for full-time and part-time family farms, arguing that "No loving husbandman can be a polygamist of many fields. The best fertilizer [remains] the shadow of the owner." Even from "an economic viewpoint," the well-managed and carefully nurtured small farm surpassed in all relevant measures the "self-styled large efficient units."[74]

The 1950s brought new challenges as well, along with a pull toward international rural affairs. But Ligutti remained faithful to his

"Agrarian Distributist" cause. Perhaps the most pressing "new" issue was the "population bomb." Neo-Malthusian propagandists, largely dormant since the 1920s in the face of withering Western birth rates, drew energy from the evident "Baby Boom" in the United States, and the surging growth of populations in the decolonizing world. Facing this assault on core ideals of family and fertility, Ligutti reminded attendees at a 1955 Missions conference that rural peoples were indeed "the nursery of the world," the ones who produce "the children of the world." He called the Malthusian message "an insult to Almighty God," who had in fact "arranged all things sweetly," including provision of the resources for life. "God has given the good earth to mankind, in abundance," he wrote. So-called overpopulation was "only a question of the improper arrangement, the ignorance of mankind, the unwillingness to follow the Divine Design, both as to the use and distribution of the land and of the fruits of the land."[75] Several years later, he accused the neo-Malthusians of being reactionaries, seeking "to continue the status quo of social injustices." Even certain "Catholic leaders and institutions" were trying to discover new paths to apostasy, what he labeled "moral pills to sooth rhythmical consciences." Old Malthus "was dead wrong" and his modern followers were just as obscurantist and unscientific. Turning to the soil, he declared: "Man is truly a beggar sitting on a chair of gold. We do not realize or appreciate the value and the secret powers of a spoonful of earth." Science, human effort, and the pursuit of social justice could easily solve the pseudo problem of overpopulation. "The most precious thing on the face of the earth," Ligutti affirmed, "is MAN with one mouth, two hands and a brain."[76]

Even as the American countryside witnessed a massive consolidation of agri-business and megafarms and a last great flow of people off the land, Ligutti remained committed to land reform and small holdings. "If the church upholds the right of private property," he reasoned, "and does nothing to make private property available to the masses it is guilty of false promises." He emphasized the need for radical change: "Christ was the Radical par excellence. Paganism, false gods, Roman materialism, Jewish formalism had to be uprooted."[77] By implication, rural activists were called to similar tasks.

Where other Agrarians were lulled into complacency by the apparent success of the postwar suburbs as nurseries for family life and children, Ligutti was less sanguine about these small subsistence homesteads that commonly exhibited few subsistence acts. On the one hand, he saw "a ray of hope" in the continued movement of urban families to the suburbs, seeking "a possibility of space, light, air, and a modicum of food production."[78] On the other hand, he knew that "America on the move" meant family turmoil and diminished family size. Ownership and permanency were far more important than "the house of 1000 gadgets" and a swarm of debt collectors.[79]

Without losing his faith in parish schools, Ligutti gave ever more attention to "the Christian family [as] a school," as "the most important educational unit in human society." The farm, in particular, was "the finest place on earth for a family to prepare for heaven." The farm home provided "a most ideal milieu" for a wider teaching and learning role for the family, where daily chores and learning-by-doing strengthened the economic integrity of the family.[80]

Still grappling with the pressures from technology, Ligutti reaffirmed his suborning of measures of efficiency to human values. "There are other values to be reckoned besides quantity o[r] even quality production," he said. "There are personal human values, family values, social values that...render man happier here below and prepare him for an eternity with God."[81] In a major 1957 paper for the Fourth International Congress on Rural Life, held in Santiago, Chile, Ligutti expanded on this *human*-centered measure of efficiency, postulating:

> Modern technology in industry, commerce, or agriculture functions more effectively and profitably in the production of goods and services when the human beings involved operate in keeping with their personal dignity, [and] welfare of the family, and when they can share in the ownership of the means of production and in its results.

Men of talent and genius fulfilled their obligations to society by envisioning new possibilities in agricultural production and new uses for agricultural products. At the same time, "most men will be found capable of ownership," and small holdings would allow them to fulfill the God-implanted "desire for creative work through productive property." Technology ought be subsumed to human ends; above all, to the welfare of the family. "This thesis is true," Ligutti concluded, "because it fulfills God's intention in man's creation, because it exhibits Christ's love for mankind, and because it furnishes all of us with the assurance of a good life here on earth and a good life for eternity."[82]

Faith and the Agrarian

The year 1959 was a difficult one for Ligutti. His growing involvement in international questions put a strain on the NCRLC. Despite generous and repeated gifts from Chauncey Stillman's Homeland Foundation (including a $50,000 challenge grant in 1958), financial pressures on the organization mounted. In 1960, Ligutti left the NCRLC to accept appointment as Permanent Observer of the Holy See to The Food and Agriculture Organization, the United Nation's agency headquartered in Rome. Stillman came to his aid again, granting $40,000 to construct "Villa Stillman" on a hill outside of Rome, as Ligutti's new residence. In this capacity and place, Ligutti emerged as "one of the foremost international churchmen"[83] of the 1960s, active not only on global food and population questions but also as a papal advisor during the critical Vatican II conclave. Albeit now largely on an international stage, he continued to press for land reform and preservation of the family unit, and to defend "the wondrous gifts" of fertility, human *and* agricultural.[84] In 1968, at the very height of the "Population Bomb" campaign, Ligutti would still give the same advice to young men that he offered to his Iowa parishioners in the 1920s: "Get married early in life; raise a big family; settle on a farm."[85]

Without his steadying, rooted presence, the NCRLC veered in new directions, losing almost complete touch with Catholic farm families and regular rural priests. During the 1960s, under the leadership of Edward O'Rourke, it became a fairly conventional social action advocacy group, focused heavily on the problems of migrant workers, with issues of family and fertility largely shelved.[86]

Without his active engagement, even the Granger Homesteads lost their way. World War II brought an end to Federal backing for this mode of living; after the war, more conventional forms of suburbanization became the favored governmental child. A contemporary visitor to Granger Homesteads will find a handful of the homes much like they were in the late 1930s, with extensive gardens and active "outbuildings." But overall, the place resembles a rural slum, supplemented by more recent "ranch style" homes built during the 1960s and 1970s by a new wave of suburbanites.[87]

Curiously, Ligutti could claim on a national level a kind of numerical success in keeping Catholics on the land. Between 1900 and 1980, the rural population of the United States fell from 60 percent to 26.3

percent. Yet among Roman Catholics, the proportion that were rural hardly changed at all, moving only from 19 to 17.7 percent, so raising the relative Catholic presence on the land.[88]

Ligutti's real legacy, however, lay in the philosophical realm, where he guided the New Agrarianism out of several intellectual cul-de-sacs. To begin with, he reattached man to the soil, refusing to accept a "land ethic" or "soil worship" divorced from intensive human settlement. Second, he escaped from Borsodi's guiding attachment to efficiency, and returned both technological innovation and the machine to positions subordinate to family life and the needs of the human personality. Finally, he boldly and correctly proclaimed the necessary bond of religious faith to any Agrarianism that might survive in the turbulent modern era.

His major error came from a failure to understand the full implications of this religious-agrarian tie. It was not enough to be in farming and to attend Mass and otherwise remain in the world. Experience would show that only a conscious, religiously motivated withdrawal from the dominant culture was adequate to the task.

Notes

1. Edwin V. O'Hara, "A Spiritual and Material Mission to Rural America," in *Catholic Rural Life Objectives: A Series of Discussions on Some Elements of Major Importance in the Philosophy of Agrarianism* (St. Paul, MN: National Catholic Rural Life Conference, 1935): 3-4.
2. O.E. Baker, "The Church and Rural Youth," in *Catholic Rural Life Objectives*, pp. 17, 29.
3. W. Howard Bishop, "Agrarianism, The Basis for the New Order," in *Catholic Rural Life Objectives*, p. 51. Another pre-Ligutti codification of similar views can be found in: National Catholic Rural Life Conference, *Manifesto on Rural Life* (Milwaukee: Bruce Publ. Co., 1939).
4. David Steven Bovee, "The Church and the Land: The National Catholic Rural Life Conference and American Society, 1923-1985," Doctoral dissertation, University of Chicago, August, 1986; p. 304.
5. Handwritten text. Lecture at Manchester College, April 14, 1958; in Box B-1, Luigi G. Ligutti Papers [hereafter LGL], Special Collections and University Archives, Marquette University, Milwaukee, WI.
6. "Manchester College"; and "These Men, This Land: The Priest with the Pitchfork," *Free America* 4 (Aug. 1940): 13.
7. "Manchester College"; emphasis in original.
8. L.G. Ligutti, "The New Ideals Come to Granger, Iowa," undated manuscript [1930s], Box B-2, LGL.
9. See: Vincent A. Yzermans, *The People I Love: A Biography of Luigi G. Ligutti* (Collegeville, MN: Liturgical Press, 1976): 31-32. A second book on Ligutti, part

simple biography and part personal reminiscence, exists: Raymond W. Miller, *Monsignor Ligutti: The Pope's County Agent* (Washington, DC: University Press of America, 1981). The volume emphasizes Ligutti's ecumenism.

10. Quotation from Yzermans, *The People I Love*, p. 32.
11. L.G. Ligutti, "A plan to solve some social, economic and religious problems by agriculture"; presentation to the Omaha Catholic Charities Conference, Omaha, NB, Sept. 25-28, 1932; Box B-2, LGL.
12. Russell Lord and Paul H. Johnstone, *A Place on Earth: A Critical Appraisal of Subsistence Homesteads* (Washington, DC: U.S. Department of Agriculture, Bureau of Agricultural Economics, 1942): 6.
13. Lord and Johnstone, *A Place on Earth*, pp. 12, 14-17, 20.
14. Ibid., pp. 21, 35, 38, 40.
15. L.G. Ligutti, "The Encyclicals and Legislation," Manuscript; Box B-2, LGL.
16. Lord and Johnstone, *A Place on Earth*, p.107.
17. Yzermans, *The People I Love*, p.33.
18. Lord and Johnstone, *A Place on Earth*, pp. 107-109.
19. "Granger Homesteads Second Anniversary Dinner," News Release, December 1937; in Box 2-B, LGL.
20. Lord and Johnstone, *A Place on Earth*, pp. 110, 115.
21. L.G. Ligutti, "Rural Sociology: The Rural Problem," Paper for the American Catholic Sociological Association, First Annual Convention, Dec. 27, 1938, p. 1; Box B-2, LGL.
22. For examples, see L.G. Ligutti, "Population Trends in Relation to Catholicity and the Landward Movement," Address to S.S. Comm. House, April 29, 1936; Box B-2, LGL.; and L.G. Ligutti, "Plowing With Angels," Lecture, May 15, 1965; Box B-1, LGL.
23. L.G. Ligutti, "Agrarianism, Cooperatives and the Bishops' Statement," Undated manuscript [1930s]; Box B-2, LGL.
24. L.G. Lugitti, "A Letter to a Contented Cow," undated manuscript [1930s]; Box B-2, LGL.
25. L.G. Ligutti, "Agrarian Distributism," Talk for WHO radio, Des Moines, IA, Oct. 2, 1937; Box B-2, LGL.
26. L.G. Ligutti, "Ideals for Rural Boys and Girls," Talk for WHO radio, Des Moines, IA, Dec. 25, 1937; Box B-2, LGL. See also: L.G. Ligutti, "The Man with a Plow," *Commonweal* (Mar. 5, 1937): 513.
27. Letter to *Des Moines Register*, July 19, 1935; Box B-2, LGL.
28. L.G. Ligutti, "Society and Agrarianism," Talk for WHO Radio, Des Moines, IA, Oct. 16, 1937, pp. 1, 3-4, 6-7; Box B-2, LGL.
29. Ligutti, "Rural Sociology," p. 6.
30. L.G. Ligutti, "A Thesis on Rural Life," undated pamphlet [1930s]; Box B-2, LGL.
31. Letter to, *Des Moines Register*, July 19, 1938; Box B-2, LGL.
32. L.G. Ligutti, "TheAgrarian Program," Talk for WHO Radio, Des Moines, IA, Oct. 23, 1937; Box B-2, LGL.
33. L.G. Ligutti, "Harvest Sunday Program," Talk for WHO Radio, Des Moines, IA, Nov. 20, 1937; Box B-2, LGL.
34. Ligutti, "Ideals for Rural Boys and Girls," pp. 2, 6.
35. Ligutti, "Harvest Sunday Program," p. 6; and Ligutti, "The Agrarian Program," p. 4.
36. L.G. Ligutti, "Urbanization and Its Effects Upon the Church," Talk for WHO Radio, Des Moines, IA, Nov. 6, 1937; Box B-2, LGL.

37. L.G. Ligutti, "What is Happening to the Catholic Population?" Undated manuscript [1930s], Box B-2, LGL.
38. L.G. Ligutti, "Planning for Youth in a Rural Parish," Lecture to N.C.C. Women, Des Moines, IA, Mar. 23, 1936; Box B-2, LGL.
39. L.G. Ligutti, "Cities Kill," *Commonweal* (Aug. 2, 1940): 301.
40. Ligutti, "Urbanization and Its Effects Upon the Church," p. 7.
41. Ligutti, "Cities Kill," p. 300.
42. Ibid.; L.G. Ligutti, "The Church and Agrarianism," Talk for WHO Radio, Des Moines, IA; Oct. 30, 1937, pp. 4-6; Box B-2, LGL; and "Cure for Communism— The Cow."
43. L.G. Ligutti, "Agrarian Lecture," Talk for WHO Radio, Des Moines, IA, Dec. 4, 1937, p. 1; Box B-2, LGL.
44. Ligutti, "Rural Sociology," p. 6.
45. Ligutii, "Ideals for Rural Boys and Girls," p. 5; also Ligutti, "Facts of Farming," undated outline for a speech [1930s]; Box B-2, LGL.
46. L.G. Ligutti, "Radio Talk," WOI, Ames, IA, Sept. 16, 1943.
47. L.G. Ligutti, "Spiritual Aspects of Rural Community Building," Banquet address for the American Country Life Association, Purdue University, Lafayette, IN, Nov. 6-9, 1940; Box B-1, LGL.
48. Ligutti, "The Church and Agrarianism," p. 7.
49. As example, see the St. Louis-based journal, *Right Spirit* 1 (October 1938); devoted to "the re-establishment of Christian rural life." Copy found in Box B-2, LGL.
50. See: John C. Rawe, "Corporations and Human Liberty: A Study in Exploitation. I. Real and Artificial Persons," *The American Review* 4 (Jan. 1935): 257-278; and John C. Rawe, "Corporations and Human Liberty: A Study in Exploitation II. Regaining the Rights of the Individual," *American Review* 4 (Feb. 1935): 473-490. Also: "The Priest with the Pitchfork," p. 13.
51. Luigi G. Ligutti and John C. Rawe, *Rural Roads to Security: America's Third Struggle for Freedom* (Milwaukee, WI: Bruce Publishing Co., 1940): xi.
52. Ligutti and Rawe, *Rural Roads*, pp. 3-6.
53. Ibid., p. 9.
54. Ibid., p. 10.
55. Ibid., p. 104.
56. Ibid., pp. 111-113, 116, 190, 200-202, 238, 313-331.
57. Ibid., p. 183.
58. Ibid., p. 185.
59. Ibid., pp. 238-251.
60. Letters, L.G. Ligutti to Bishop Vincent J. Ryan, December 23, 1940; and L.G. Ligutti to Bishop Vincent J. Ryan, April 3, 1941; in Box D-2, LGL.
61. See: Bovee, "The Church and the Land," pp. 319-323.
62. L.G. Ligutti, "The Spirit of Sacrifice in Christian Society," Liturgical Week Conference, October 13, 1943, Chicago, IL; Box B-1, LGL.
63. Ligutti, "The Spirit of Sacrifice."
64. From the *Motu Propio*, Sept. 15, 1802; cited in L.G. Ligutti, "The Popes and Agriculture," *Commonweal* (March 1, 1940): 3.
65. Letter, L.G. Ligutti to Charles Johnson, January 3, 1941; in Box D-2, LGL.
66. Letter, L.G. Ligutti to Clyde Herring, Jan. 13, 1941; Box D-2, LGL.
67. Letter, L.G. Ligutti to Senator Guy Gillette, March 24, 1942; Box D-2, LGL.
68. L.G. Ligutti, "Rural Church—A Factor in National Defense," Address to the First Regional Conference, Confraternity of Christian Doctrine, Lincoln, NB [1942-?]; in Box B-1, LGL.

69. Letter, Luigi Ligutti to Editor, [Des Moines] *Register-Tribune*, Jan. 27, 1940; Box D-2, LGL.
70. On the background to the statement, see: Benson Landis, "The Declaration of Economic Justice," *Free America* 10 (Autumn 1946): 6-8.
71. *Man's Relation to the Land: A Statement of Principle, Which Shall Underlie Our National, State and Individual Actions* [1946], Distributed by the National Catholic Rural Life Conference, Des Moines, IA.
72. L.G. Ligutti, "Christ to the Country—The Country to Christ," Radio broadcast, CBS "Church of the Air" Program, Nov. 30, 1947; in Box B-1, LGL.
73. "Christ to the Country—The Country to Christ," op. cit.
74. L.G. Ligutti, "In My Opinion," Radio broadcast, KSO, Des Moines, IA, Feb. 14, 1948; Box B-1, LGL.
75. L.G. Ligutti, "World Problems of Rural Social Action," Address to the Fordham Mission Institute, Jan. 23, 1955; Box B-1, LGL.
76. L.G. Ligutti, "How Can We Support an Increasing World Population?" Address to the Charles Carroll Forum, Chicago, March 8, 1959; Box B-1, LGL.
77. L.G. Ligutti, "The Chruch and Agriculture," Address to the National Catholic Rural Life Conference, Belleville, IL, Oct. 16, 1950; in Box B-1, LGL.
78. L.G. Ligutti, Address in Fort Wayne, IN, Oct. 28, 1958; Box B-1, LGL.
79. L.G.Ligutti, "The Ideal Home—Now," Address to Notre Dame High School, Chicago, IL, Feb. 14, 1950; Box B-1, LGL.
80. Ligutti, "Fort Wayne," p. 4; and Ligutti, "The Church and Agriculture," p. 6.
81. Ligutti, "Fort Wayne," p. 6.
82. L.G. Ligutti, "Human Dignity and Human Love," Paper presented to the Fourth International Congress on Rural Life, Santiago, Chile, April 1-6, 1957; published as appendix I in Yzerman, *The People I Love*, pp. 297-313.
83. Bovee, "The Church and the Land," p. 304.
84. See: Ligutti, "Plowing with the Angels"; L.G. Ligutti, "Ethical and Social Principles, Basic to Land Reform," Address to the FAO Assembly, Santiago, Chile, March 1965; in Box D-2, LGL.
85. L.G. Ligutti, "Msgr. Ligutti Advises Young Men," *Catholic Bulletin* [New Ulm, MN], Jan. 26, 1968, p. 2.
86. Bovee, "The Church and the Land," pp. 515-516.
87. Impressions from a visit by the author to Granger Homesteads, Iowa; July 12, 1998.
88. The Catholic figures are from 1920 and 1974, respectively. See: Bovee, "The Church and the Land," p. 514.

8

The Agrarian Elegy of Wendell Berry

Born two years before Lincoln's first presidential election, Liberty Hyde Bailey would craft the themes of the New Agrarianism. The generation born between 1885 and 1905—Zimmerman, Borsodi, Bromfield, Owsley, Lytle, Agar, and Ligutti—produced the great flowering of new agrarian ideas at mid-century. Standing almost alone as a public voice after 1960 would be their reluctant heir, Wendell Berry.

In Berry, the Highland Southerners—celebrated by the whole cast of twentieth-century agrarian writers—found their most versatile and creative native voice. He was, in a sense, a full-blooded representative of and advocate for Zimmerman's "stem family" and Agar's "culture man," here come to life. Born 1934 in the Kentucky hills along the Ohio River, Berry represented the fifth generation of his family on his mother's side to farm in Henry County. He published his first short story in 1955, his first poetry two years later, and his first novel in 1960. Nonfiction essays on the agrarian problem began appearing in profusion during the mid-1960s. By 1998, the books would number thirty-four. Between fellowships and teaching appointments in Europe, New York, and California, Berry farmed the family homestead in 1960-61 and resumed full-time residence in Kentucky in 1964, eventually carving out an eighty-five-acre hillside farm.

In a manner unlike that of any other recent American writer, Berry's poetry, fiction, and essays would share common themes, more or less unchanged from the beginning. They mutually reinforced what he called an "Agrarian Traditionalism," focused on family integrity, the power of the domestic economy, the reality and the metaphor of marriage, the importance of fertility, the necessity of a broad distribution

177

of property, the value of subsistence farming, and the foundation for community.

Berry was somewhat coy about his intellectual pedigree. Relative to literature, he openly stood as a student of Wallace Stegner, the "regionalist" author who taught a graduate seminar in creative writing at Stanford University, in which Berry participated in 1958-59.[1] He cited William Carlos Williams as the poet who most inspired him, particularly through the New Jerseyan's ability to find poetic material in his own urban place. Berry's agrarian roots, though, are more obscure. He had read at least the more literary works of Liberty Hyde Bailey, and had especial praise for *The Holy Earth* (calling it a "remarkable title") and *The Outlook to Nature*. Berry particularly admired the way in which Dean Bailey had integrated "the necessary pursuits of human economy" into a "harmony with nature, which he understood as their source and pattern."[2] Berry was also aware of, and learned from, the work of Louis Bromfield, sharing in the latter's admiration for the gardeners of France, who had turned small home plots into a source of both security and independence.[3]

The Kentuckian's most direct and complex relationship, though, lay with the Southern Agrarians. On the one hand, he sought to distance himself from the Vanderbilt group. He criticized their attachment to the "false and destructive" conventions of Southern regionalism, which had resulted in a kind of chauvinism or nationalism that violated real attachment to a place. He also rejected their apologetics for slavery and segregation and their "Eurocentrism." Berry added that "the withdrawal of the most gifted of these people" to Northern colleges and universities after 1940 had "invalidated their thinking," leaving it a merely "theoretical" agrarianism. On the other hand, he also later apologized to a degree for these harsh judgments, and admitted that the effect of the Twelve Southerners "on me has been large." He dedicated poems to Allen Tate and Robert Penn Warren and wrote that "the cause for which the Twelve Southerners spoke," in their statement of common principles, "was not a *lost* but a *threatened* cause: *the cause of human civilization*."[4] In explaining the agrarian "succession" itself, from Jefferson through Bailey to twentieth-century authors, Berry suggested that a "series of agricultural writers" might be a more accurate phrasing:

> I say "series" rather than "succession" because I don't know to what extent these people have worked consciously under the influence of predecessors. I suspect that

the succession, in both poetry and agriculture, may lie in the familial and communal handing down of *the agrarian common culture*, rather than in any succession of teachers and students in the literary culture or in the schools.[5]

This reluctance to acknowledge intellectual debt had its source as well in Berry's own declaration of independence. Like the farmers he admired, Berry usually refused to be drawn into any intellectual or political camp; or, once brought in, he would usually embarrass his ideological hosts. In one early essay, he labeled himself "melancholic and rebellious."[6] In another, he admitted to his own "badness," which he traced to a youthful dislike of all institutions: "School and Sunday school and church were prisons to me."[7] So were modern ideological constraints.

Berry also refused to be labeled as a conventional "regionalist," a style of interpretation which he thought relied too much on myths and stereotypes. Instead, he rooted his work on the principle of local life aware of itself, bearing a special knowledge "of the life of a place one lives in and intends to *continue* to live in." Where most American writers—indeed, most Americans—were "displaced persons," he reported, "I am a placed person. For longer than they remember, both sides of my family have lived within five or six miles of this riverbank...where I sit writing now." For him, it was never an issue of finding a subject, but rather one of "learning what to do with the subject I...could not escape."[8]

Berry broke with the "expatriated" Southern Agrarians in another important way as well. For the latter, the Civil War—or War Between the States, as they preferred—was the central historical event, the great tragedy that had befallen agrarian America. In contrast, Berry gave the events of 1861-65 little attention. Instead, he saw the 1940-1945 period, or the experience of World War II, as the great and terrible watershed in American history. Where the earlier generation of New Agrarians had cast the 1930s that they had lived in as a time of agrarian troubles, Berry saw it as "a golden age," at least in comparison to what came later. "The economies of many households were [then] small and thorough," he wrote. These folks "practiced household husbandry," tended gardens, "fattened meat hogs, milked cows," kept flocks of chickens, used horses for field work, and employed "little children" in their labors. These enterprises "comprised the direct bond between farm and household."[9] It was global war, he held, that had destroyed this harmony. World War II would form the subtext for much of Berry's fiction, particularly for his most ambitious novel, *A Place on Earth*. In it, the passing of the seasons in 1944-45 was contrasted with the war-induced unraveling of Port William, the small farming village that was the locale for all of his fiction. As they saw their sons go off to fight and—in some cases—to die, the characters came to understand the small world that they had known was passing away: "Something would be lost, was in the process of being lost, and they dreaded to ponder what."[10] As one of Berry's best drawn characters, Old Jack Beechum, thought about it: "There is too much dying. Too many young men dying. He mistrusts what he reads in the papers. The war is more serious, it seems to him, than the papers make it out to be."[11]

Indeed, Berry would confirm the worst fears of anti-interventionist agrarians such as Davidson and Ligutti. With war's end, the Kentucky countryside joined all of rural America in rapidly embracing mechanized farming: "People...began to move to the cities, and the *machines* moved from the cities into the fields." Soon, the tractors were ubiquitous, and the few horses and mules left were sentimental remnants.[12] Within three decades, the farmland itself was in decline: "fields and whole farms abandoned, given up with their scars unmended; washing away under the weeds and bushes; fine land put to row crops year after year, without rest or rotation; buildings and fences going down; good houses standing empty, unpainted, their windows broken."[13]

Home, Family, and Fertility

Despite this specter of decay and decline, Wendell Berry presented in his work the most integrated and in some respects the most beautiful and compelling case for the building of an agrarian society. At the core or foundation of this vision, he held, lay the domestic or family economy. He complained that in their postwar embrace of rampant consumerism, Americans had nearly destroyed private life: "Our people have given up their independence in return for the cheap seductions and the shoddy merchandise of so-called 'affluence.'"[14] The natural cultural centers of community and household had succumbed to this invasion of commerce through their own failure as economies. This had left family members and neighbors of little use to each other. And so, the "centripetal force of family and community" had failed, and isolated individuals fell under the sway of "exterior economies" and "professionals."[15] Accordingly, the first goal must be to reunite the place of residence with the place of work, and so restore the working home. "If we do not live where we work, and when we work," Berry explained, "we are wasting our lives, and our work too."[16] In one of his best short stories, "A Jonquil for Mary Penn," Berry showed how a young bride was introduced by her neighbors to the profound importance of "the economy" that she and her husband were building:

> She had learned to think of herself as living and working at the center of a wonderful provisioning: the kitchen and garden, hog pen and smokehouse, hen house and cellar of her own household; the little commerce of giving and taking that spoked out along the paths connecting her household to the others....She loved her jars of vegetables and preserves on the cellar shelves, and the potato bin beneath, the cured hams and shoulders and bacons hanging in the smokehouse...the egg basket and the cream bucket slowly filling, week after week.[17]

Berry insisted that any hope for rebuilding American life on principles of liberty and private life depended on refunctionalizing households. "We are going to have to gather up the fragments of knowledge and responsibility" that had been turned over since 1945 to governments, corporations, and specialists, and "put those fragments back together again in our own minds and in our families and households and neighborhoods." Berry suggested that Americans concerned about environmental deterioration first seek solutions by starting their own gardens, so beginning again the "great provisioning" of their homes in an ecologically sound way.[18] He also saw and celebrated the breastfeeding of babies as a hopeful sign, calling it the "last form of home production," one which women wisely refused to surrender.[19]

This focus on true home economics inevitably set Berry at odds with the philosophically liberal faction of modern feminism. He saw the "off farm" employment of rural women not as a gain, but as "a symptom of economic desperation and great unhappiness." He identified a close connection "between the oppression of women and the general contempt for household work." Women who labored for corporations did not gain "freedom." Rather, they combined "feudal submissiveness" with "modern helplessness." In leaving their homes for office and factory, they had doomed the productive household and contributed directly to "the disintegration of their families and communities" and "to the desecration and pillage of their country." He also concluded that women had not changed corporate culture; "To have an equal part in our juggernaut of national vandalism is [still] to be a vandal." Instead, Berry insisted on the continued possibility of a working home, rooted in the tasks of both husbandry and housewifery, where the couple "makes around itself a household economy that involves the work of both wife and husband, that gives them a measure of economic independence and self-protection...of self-employment...of freedom."[20]

Such a home also reinforced the bonds of kinship, of the generations. In his first novel, *Nathan Coulter* (1960), Berry used the image of a spring running alongside the homestead through all time: when the Indians had hunted the land; when the fictional boy's own people "came and took the land away from them and cleared it"; when his "Grandpa's grandfather" and his father got old and died; and "while Grandpa drank its water and waited his turn." The boy now waited his own turn, as well, in obedience to a shared familial attachment to this particular soil. In *A World Lost*, Berry returned to the image of the spring, describing a line of these natural water spouts lying in his country, and each carrying the names of families—"Chatham and Beechum and Branch and Bower and Coulter"—*his* families.[21] Another fictional character, Old Jack, "felt over and around him the regard of that fellowship of kinsmen and friends," watching, encouraging and instructing him "because in him, they see, come back again, traits and features of dead men they loved."[22]

At the heart of the true working home lay a marriage, and few modern American writers have given as much attention to the mysteries and importance of the marital bond as Berry. One of his most powerful metaphors emphasized the tie of marriage and farm: "A man planting a crop is like a man making love to his wife, and vice versa; he is a husband or a husbandman."[23] Proper marriage was a sexual *and* economic union; and the former without the latter became ruinous, with "degenerate housewifery" and "degenerate husbandry" the result. When brought together, though, the consequence was beauty. As Berry explained in his poem, "The Country of Marriage":

> Our bond is no little economy based on the exchange
> of my love and work for yours, so much for so much
> of an expandable fund. We don't know what its limits are—
> That puts it in the dark. We are more together
> than we know, how else could we keep on discovering
> we are more together than we thought![24]

Marriage, so understood, was an economy of joy. Berry's fictional Mary Penn described how, with "a joyous ache," she knew that she "completed" her husband, as he "completed" her: "When had there ever been such a yearning of halves toward each other, such a longing, even in quarrels, to be whole? And sometimes they would be whole. The wholeness came upon them as a rush of light...so that she felt they must be shining in the dark."[25] Marriage was in fact a "great power" able to transform not only people, but the world. As the author's fictionalized persona, Andy Catlett, thought the matter out, it "was as though grace and peace were bestowed on them out of the sanctity of marriage itself." They did not "make" a marriage so much as find themselves "being made by it." Held in its grip, time flowed over them "like swift water over stones," smoothing and shaping them to "fit together in the only way that fragments can be rejoined."[26]

But the Country of Marriage, at times, also brought pain. Berry termed it "a perilous and fearful effort," in which "there can't be enough knowledge at the beginning." Ignorance and errors would mark the way, even in the best of circumstances.[27] Complete failure could also occur. Some of the most poignant pages in all of Berry's fiction describe the courtship and marriage of Old Jack Beechum to Ruth: "He won her with his vices, she accepted him as a sort of mission field, and it was the great disaster of both their lives." Together, they were unable to complete each other or craft a meaningful working home. Old Jack's failure, Berry explained, was that "he had not united farm and household and marriage bed, and he could not." Tragedy followed.[28]

Attention to the marriage bed also led to Berry's celebration of fertility, another recurring agrarian motif. Among Berry's earliest poems was "The Broken Ground," a sensuous description of the plow in the furrow:

> The opening out and out,
> Body yielding body:
> the breaking
> through which the new
> comes, perching
> above its shadow....
> bud opening to flower
> opening to fruit opening
> to the sweet marrow
> of the seed[29]

Berry's descriptions of the country women he admired also emphasized an exuberant, purposeful sexuality. In *The Memory of Old Jack,* he wrote of young Hannah: "She feels good. She feels full of the goodness, the competency, of her body that can love a man and bear his children, that can raise and prepare food, keep the house, work in the field."[30] In *A World Lost*, he described Minnie Branch, "a large, muscular, humorous" women who could split firewood, butcher hogs, raise a garden, shoot a fox, and wring a hen's neck; and who "conceived and birthed as faithfully as a good brood cow, welcomed each newcomer without fuss, prepared without complaint for the next."[31]

Writing during the years of the birth control pill, the "population bomb," and the legalization of abortion, Berry remained faithful to the pro-natalist position, to the undoubted discomfort of many of his more progressive readers. He termed the casual use of birth control "horrifying," and indicted "the evangelists, technicians, and salesmen of birth control" for undermining the ability of Americans "to see any purpose or virtue in sexual discipline." He saw artificial birth control as an example of industrial-chemical warfare on humankind, and endorsed instead maternal nursing and forms of culturally inspired sexual restraint.[32] The history of the sexual revolution, he insisted in a commentary on "the pill," turned out to be "a history of increasing bondage to corporations."[33] Berry simply rejected the argument that "there are too many people." He was sure this was not true of the United States, and he feared for the implications of the statement. To accede to such an argument, he explained, was implicitly to call for a dangerous determination of "who are the surplus." More broadly, the problem was not "human fecundity." Rather, he said that "technological multipliers" were artificially magnifying the negative impact of some peoples on the world, and he urged a redirection of attention here.[34] The author also labeled abortion as part of a "general warfare against children." He rejected the argument that a woman should be allowed to "control her own body" by noting "that if you can control your own body only by destroying another person's body, then control has come much too late." He also denied the contention that a fetus was not a human until it could claim "viability" outside the womb. "If we are unworthy to live as long as we are dependent on [others], then none of us has any rights." Giving the argument an agrarian twist, he added: "I would not try to convince any farmer or gardener that the planted seed newly sprouted is not a crop."[35]

Along with family and fertility, Berry favored the widespread ownership of productive property. He paid homage to Thomas Jefferson for advancing "the idea that as many as possible should share in the ownership of the land" and so be bound to it by material interest, "by the investment of love and work," and by family bonds, memory, and tradition. This old ideal was "still full of promise," "potent with healing and with health." He yearned "with a kind of homesickness" for the "naturalness of a highly diversified, multi-purpose landscape, democratically divided," and "hospitable to the wild lives of plants and animals and to the wild play of human children." This, Berry insisted, was "the kind of country we had from the Revolution through World War II." And this, alone, held promise for "a defensible" national future.[36] Sharing the view of Ralph Borsodi and Father Rawe, Berry traced the abuse of property to the legal fiction that treated corporations as "persons," allowing them to accumulate vast tracts of land.[37] Drawing directly from Allen Tate, Berry noted how in the Old South the presence of black slaves had separated white "owners" from real contact with the soil, which undermined the possibility for a stable antebellum agrarian order. White society had been cut off from any true cultural roots; while blacks had been denied the real ownership that marked a free peasantry. Although the "transition from slave to citizen" was "good," the transformation of African Americans from "useful and therefore valuable slave" to "useless and therefore costly economic dependent" was simply "bewilderment."[38]

Berry also shared the related agrarian enthusiasm for subsistence farming. "Commercial farming must never be separated from subsistence farming," he wrote. "[T]he farm family should live from the farm."[39] It was this commitment to sufficiency that defined the yeoman tradition and protected farmers from dangerous over-extension, and a loss of independence. Indeed, it was such attachment to the modest-sized acreage that could excite a man "until he could not sleep: Like a woman!"[40] Berry was sure as well that the subsistence principle—"the use of the product by the producers"—alone was a guarantee of quality production.[41] Echoing Louis Bromfield's fictionalized Maria in *The Farm*, Berry saw commitment to "subsistence" as in practice largely a matter of spirit and will, rather than mere economics. His Old Jack watched his young tenants, and smiled: "These people are not the kind who will be running to the grocery store to buy all they eat. That means a great deal, to Old Jack's way of thinking."[42] It was in the acts of self-sufficiency that Berry's poetic persona, "The Mad Farmer," found his satisfactions:

> ...the early garden: potatoes, onions,
> peas, lettuce, spinach, cabbage, carrots
> radishes, marking their straight rows,
> with green, before the trees are leafed
>
> raspberries ripe and heavy amid their foliage,
> currents shining red in clusters amid their foliage,
> strawberries red ripe with the white
> flowers still on the vines—picked
> with the dew on them, before breakfast...."[43]

Even the killing of hogs on the subsistence homestead took on poetic meaning:

> ...let this day begin again the change of hogs into people, not the other way around,
> for today we celebrate again our lives' wedding with the world,
> for by our hunger, by this provisioning, we renew the bond.[44]

On the subsistence farm, Berry argued, a man found purpose as well: "Every fold of the land, every grass blade and leaf of it gave me joy, for I saw how my own place in it had been prepared...." Or as he wrote about his aging characters, Mat and Margaret Feltner: "She pleased him, and the garden pleased him. After even so many years, he still needed to be bringing something to her."[45]

The subsistence farm also had the broader effect of securing liberty and democracy. At the household level, it provided the material basis for real freedom. As the character Nathan Coulter paraphrased his Daddy: "when we finally did get the farm paid for we could tell everybody to go to hell. That was what he lived for...."[46] Men would be free only when they were "equal to their own needs."[47] The *hard* work and the *hand* work on the small, diversified farm was "the source of a confidence and an independence of character that can come no other way, not by money, not by education."[48] With the whole array of agrarians, from Jefferson forward, Berry agreed that the presence or absence of subsistence family farms would determine the question of who would own, and run, the country: the moneyed interests or the plain people themselves?[49]

Berry also displayed a passion for community. Bonds of kinship, friendship, and neighboring, and other forms of "homemaking" in a place, were "the rites by which we solemnize and enact our union with the universe."[50] The true community balanced change with constancy, placing high value on love of neighbor, marital fidelity, local loyalty, family integrity, respect for the aged, and instruction of the young. A vital community avoided money and the rule of competition, preferring nonmonetary exchanges. A strong community implied—indeed rested on—such a strong local economy. The "beloved community" meant "common experience and common effort on common ground."[51] Viable rural communities held people who "had worked together a long time," who "knew what each one was good at." Even the landscape would be transformed by the signs of real community: "on rises of ground or tucked into folds were the grey, paintless buildings of the farmsteads, *connected to one another by lanes and paths.*"[52] In his fiction, Berry took to describing the Port William community as "the worn and wasted, sorrow-salted ground, familiar as if both known and dreamed," a membership that "he did not make, but has chosen, and that is death and life and hope to him."[53]

Suburbs, Peasants, and Monster Technology

Wendell Berry lived through the post-World War II decades, and so—through simple observation—escaped several of the illusions that had drawn earlier New Agrarians down unfruitful paths. To begin with, he never described the postwar suburbs as a "solution" to the moral, material, and biological problems of America. The "domestic economy" proper to farming life was fundamentally different from that found in "the industrial suburbs," he said. Despite the hopes of many in the 1930s and 1940s, suburban Americans proved to have little interest in subsistence gardens and chicken houses. Instead, their homes became centers of conspicuous industrial consumption.[54] Accordingly, he reasoned that the flow of city-people to the suburbanizing countryside was no compensation for the accelerated movement of country-people cityward: they "are hardly the same people."[55] Rather, the rural life had been "defeated" for the benefit of the "victorious" suburban housing developments, those places where the "winners" in the industrial economy resided. These affluent suburbs, "like ringworm," ate their way outward, consuming good land and leaving the old central cities "desolate, filthy, ugly, and dangerous."[56] Berry described the process in his poem, "The Clearing":

> ....the farm dismembered,
> sold in pieces on the condition
> of the buyer's ignorance,
> a *disorderly town*
> of 'houses in the country'
> inhabited by strangers....[57]

Berry also took to task the values of suburbanized America, including "marriage without love; sex without joy; drink without conviviality; birth, celebration, and death without adequate ceremony; faith without doubt or trial; belief without deeds; [and] manners without generosity."[58]

In contrast with most New Agrarians, and as with Father Ligutti, Berry praised the "peasant" style of life. His chief criticism of the Old South was its denial to black families of "the peasant's sense of a permanent relation to the earth."[59] From William Carlos Williams, he drew a positive assertion of "the importance of peasant tradition" to his own time.[60] In his commentaries on Amish settlements in Indiana, Ohio, and Pennsylvania, Berry praised a landscape "vibrantly populated" with busy people, animals, and "the voices of children," all living in village-like proximity to each other and exhibiting peasant folkways.[61]

On the theoretical level, at least, Berry also claimed to oppose government intervention. While holding a sentimental attachment to parts of the New Deal (and particularly to the tobacco allotment program that his own father had helped to construct), Berry was more influenced here by the obvious failure of the federal land grant schools to help family farming. The Colleges of Agriculture, he argued, had "presided over the now nearly complete destruction of their constituency." Founded to assure agriculture an "equal footing with industry" and to promote the rural home, the Land Grant system had been captured by corporate interest and careerists, and now served the goals of agribusiness alone.[62] As a country lawyer explained to a city detective in the story, "Fidelity": "we know that for a hundred years, the chief clients and patrons of that state of yours have been in the business of robbing and impoverishing the country people."[63] In Berry's mind, the great enemies of freedom were the alignment of political power with wealth, and the dispossessing of real property from the people. Since the 1940s, he said, the U.S. government had consciously sought "the removal of the vast majority of all races from the independent use or ownership of land." State espousal of "economic and technological determinism" had "virtually destroyed community life and community economy" in all parts of the country. He concluded by rejecting legislative solutions to moral and social problems,[64] calling "only" for "negative government," meaning the protection of small communities from invasion, armed or economic.

In line with this rejection of state control, Berry took frequent aim at the claims of public education at the elementary and secondary levels. In *What Are People For?*, he argued against the "powerful superstition of modern life" that people "are improved inevitably by education." In fact, he asserted that the purpose of state education had long been to teach country folk to leave the country and to "take their place" in industrial society. Public schools were no longer oriented to a cultural inheritance, to be passed on unimpaired. Rather, they focused on the career, or the "future" of the child. Such schools innovated "as compulsively and as eagerly as factories." Under such circumstances, educators logically saw parents as "a bad influence" on the children. And many parents, in turn, had no useful work for their children to do, and so were eager to turn these encumbrances "over to the state for the use of the future." As Berry summed up the situation: "The local schools no longer serve the local community; they serve the government's economy and the economy's government."[65] Indeed, even busing as "a cure" for desegregation was better seen as another stage in school consolidation, in the loss of neighborhood identity, and in enhanced central control of the children.[66] Unfortunately, Berry never quite decided where to go for an alternative. He had praise for both formal and informal apprenticeships.[67] He suggested, at one point, that if technological innovation had been differently directed after 1945, "they might have used it to improve the homelife and the home instruction of children."[68] And Berry even opined that "our schools...should offer a major in homecoming."[69] But he chose, for unstated reasons (perhaps his distrust of "movements"), not to give his direct blessing to home schooling as a universal option.

Most dramatically, Berry broke with most New Agrarians in his assessment of technology. On a few occasions, Berry would sound a Borsodi-like note, as in his call for "a system of decentralized, small scale industries" to process rural products, or in his praise of the Amish as "the truest geniuses of technology," or in his contention that the triumph of agribusiness over subsistence farming was not due to greater efficiency, but rather to "a deliberate policy to allow the big to grow bigger at the expense of the small."[70] But his dominant message was an overwhelming hostility to technological innovation. Despite "all the scientific agricultural miracles," he wrote, farmers were still poorer than those folks in the city. "The machine" allowed humankind to ignore fear, awe, reverence, humility, or delight, sentiments that might have restrained human ambitions. Indeed, the machine had become an agent of release from the constraints of the Creation. The farmer, already reeling from the industrial revolution, was easily sucked in by the promise of a better tomorrow. Under the banner of "efficiency," even "the monster technology" of the machines called "acre-eaters" would spread across the land, destroying what was left of rural life. In a sharp break with Borsodi-doctrine, Berry termed the sciences neither positive nor neutral, but "destructive," because they worked, "by principle," outside the demands and controls of human affection. Industrialism, by its very nature, transformed crops, animals, and even people into machines, without spirits or souls. He concluded: "I hope that my country may be delivered from the remote, cold abstractions of university science."[71]

In this "insidious" process, there could be no easy place of rest: "The revolution that began with machines and chemicals proposes now to continue with automation, computers, and biotechnology." Over a dozen pages in *The Unsettling of America*, Berry chronicled with mounting horror the visions of a "dream farm" developed under USDA tutelage in the 1970s: bubble-topped control towers with computers and minute-by-minute stock reports; remote-controlled tiller-combines in ten-mile-long wheat fields: jet-powered helicopters spraying insecticides; and fifteen-story "livestock buildings" containing 20,000 large animals. Binding all of them together was one quality: the absence of people. "There will be no singing in those fields," Berry wrote. "There will be no...neighbors laughing and joking, telling stories, or competing at tests of speed or strength or skill."[72]

Modern electronics drew Berry's particular opposition. In the poem, "The Record," he noted the need to save the vital knowledge of the old ways:

> As the machines come and the people go
> the old names rise, chattering, and depart.

But the poet was resolute in rejecting use of a tape recorder:

> [K]nowledge of my own going into old time
> tells me no. Because it must be saved,
> *do not tell a machine to save it.*[73]

In a famous article appearing in *Harper's Magazine*, Berry also rejected the use of computers for word processing. He reported that he wrote all his books, essays, and poems by hand, which were then typed up by his wife on a 1956 Royal Standard. "I do not see," he continued, "that computers are bringing us one step nearer to anything that does matter to me: peace, economic justice, ecological health, political honesty, family and community stability, good work." Writers who used computers, he added, dangerously flirted with "a radical separation of mind and body."[74] With "forty-odd years" as evidence, Berry also concluded that television, "far from proving a great tool of education, is a tool of stupefaction and disintegration."[75] Quite simply, the higher aims of "technological progress" were money and luxury, from which no good would come.

Radical Change and the God of Nature

In other ways, though, Wendell Berry carried to century's end the distinguishing New Agrarian themes. His attack on the principles of industrial capitalism, for example, was radical indeed, moving beyond that of Herbert Agar and the Distributists. To begin with, Berry indicted the industrial economy's "characteristic division between life and work," or the institutions of office and factory that pulled working adults out of their homes and away from their children.[76] He also denounced the "standard of efficiency" for its non-attention to the best traditions of husbandry and for having encouraged the "potentially catastrophic" industrialization of agriculture.[77] He ridiculed "the falseness and silliness of the economic ideal of competition," which was untrue toward and destructive of both nature and human nature. The Kentuckian rejected specialization for having fragmented knowledge, and so become a destructive force.[78] Indeed, the division of labor—the very heart of classical liberal economics—had dehumanized home and family life, in his view. "For all his leisure and recreation," Berry wrote, the modern *specialist* "feels bad, he looks bad, he is overweight, his health is poor....He does not know why his children are the way they are. He does not understand what they say."[79] The family farm failed because of the overriding assumption that "value equals price,"[80] an equation which did not take human, family, or community values into account. Indeed, Berry saw industrial capitalism as "the economy of the bulldozer," seeking to level the economy of nature or "the economy of God." The system sought to make everyone and everything a commodity, to be bought or sold, so that "not one free-standing tree or household or man or woman would remain."[81] Indeed, the seven deadly sins—especially envy, gluttony, lust, pride, and sloth—could be easily construed as the guiding principles of the official economy.[82] The Vietnam War had been a perfect example of this, he opined, where the products of advanced industrial technology were employed to destroy peasants, women, and children.[83] Put another way, the American system was "a farmer-killing and a land-killing economy."[84]

Berry also documented the perverse way in which this industrial economy encouraged family disintegration. He referred to a happily married husband and wife, who produced most of what they needed on their small farm, and who therefore had "work at home for children" and a true and complete household. But they consumed very little that had been produced by the money economy, and so were of little consequence to the state or to business. Yet once divorced, "their contribution to the economy would increase spectacularly"; their worth to both tax collector and corporate chieftain would grow, giving these professionals a positive interest in the breaking apart of homes.[85]

In 1988, Berry added up the consequences of the dominant industrial economy, counting: "divorce, venereal disease, debt, bankruptcy, pornography, soil loss, teenage pregnancy, fatherless children, motherless children, child suicide, public child-care, retirement homes, nursing homes, toxic waste…government lying, government crime…sexual promiscuity…the explosion of garbage, hopeless poverty…."[86] Cities sucked the life out of the countryside and even lost their own distinctiveness, becoming "Anywherevilles" in the global industrial megalopolis.[87] Vast agribusiness corporations operated where twenty-five family farms might have thrived.[88] Captives of television and salesmen, country people more and more lived like city people, from whom they absorbed their social and economic fashions. In the end, Berry reported, rural Kentucky garbage "mingles with New Jersey garbage in the local landfill, and it would be hard to tell which is which."[89]

Even the remaining farmers themselves were a problem. From the beginning, American agriculture had been overly obsessed by growth, greed, and abundance, a legacy of the "get rich quick" schemes of the first explorers on the new continent. Berry cast his fictional Hample family as fairly typical of the breed, who practiced a style of farming that

had destroyed, "maybe forever," the fertility of their land.[90] Other farmers crossed the dividing line between true community and submission to
industry on that day they decided "it would be better to own a neighbor's
farm than to have a neighbor."[91] Still others moved into agribusiness
themselves, and became farmers in name and memory only.

So what could one do? In the midst of this social catastrophe, given
his economic analysis and despite his desire to avoid big government,
Berry turned from raw necessity to massive social and economic engineering. Although referring to technology, he probably had a broader
lesson in mind when he wrote: "if we are ever again to have a world
fit and pleasant for little children, we are surely going to have to draw
the line where it is not easily drawn."[92] At the thematic level, he
called for an economy focused, not on production, but on reproduction, where the aim was "not to happen once, but to happen again and
again," so seeking "a balance between saving and spending" and a
proper use of energy.[93] He called for building the "Great Economy,"
one derived from the Kingdom of God, where there would be no
division or specialization, where all things would fit together.[94] Berry
said that the fundamental difference of agriculture from other forms of
human productive behavior must be recognized. In farming alone, he
argued, abundance destroyed its producers.[95] This meant that farming
had to be lifted completely out of the competitive industrial economy.[96]
Specific recommendations to that end, drawn from several of his books,
included:

●the elimination of national and international markets in food and
fiber, so that local producers would grow for local use;

●the elimination of local markets, as well, since no market mechanism could value items such as topsoil, ecosystem, farm family, or
community;

●the use of differential taxation to insure the wide distribution of
property;

●government-subsidized loans for the purchase of farms by property-
less families;

●national controls on production;

●governmental controls on commodity prices to ensure a fair balance
between farming income and necessary expenses;

●state-imposed limits on the application of technology to farming;

●tariffs on food and fiber commodities high enough to discourage
import of products that could be grown locally;

•the declaration of a "right" to be a small farmer, within "limits" that were obvious and reasonable;

•the creation of a new kind of money that "does not lie about value," but rather created "a decent balance between what people earn and what they pay";

•and [perhaps most realistically], a change in the way professors of agriculture were paid, where half of their compensation would come from produce off a grant of land for their own productive use.[97]

While perhaps never intended to be brought together, this list implies a level of state intervention that could properly be labeled a "command economy," one that even Berry himself would have recognized as the very negation of the liberty he sought to preserve.

Berry also exhibited the characteristic New Agrarian attitude toward religion generally, and Christianity in particular. With special power in his poetry, Berry did employ moving Christian imagery. In "The Way of Pain," for instance, he wrote:

> I read of Christ crucified,
> the only begotten Son
> sacrificed to flesh and time
> and all our woe. He died
> and rose, but who does not tremble
> for his pain, his loneliness,
> and the darkness of the sixth hour?
> Unless we grieve like Mary
> at His grave, giving Him up
> as lost, no Easter morning comes.[98]

Or consider his extraordinary retelling of the Christmas story, set in rural Port William, among farmers birthing their sheep:

> He said:
> "It's the old ground trying it again
> Solstice, seeding and birth—it never
> gets enough. It wants the birth of a man
> to bring together sky and earth, like a stalk
> of corn."[99]

In the novel, *A World Lost*, Berry described wonderfully a vision of Paradise, in which the dead, "waking, dazed, into a shadowless light," were "loved completely, even as they have been, and so are changed into what they could not have been but what, if they could have imagined it, they would have wished to be."[100]

Yet the dominant force of his nonfictional analysis was hostile to aspects of Christianity, both in organization and theology. Relative to the former, he condemned the "organized church" for making its peace "with a destructive economy" and for divorcing itself "from economic issues." He decried "the evident ability of most churches leaders to be 'born again in Christ,'" without questioning their faith in the industrial economy.[101] While "saving the souls of pagans" on other continents through "the gleeful imperialism of self-righteousness," the American churches were at home little more than fashion shows, women's clubs, moral pain killers, "soporific."[102] Berry repeatedly blasted national churches that used rural parishes as practice grounds for new preachers. In a judgment reminiscent of Bromfield's quip that the best farmers didn't go to church, Berry labeled the character Old Jack as "not a churchly man" but rather "a man of unconfining righteousness."[103]

On the more important questions of theology, Berry suggested that if one "is living by the tithes of history's most destructive economy, then the disembodiment of the soul becomes the chief of worldly conveniences."[104] For Berry, the radical dualism of Christian eschatology—the opposition of this world to the next world—was the source of both agricultural and environmental crises. Given the Christian instinct to devalue the physical world, exploitation of that worldly environment logically followed: "If Christianity is contained within churches, which are the only holy places, then Christians are free to desecrate the rest of Creation." By becoming a "specialist" creed focused on the saving of souls and lifting folks into heaven, Christianity connived "directly in the murder of Creation."[105]

Berry also criticized orthodox Christianity for not providing "a precise enough understanding of the commonplace issues of livelihood." While one could find, particularly in the Old Testament, a "divine mandate to use the world justly and charitably," this stewardship was "meaningless" unless it also involved "long-term courage, perseverance, devotion, and skill." Here, in Berry's understanding, the Judeo-Christian tradition failed, trumped again by the "other worldly philosophy." Berry also disliked the motif of heroism found throughout Scripture, which to his mind encouraged both hubris and abstraction in human affairs.[106] More generally, he denounced "the doctrinal arrogance" and "the witless piety" to be found in the American churches.[107]

Berry differed from agrarians such as Bailey and Bromfield in the respect he held for certain sects. For example, he thought that the Shakers had found a proper resolution of the livelihood problem in their view of work as prayer.[108] And he shared with Wallace Stegner an admiration for the Mormons, praising Mormon philosopher Hugh Nibley's admonition that "man's dominion is a call to service, not a license to exterminate."[109]

Above all, Berry looked to the Amish as examples of the better way. "They alone," he reported, "have carefully restricted their use of machine-developed energy, and so have become the only true masters of technology." They also "may well be the last surviving white community of any considerable size in this country."[110] Berry acknowledged that part of their secret lay in the exercise of "spiritual authority." Yet curiously, he subtly shifted the terms of his analysis away from the basic Amish religious principle of "separation from the world." Indeed, of all the Christian sects in America, the Amish held to perhaps the most radical division between "the church" and the rest of "the world." This, together with the practice of *gelassenheit* (submission) and insistence on strict obedience to church authority, largely accounted for Amish survival.[111]

Yet these qualities of radical separation, submission, and obedience did not quite fit into Berry's broader critique of Christianity. So he simply glossed them over. In *The Unsettling of America*, for example, Berry described the Amish as "a religion unusually attentive to its effects and obligations *in the world,*" where in practice, the Amish religion was first and foremost about the next world. In *The Gift of Good Land*, he attributed Amish behavior to the principle of loving one's neighbor, not mentioning the radical Amish eschatology of division between "the church" and "the world." In *Home Economics*, he listed the many admirable Amish principles of life (e.g., lively practice of the domestic arts and the rearing of their children at home), but relegated their religion to a status merely equivalent to cultural, family, and communitarian goals. Berry also attributed Amish respect for "good work" to a "respect for nature,"[112] although the more accurate sources were obedience to "a calling from God" and preparation for eternity.[113]

These subtle, but critical differences in interpretation of Amish theology took on further significance in light of Berry's occasional effort to craft a version of nature worship. Veering close on these occasions to the work of Liberty Hyde Bailey, he found comfort and meaning in phrases such as "the circle of life" and "sacred groves," the latter defined as wilderness places, large and small, left alone "because we do not" understand what happened there.[114] In *A Continuous Harmony*, he argued that there was "only one value," namely "the life and health of the world."[115] Agriculture, he noted elsewhere, had the same root as the word, "cult," leading him to conclude that "[t]o live, to survive on the earth, to care for the soil, and to worship, all are bound at the root to the idea of cycle." Adding to this de-anthropomorphization of God, Berry stated that "the absolute good...is health," not so much of the individual body, "but the health, the wholeness, finally *the holiness* of Creation, of which our personal health is only a share."[116]

A World Lost

Alas, Berry's effort at agrarian reconstruction—social, economic and spiritual—kept colliding with the reality of the rapid disintegration of rural America. Berry himself noted that the farm population fell from 31 million in 1940 to 23 million in 1950 to 4.6 million by 1970. In 1993, Berry woefully reported, the U.S. Census Bureau had announced that it would "no longer count the number of Americans that lived on farms," so small had their numbers become.[117]

The years 1944-45, Berry wrote, "seem to me now to have been a kind of ending, not just of lives but of a kind of life and a kind of world."[118] Soldiers trained in war to use machines returned to the fields with tractors in tow, eager to continue in the modern ways. The old and the children vanished as well. In the words of the fictional Burley Coulter:

> They began to go and not come back....The old ones dead and gone that won't ever be replaced, the world they were made in done throwed away, and the young ones dead in wars or killed in damned automobiles, or gone off to college and made too smart ever to come back, or gone off to easy money and bright lights.[119]

The radical nature of Berry's political program and his desperate effort to craft a direct religious land ethic might be explained by this sense of the terrible shortness of the hour. Already, in 1976, Berry warned that only "the sad remnants" of rural communities remained. "If we allow another generation to pass" without reversing the course, he added, "we will lose it altogether."[120] A generation later, Berry admitted to this failure: "the fact is that we have nearly destroyed American farming, and in the process have nearly destroyed our country" [1989];[121] or "one...had better understand that there may, after all, be nothing left to save""[1988];[122] or "these figures [on rural depopulation] describe a catastrophe that is now virtually complete" [1995].[123]

In response, Berry increasingly turned his writing into a kind of elegy for the dead, seeking to capture in words the thoughts, feelings, customs, and attitudes of an agrarian people virtually gone, their ways no more familiar to living Americans than the folkways of the Kalahari Bushmen. As early as the Revised version of *A Place on Earth* [1983], Berry brought the novel to resolution when Mat Feltner, his only son killed in the war, realized that his farm would soon pass away: "Although the meanings of those clearings and his devotion to them remain firm in his mind, he knows without sorrow that they will end, the order he has made and kept in them will be overthrown, the effortless order of wilderness will return."[124] Subsequent fiction, such as *A World Lost* (1995) and *Watch With Me* (1994), could also be read as a kind of anthropological record of a way of life that had passed, forever.

To the century's end, though, Berry would still try on occasion to find hope. Perhaps "somewhere the agrarian dream survives."[125] Just "*one* revived rural community" would do more good than all the government and university programs of the last half century. Or perhaps it was enough just to testify to the truth, in "the hope of preserving qualities in one's own heart and spirit that would be destroyed by acquiescence."[126]

And so, a project that began with the goal of building a Great Rural Civilization in America's vast Mississippi Valley, ended as a personal witness to a largely vanished way of life. In Wendell Berry, the New Agrarian Mind came to a kind of endpoint.

Notes

1. See Andrew J. Angyal, *Wendell Berry* (New York: Twayne, 1995): 15.
2. Wendell Berry, *What Are People For?* (San Francisco, CA: North Point Press, 1990): 103.
3. Wendell Berry, *A Continuous Harmony: Essays, Cultural and Agricultural* (San Diego, CA and New York: Harcourt Brace Jovanovich, 1972, 1970): 83.

4. Berry, *A Continuous Harmony*, pp. 66-67, 120-121; Wendell Berry, "The Clear Days" and "The Wheel," in *Collected Poems, 1957-1982* (San Francisco, CA: North Point Press, 1984): 165, 261; and Wendell Berry, *The Hidden Wound* (San Francisco, CA: North Point Press, 1969; 1989): 105.
5. Berry, *What Are People For?*, p. 105. Emphasis added.
6. Wendell Berry, *Recollected Essays, 1965-1980* (New York: Farrar, Straus and Giroux, 1981): 31.
7. Berry, *What Are People For?*, p. 71.
8. Berry, *A Continuous Harmony*, p. 67; and *Recollected Essays*, pp. 42, 52.
9. Berry, *The Gift of Good Land*, pp. 98-99.
10. Wendell Berry, *A Place on Earth—Revision* (New York: North Point Press, 1983): 11.
11. Berry, *A Place on Earth*, p. 50.
12. Berry, *The Hidden Wound*, p. 55.
13. Wendell Berry, *The Unsettling of America: Culture and Agriculture* (New York: Avon, 1977): 108.
14. Berry, *A Continuous Harmony*, p. 76.
15. Berry, *What Are People For?*, p. 164.
16. Berry, *The Unsettling of America*, p. 79.
17. In Wendell Berry, *Fidelity: Five Stories* (New York & San Francisco, CA: Pantheon Books, 1992): 74-75.
18. Berry, *A Continuous Harmony*, pp. 79, 82.
19. Berry, *The Unsettling of America*, p. 115.
20. Berry, *What Are People For?*, pp. 111, 180, 184; and *The Hidden Wound*, p. 113.
21. Wendell Berry, *A World Lost* (Washington, DC: Counterpoint, 1996): 8.
22. Wendell Berry, *Nathan Coulter* (San Francisco, CA: North Point Press, 1960; 1985): 179-180; and *The Memory of Old Jack*, p. 140.
23. Berry, *A Continuous Harmony*, p. 159.
24. Berry, "The Country of Marriage," *Collected Poems*, p. 147; also *The Unsettling of America*, pp. 116-118.
25. Berry, *Fidelity*, p. 79.
26. Wendell Berry, *Remembering: A Novel* (San Francisco, CA: North Point Press, 1988): 34, 113.
27. Berry, *Recollected Essays*, p. 37.
28. Berry, *The Memory of Old Jack*, pp. 51, 165-166.
29. "The Broken Ground," in Berry, *Collected Poems*, p. 25.
30. Berry, *The Memory of Old Jack*, p. 103.
31. Wendell Berry, *A World Lost* (Washington, DC: Counterpoint, 1996): 55.
32. Berry, *The Unsettling of America*, pp. 131-135.
33. Berry, *Home Economics*, p. 120.
34. Wendell Berry, *Home Economics* (San Francisco, CA: North Point Press, 1987): 149-150.
35. Wendell Berry, *Another Turn of the Crank* (Washington, DC: Counterpoint, 1995): 79-81; also, *The Unsettling of America*, p. 133.
36. Berry, *Home Economics*, pp. 103-106, 151; *The Unsettling of America*, pp. 13-14; *A Continuous Harmony*, pp. 103-105.
37. Berry, *Another Turn of the Crank*, p. 51.
38. Berry, *The Hidden Wound*, pp. 79-119.
39. Berry, *Home Economics*, pp. 124-125.
40. Berry, *A World Lost*, p. 64.
41. Berry, *The Gift of Good Land*, p. 24.

42. Berry, *A Place on Earth*, p. 203.
43. Berry, "The Satisfactions of the Mad Farmer," in *Collected Poems*, pp. 132-133.
44. "For the Hog Killing,' in Berry, *Collected Poems*, p. 200.
45. Wendell Berry, *The Wild Birds: Six Stories of the Port William Membership* (San Francisco, CA: North Point Press, 1986): 88, 102.
46. Berry, *Nathan Coulter*, p. 8.
47. Berry, *A Continuous Harmony*, p. 130.
48. Berry, *The Hidden Wound*, p. 72.
49. Berry, *Home Economics*, p. 165.
50. Ibid., p. 118.
51. Ibid., p. 190; and Berry, *What Are People For?* pp. 85-86, 135.
52. Berry, *Fidelity*, p. 74; emphasis added.
53. Berry, *Remembering*, p. 65.
54. Berry, *Home Economy*, p. 177.
55. Berry, *The Unsettling of America*, p. 63.
56. Berry, *What Are People For?*, pp. 137, 155.
57. "The Clearing," in Berry, *Collected Poems*, p. 180.
58. Berry, *The Hidden Wound*, p. 67.
59. Ibid., pp. 106-107.
60. Berry, *A Continuous Harmony*, p. 61.
61. Berry, *The Unsettling of America*, p. 212; and *Remembering*, pp. 78-81.
62. Berry, *What Are People For?*, p. 132; and *The Unsettling of America*, pp. 143-149.
63. Berry, *Fidelity*, p. 165.
64. Berry, *The Hidden Wound*, pp. 104, 118, 127, 135.
65. Berry, *What Are People For?*, pp. 25-27, 162-164.
66. Berry, *The Hidden Wound*, pp. 132-134.
67. Berry, *A Place on Earth*, p. 173; and *Home Economics*, p. 83.
68. Berry, *The Gift of Good Land*, p. 110.
69. Berry, *Another Turn of the Crank*, p. x.
70. Berry, *What Are People For?*, p. 113; *The Unsettling of America*, pp. 212, 218.
71. Berry, *The Unsettling of America*, pp. 40, 43, 53-56, 61, 63, 91; and *What Are People For?*, pp. 115.
72. Berry, *The Unsettling of America*, pp. 63-74.
73. Wendell Berry, *Entries* (Washington, DC: Counterpoint, 1994, 1997): 9-10; emphasis added.
74. Berry, *What Are People For?*, pp. 171-172.
75. Ibid., p. 187.
76. Berry, *What Are People For?*, p. 139.
77. Berry, *A Continuous Harmony*, p. 94.
78. Berry, *What Are People For?*, p. 130.
79. Berry, *The Unsettling of America*, pp. 19-21.
80. Berry, *Home Economics*, p. 168.
81. Berry, *Remembering*, p. 96.
82. Berry, *Home Economics*, p. 169.
83. Berry, *A Continuous Harmony*, pp. 48, 72-73.
84. Berry, *The Gift of Good Land*, p. x.
85. Ibid., p. xiii.
86. Berry, *The Hidden Wound*, p. 131.
87. Berry, *The Unsettling of America*, p. 137; and *Home Economics*, p. 44.
88. Berry, *Remembering*, p. 84.

89. Berry, *What Are People For?*, pp. 156-157.
90. Wendell Berry, *Watch With Me, and Six Other Stories of the Yet-Remembered Ptolemy Proudfoot and His Wife, Miss Minnie, nee Quinch* (New York: Pantheon, 1994): 156.
91. Berry, *Home Economics*, p. 173.
92. Berry, *What Are People For?*, p. 196.
93. Berry, *The Unsettling of America*, pp. 81-85, 217.
94. Berry, *Home Economics*, p. 56.
95. Berry, *The Unsettling of America*, p. 42.
96. Berry, *Home Economics*, pp. 123, 176.
97. On the above, see: Berry, *The Unsettling of America*, pp. 218-221; *Home Economics*, pp. 124-128, 174-176; *The Gift of Good Land*, pp. 94-95, 111-112; and *Another Turn of the Crank*, pp. 13-15.
98. "The Way of Pain," in Berry, *Collected Poems*, p. 210.
99. "The Birth (Near Port William)," in Berry, *Collected Poems*, p. 127.
100. Berry, *A World Lost*, p. 151.
101. Berry, *What Are People For?*, pp. 95, 98.
102. Berry, *The Hidden Wound*, p. 66.
103. Berry, *The Memory of Old Jack*, p. 198.
104. Berry, *What Are People For?*, p. 96.
105. Wendell Berry, *Sex, Economy, Freedom and Community* (New York: Pantheon, 1992/1993): 114.
106. Berry, *The Gift of Good Land*, pp. 269-278.
107. Berry, *What Are People For?*, pp. 66-67.
108. Berry, *Sex, Economy, Freedom and Community*, p. 111.
109. Berry, *What Are People For?*, pp. 98-99; and *Another Turn of the Crank*, p. 69.
110. Berry, *The Unsettling of America*, pp. 95, 210.
111. See: Donald B. Kraybill, *The Riddle of Amish Culture* (Baltimore, MD: Johns Hopkins University Press, 1989): 25-38.
112. Berry, *The Unsettling of America*, p. 211; *The Gift of Good Land*, p. 261; *Home Economics*, pp. 177-178, 188-189.
113. Kraybill, *The Riddle of Amish Culture*, pp. 38-40.
114. Berry, *What Are People For?*, p. 12; and *Home Economics*, p. 17.
115. Berry, *A Continuous Harmony*, p. 164.
116. Berry, *The Unsettling of America*, pp. 87, 222.
117. Berry, *Another Turn of the Crank*, p. 8.
118. Berry, *A World Lost*, p. 79.
119. Berry, *The Wild Birds*, p. 135.
120. Berry, *The Unsettling of America*, pp. 43-44.
121. Berry, *What Are People For?*, p. 205.
122. Ibid., p. 102.
123. Berry, *Another Turn of the Crank*, p. 8.
124. Berry, *A Place on Earth*, p. 317.
125. Cited in Angyal, *Wendell Berry*, p. 127.
126. Berry, *What Are People For?*, pp. 62, 169.

9

Lessons from the Plain People

The failure of the New Agrarian project in the twentieth century could, perhaps, be laid at the feet of economic determinism. It might be argued that no human action could have halted the industrialization of agriculture, and the consequent displacement of human labor by capital in alliance with technology. The same process, it might be said, inevitably tore apart the working home as well, displacing economic generalists known as husbandmen and housewives with professional experts and factory-based production. This interpretation would emphasize that, despite frequent claims to the contrary, the production of food, fiber, or children is no different than the production of any other commodity. The New Agrarian effort to protect the farm family, through special treatment of the farm economy, could be seen as an admirable exercise in sentimentality, but one with no prospect of long-term success. Even the oft-cited "Scandinavian model" in Denmark and Sweden, involving sophisticated forms of government protection of the small-farm sector, tight controls on joint-stock companies, preferences for decentralized industry, and conscious programs of family policy, has broken down since 1970. It could not survive the relentless pressures of international competition, finite governmental resources, and ideological drift. Industrial capitalism, quite simply, might be judged the preordained victor and the New Agrarians merely a sad, if noble, band of reactionaries swept aside by the winner's characteristic "creative destruction."[1]

The problem with this interpretation is that while it explains many of the historical facts, it does not quite explain them all. It would account for the consolidation of American farms from 6 million in

1900 to 2 million by the end of the century, and for the decline in the total number of people on farms from 30 million to under 5 million over the same period of time. It would explain the collapse of a distinctive rural fertility toward modern American norms. It would allow for the failure of most new "subsistence homestead" projects, such as those undertaken by the disciples of Ralph Borsodi in the 1930s or the followers of Wendell Berry in the 1970s. This interpretation would also explain why most "real farmers" paid little attention to the New Agrarian campaign: they were either caught up in the inevitable need to modernize and grow or driven to surrender their land to their bolder and luckier neighbors and find a less stressful, more remunerative way of life.

However, this explanation does not account for certain events on the margins of twentieth-century experience. It cannot explain, for example, how sectarian groups rooted in subsistence agriculture could grow: the Old Order Amish, from 5,000 in 1900 to 150,000 at century's end; the Hutterites from 2,000 to 40,000 over the same time span; and the emergence of other growing subsistence farming communities, such as the Brazos de Dios Homesteads in Texas, an Anabaptist community first organized in Manhattan's Hell's Kitchen. It is by examining *these* rural groups, which have successfully run *against* the grain of the twentieth century, that we can isolate some of the true missteps taken by the New Agrarians.

To begin with, they were mistaken about the nature of science and the promise of technology. There is something peculiarly American about faith in the scientific way and the mantle of technology. Early twentieth-century progressivism did not so much create these views as reflect them. So too with the New Agrarians. Starting with Liberty. Hyde Bailey—and excepting only two of the Twelve Southerners (Lytle and Davidson) and Wendell Berry at the end—the common orientation was to embrace scientific and technological advance as a vital part of their project. This is why the experiments in home production of Ralph Borsodi made so deep an impression on the cause, and why his celebration of the decentralist potential in electric and gasoline power so shaped their perceptions of future possibilities and policies. The arguments of the New York economist allowed the Agrarians to embrace the gadgets and innovations of modern technology—indeed, to claim a place on the technological cutting edge—while still holding to the themes of tradition, stability, and family. It allowed them to claim that the material movement of history was on their side, if only the obstructions of mega-corporations and bureaucrats could be pushed away.

In fact, the whole logic of the tool—of every tool—is to augment human energy, to create the same amount of product by reducing the necessary input of human labor. The machine tool adds external sources of power—animal, steam, electric, water, or fossil fuel—under the guidance of human intelligence and will. It is part of human nature, moreover, to tinker with, and "improve," such devices. This was as true of the first animal-drawn stick thrust into the ground for a primitive plow as it is of the massive contemporary diesel tractor pulling a computer-guided twenty-four-bottom plow. The electric and internal combustion engines did not negate these generalizations, as Borsodi implied. Instead, they *accelerated* their application. To choose just one prominent example, it was the linkage of the small two-cylinder gasoline engine to traction power, in mass-produced form, that brought the victory of the tractor over the horse and mule, and sharply reduced the human labor hours needed per bushel of product. In 1900, it took approximately 150 man-hours of labor to produce 100 bushels of corn. By the end of the century, it took only three hours. With all else equal, this meant the displacement of forty-nine out of every fifty farmers. As engineers found new ways to apply the small tractor and other new techniques to additional uses, real prices for the affected commodities steadily fell, driving the surviving producers into the hands of the new technologies and the others off the farm altogether. The full application of electricity also undermined the home economy, destroying the useful places of sons in the barns and out-buildings, and of daughters and wives in the productive home, a consequence that only Andrew Lytle among the New Agrarians seemed able to flag and understand.

Again, by definition, gains in efficiency mean less labor expended in creating the same level of output. This is no trick of capitalism. It is simply the consequence of human action. To accept efficiency as a guiding value in human affairs, as most of the New Agrarians did, is to accept the inevitable displacement of human labor in creating existing products: in the middle and long run, there can be no other result. Despite its celebration of innovation, the Borsodi argument actually presumed that future technological progress would be very modest. But the writer provided no mechanism to produce this end. Quite the contrary, Borsodi's fierce opposition to both governmental and religious authority eliminated the only forces capable of creating such controls within communities.

There are human societies, in our time, where the state plays the role of restricting innovation: the recent or current regimes in Cambodia and Afghanistan offer extreme examples; the "green" social democracies of Northern Europe more modest ones. In a liberal democracy, however, the record suggests that only religious devotion and obedience are strong enough to produce effective *voluntary* restraints on technological advance. The most established and ingenious example of this process is found among the Old Order Amish. Their secrets are simple: "efficiency" is commonly subordinated to the preservation of certain forms of human labor; tools remain bound to the idea of personal craft; and technological innovation is usually subsumed to the preservation of community. Religious obedience, in turn, makes bearable the psychological price of renouncing the symbols and products of intensive consumerism and a highly refined division of labor.

As an example of their first secret, Amish elders have allowed the use of gasoline-powered hay balers, but with two provisos: the baler must be pulled by horses; and the newly packed bales must be hand-tossed from baler to wagon. The "innovation" eased the difficult task of making hay and improved the prospects of Amish farmers for making a living; while the provisos preserved both the community commitment to true horsepower in the field and a job commonly done by the older boys. As an example of the subordination of technology to the preservation of the community, the clearest example is the Amish treatment of horse and automobile. The Amish themselves may travel only by horse, or horse and buggy, which limits the distance they can move each day to about twenty miles. This holds individuals close to their rural neighborhood; and it protects them from "worldly" contamination. At the same time, the elders allow the Amish families to hire drivers-with-car. This permits emergency, special, and job-related trips, but always with a clear calculation of cost and gain.[2] Most such rules create inconveniences, relative to what might be. But the values of separation from the world and obedience to religious authority allow individuals psychologically to override those inconveniences, for the sake of a greater good.

Further, the Plain People adhere to a sense of personal responsibility, which translates into altogether different measures of value. As the Brazos de Dios homesteaders explain, "the essential beauty and perfection of, say, the work put into a handmade chair comes from the craftsman's response to the highest calling, to the love of God, to which the chair then bears witness." Supply and demand have no determining place in the calculations of "people whose vision is directed heavenward." Efficiency is also, quite simply, irrelevant. The beauty and utility of things well made are instead thank offerings to God, true products of the economy of the Kingdom of God.[3] That·they also usually command "above market" prices in homesteader shops points to the limits of conventional economic assumptions.

In sum, the negative and positive lessons of twentieth-century America suggest that *a sustainable rural community and a subsistence farm economy can survive in democratic society only within a strong religious context.* Beyond the common guiding hand of faith and religious discipline, though, the possible accommodations with technology are quite varied. The Old Order Amish combine the use of hydraulic power, hand-held calculators, and portable gasoline engines with horse-drawn plows and oil lamps. The Brazos de Dios homesteaders count horse-drawn cultivators, subsistence gardens, and handmade furniture along with trucks, cellular phones, and air conditioned houses. In both cases, religious authority guides the human compromises with the machines, in order to sustain the human community. Prayer and "submission" undergird the results.

Second, the New Agrarians never satisfactorily resolved their simultaneous calls for "strong individualism" and "strong community." Liberty Hyde Bailey praised the freestanding farm family on the normative 160-acre farm as the American ideal and he deplored examples of communitarian, peasant-like existence. His Country Life colleagues denounced continuing "ethnic" associations in the countryside, which they said undermined the "needed" forms of democratic association. Most later Agrarians, from Borsodi and Bromfield to Agar and Berry, reflected a related admiration for the antistatism and the anticlericalism of the ruggedly independent, freethinking yeoman farmer.

At the same time, though, they all called for a countryside filled with strong communities. Shared values and communal experiences of the right sort, they held, should weave these rural folk together into sustainable social constructs, ranging from neighborhoods to a civilization.

But can "rugged independence" and "strong communitarianism" co-exist? Outside agrarian mythology, it seems unlikely, almost by definition. Even in the pre-1840 period, American agrarianism had a far stronger rootedness in religious and ethnic bonds than usually admitted. Denominational differences carried into farming and inheritance patterns, while ethnic connections strongly influenced business transactions, belying the "independent yeoman" legend.[4]

The counterpoint to the "rugged yeoman" line of argument came from those (somewhat fewer) New Agrarians who were more attached to European communalism, notably Zimmerman and Ligutti. They recognized, at least implicitly, that the rooting of farm families in ethnic or religious community would be necessary for rural survival in the modern age. Put another way, the isolated modern nuclear family, even when on a farm, would by itself be incapable of weathering the gale of the urban-industrial revolution. The support and shelter provided by strong communal bonds must also be there.

Beyond the already-cited example of the survival of the Plain People, there is other evidence that Zimmerman and Ligutti were closer to the truth. In her careful study of seven modern Illinois commercial farm communities, sociologist Sonya Salamon has shown that it has been families of German ancestry that have been successful in passing farms across the generations of a family. This has been is in marked contrast to "Yankee" operated farms, peopled by descendents from the "old stock" Anglo-Americans, where there has been significantly less transfer of farm title from one generation to the next. She attributes this difference to the stronger communal attachments of the German-Americans.[5]

Third, the New Agrarians grievously misunderstood the nature of the modern suburb. The normal refrain of the New Agrarians was that suburbanization was a positive gain, part of their project for a decentralized America. These were new communities, built by Americans who sought a home on a piece of land, where subsistence gardening and a chicken house would allow urban workers to keep one foot on the farm. Among some Agrarians, such as Zimmerman and Bromfield, the suburbs became even more important. For the sociologist, these "rurban" centers were the new nurseries for the American population, taking over the necessary task of replacing the population with a crop of babies, following the decline of rural fertility. For the novelist, the suburbs were the place where "farming as a way of life" could survive as an ideal, while real farming became an elite scientific and conservation-oriented project.

But the reality of suburban life was very different. While simple landscaping, lawn care (e.g., The "John Deere" riding mower), and the keeping of a dog, became aspects of the common life for suburbanites, subsistence gardening and animal husbandry did not. It is true that Rodale-published magazines, such as *Organic Gardening*, found a modest following in suburban climes. But such a commitment was never normative. The architectural plans for the "Productive Home," compiled by Ralph Borsodi and the other editors of *Free America*, stand as haunting examples of what might have been, but they never bore any reality. Instead, the post-1945 suburbs were the product of conventional mass developers, usually sharing a limited sense of aesthetics, in union with federal government subsidies. They did represent a state-induced form of "decentralization," but primarily as an expression of national defense in the "atomic age," a plan to disperse the population as a countermeasure to possible nuclear attack.[6]

Moreover, Zimmerman's celebration of the postwar suburbs as "a new family form" capable of achieving positive population growth simply proved to be wrong. To begin with, the "baby boom" that began in the mid-1940s was time-limited. It came to an end in the mid-1960s. Indeed, a decade later, it had been replaced by a "baby bust," with the U.S. total fertility rate falling from a high of 3.6 children per completed family in 1957 to 1.7 in 1976, a level well-below the "zero growth" figure of 2.1. As such, Zimmerman's new family model proved to be without social substance. It was ephemeral, the product of a single generation, people who were unable to pass on values regarding fertility to their children.

Other evidence suggests that the baby boom itself was not a product of secular forces. Instead, it appears to have been largely a Roman Catholic event. The total fertility rate for non-Catholics was 3.15 children per woman in 1951-55 and 3.14 in 1961-1965. But for Catholics, the figures were 3.54 and 4.25. Similar evidence confirms that the "return" of large families in the suburbs was heavily concentrated among Catholics. A survey from 1952-55 found only 10 percent of Catholics under age forty having four or more children, a number close to the 9 percent for Protestants. By 1957-59, the Protestant figure was unchanged. However, the proportion for Catholics had soared to 22 percent. The research also shows that this "Catholic fertility" event was tied to more frequent attendance at Mass, and to prior attendance of the mothers at Catholic parochial schools, colleges, and universities. Pope Pius XII and the whole "teaching church" gave much more frequent attention in these years to the nature of the Christian family and to the large family as a sign of obedience to God's will.[7] Simply put, it seems fair to conclude that the positive relationship between fertility and suburbanization was secondary; the real source of the baby boom lay in the effects of particular religious devotion and authority on the lives of particular adherents for a limited period of time.

Indeed, it is the Plain People of the late 1990s, living on subsistence farms, that almost alone among Americans continued to show high levels of community-wide fertility. Doctrinal opposition to the use of birth control has combined with the fact that a large number of children "are an asset to the Amish farm economy" to produce families averaging between seven and nine children.[8] Among the Hutterites, average completed family size sometimes reaches ten children. At Brazos de Dios, a Christian community founded in 1973 in a drug- and prostitute-ridden New York City neighborhood now produces strong marriages and an abundant crop of beautiful children.[9] The lessons seem clear: the "economic gain" provided by children on the subsistence farm is, by itself, not strong enough to overcome the more general anti-natalism of industrialized society; submission to religious authority is also necessary.

Fourth, the New Agrarians mistakenly placed their faith in aggressive social engineering, be it through governmental power or the quasi-governmental coercion of "superior men." The twentieth century bears terrible witness to the repeated failure of secular social engineering, whether the project be creating the "New Soviet Man" of the Bolsheviks, the "New Aryan Man" of the National Socialists, the "New Cooperative Man" of the Scandinavian Social Democrats, or the "New Farmer" of the twentieth-century Agrarians. Despite the vast differences in the moral quality and political consequences of these programs, they failed for common reasons: reliance on coercion, rather than conscience, for their implementation; violation of both the authority of tradition and the reality of human nature; and denial, by definition, of the imperative of liberty. Even the quest for the "New Farmer," the most benign and virtuous of these projects, commonly involved the harsh condemnation of existing farmers, the projected use of governmental powers of differential taxation, subsidy, and confiscation to achieve ideological goals, the creation of a command

economy as a substitute for markets in food and fiber, the indoctrination of a new breed of farmers into compatibility with the ideal vision,
and the forcible displacement of farmers who stubbornly held to rival
visions of agriculture.

This is not to dispute the value and real power of a certain kind of
social engineering. Kraybill makes the case that the Old Order Amish
are in fact master social engineers.[10] The difference is that the Plain
People refuse to apply the coercive power of the state to achieve their
ends. To the contrary, they rely on voluntary adherence to the community by their members, the purposeful socialization of their children,
and the application of informal social controls, such as shunning, to
achieve their ends. The Amish have indeed engineered a novel, progressive existence, sustaining family and neighborhood, without the
aid of (and oftentimes, in opposition to) the state authority. Their
achievement is compatible with human liberty; in this respect, the
New Agrarian project was not.

*Fifth, the New Agrarians erred deeply in their opposition to sectar-
ian, other-worldly Christianity.* Liberty Hyde Bailey and the other
Country Life leaders complained bitterly about the growth of the sectarian, fundamentalist, "gospel splitting" denominations. Only Carle
Zimmerman looked with real favor on Old World Lutheranism and
Catholicism. Ralph Borsodi condemned all devotion to otherworldly
gods. Louis Bromfield mocked fundamentalisms and said that the
"best farmers" would seldom be found in churches. The Southern
Agrarians were embarrassed by the Baptists and fundamentalists in
their midst. The American Distributists, exemplified by Herbert Agar,
also saw the rural Protestant churches as symbols of failure. Even
Wendell Berry, who admired the farming practices of some of the
separatist sects, condemned "otherworldly" Christianity as a cause of
rural degradation.

The surprising reality, though, is that the virtues of family, fertility,
neighboring, and autonomy would survive together only among American sectarians in the universally condemned Anabaptist, fundamentalist, Pentecostal, and monastic dispensations. Only a commitment to a
radical "separation from the world," with eyes firmly fixed heavenward, gave sufficient power to individuals in communities to overcome the lures, appetites, and pressures of the full industrialization of
life and to motivate rural dwellers to become good stewards of both
land and community. Even in American Judaism, strong families and

high fertility in the late twentieth century would be found primarily among the mystical, otherworldly, separatist Hassidic groups.[11]

By way of contrast, the mainline Protestant faiths, on which Bailey fixed so much hope, failed completely as protectors and nurturers of rural life. They moved instead into a social radicalism that questioned the worth of the traditional family, opposed high fertility, and embraced most aspects of the sexual revolution.[12] Even the rich theological argumentation of Luigi Ligutti failed to provide a utilitarian basis for the long-term preservation of a Catholic rural community, aware of itself. The Granger Homesteads were disordered by war and loss of clerical leadership. The demise of the fine lay Catholic agrarian journal, *Caelum et Terra*, in 1995 was only the most recent example of this weakness. The exceptions proving the rule have been unofficial Catholic and "High Protestant" communities organized on a quasi-monastic model, where subsistence agriculture and craftsmanship actually thrive within the context of vows of poverty, obedience, charity, and marriage. Such informal religious "family" communities exist, and grow, in Wisconsin and Massachusetts. Here, too, the guiding assumption has been separation from the world, an all-consuming focus on the next life, which paradoxically energizes self-sufficient farming, human fertility, ecological awareness, and the creation of working homes in this life.

Sixth, the New Agrarians either denied or ignored the one "secular" change that could invigorate working homes: namely, home schooling. From Bailey and Zimmerman through Agar and Berry, the agrarian imagination faltered on the question of education. They all understood that the primary source of family weakness came from the stripping away of functions from the household, from the steady transfer or surrender of parts of the home economy to governments, corporations, and paid specialists. They also properly understood that the rebuilding of strong families would require the return of at least some of these productive functions to the household. But, with the limited exception of Father Ligutti, they could never really imagine that this might begin with the return of primary and secondary education to the home. Even Ralph Borsodi, who successfully "home schooled" his own children, and Wendell Berry, who witnessed the rapid growth of home schooling in the 1980s and 1990s, failed to understand its real potential. Fixated on agricultural and other physical matters, all the New Agrarians sought to recreate functional homes using the existing, and largely government-operated, schools or elite-run projects such as the Extension Service and Borsodi's School of Living. Curricular reforms, school consolidation or deconsolidation, and the training of a new breed of teachers were among their other preferred educational solutions, none of which produced desired results. Rather, it would be the radical, albeit simple, act of parents teaching their own children in their own dwellings that would turn out to be the key to recreating working homes.

At least this is what the evidence suggests. Using the measure of success most widely accepted by the New Agrarians—namely fertility—data from the United States show that the average number of children born into home education families was 3.43 in 1991, compared to two for the nation-at-large. In Canada, average family size for home educators was 3.46 children, more than double the national mean.[13] We may conclude that refunctionalized families are indeed stronger and more fertile, just as the New Agrarians had always presumed. Their mistake was to seek revitalization first through the subsistence garden and the keeping of chickens. It would be in the home school room, or around the humble kitchen table, that renewal would actually begin. Embracing an estimated 20,000 children in 1970, home schooling counted nearly two million American children at the century's end, a hundred-fold increase. Moreover, it has been out of home education that commitments to other forms of family production have grown: including, most particularly, subsistence gardening and the keeping of simple livestock. The procession of reclaimed functions among the Brazos de Dios community may serve as a paradigm here. They discovered "home births" in the mid-1970s. Several years later, they began "home schooling." "Urban gardens" came next, followed by a migration of the congregation to rural settlements in Colorado and Texas, where they were joined by kine, fowls, and work horses.[14] It seems that once having tasted household freedom in the act of home education, the family looks for other ways to grow into autonomy. Its members have come to know what it feels like to be "refunctionalized," and they seek more.

So perhaps we may also conclude that the "New Agrarian" project has not wholly disappeared. If understood at its core as the effort to rebuild working homes sheltering fertile and economically autonomous families, then the New Agrarian vision survives and even expands on the social margins at this century's end: in the separatist, other worldly, pietistic fundamentalisms of Christianity and Judaism; and in the revolutionary cells that constitute home schools. The irony is that these were perhaps the very last places that the New Agrarians thought to look for answers.

Notes

1. A phrase borrowed from economist Joseph Schumpeter.
2. See Donald B. Kraybill, *The Riddle of Amish Culture* (Baltimore, MD: Johns Hopkins University Press, 1989): 168-171, 178.
3. Blair Adams, *Craft: The Art of Work* (Austin, TX: Colloquium Press, 1996): 6-7.
4. See John Demos, *A Little Commonwealth: Family Life in Plymouth Colony* (New York: Oxford University Press, 1970): 77-78; Daniel Snydacker, "Kinship and Community in Rural Pennsylvania," *Journal of Interdisciplinary History* 13 (Summer 1982): 41-61; and Dennis P. Ryan, "Six Towns: Continuity and Change in Revolutionary New Jersey, 1770-1792," doctoral dissertation (New York: New York University, 1974): 57-71.
5. Sonya Salamon, *Prairie Patrimony: Family, Farming & Community in the Midwest* (Chapel Hill and London: University of North Carolina Press, 1992).
6. See chapter 3, "The Suburban Strategy," in Allan Carlson, *From Cottage to Work Station: The Family's Search for Social Harmony in the Industrial Age* (San Francisco, CA: Ignatius, 1993): 65-84.
7. See: William D. Mosher, David P. Johnson, and Marjorie C. Horn, "Religion and Fertility in the United States: The Importance of Marriage Patterns and Hispanic Origin," *Demography* 23 (Aug. 1986): 367-369; Gerhard Lenski, *The Religious Factor: A Sociologist's Inquiry* (New York: Doubleday, 1961): 39-40; Lincoln H. Day, "Natality and Ethnocentrism: Some Relationships Suggested by an Analysis of Catholic-Protestant Differentials," *Population Studies* 22 (1968): 27-30; and Leon Bouvier and S.L.N. Rao, *Socio-religious Factors in Fertility Decline* (Cambridge, MA: Ballinger, 1975): 1-4, 84-91, 156-158.
8. John A. Hostetler, *Amish Society*, revised edition (Baltimore, MD: Johns Hopkins University Press, 1968): 81-83.
9. See *A Glimpse of Brazos de Dios* (Elm Mott, TX: Heritage Homestead, n.d.); and Lana Robinson, "Simple Gifts," *Texas Highways* 43 (Nov. 1996): 36-41.
10. See Kraybill, *The Riddle of Amish Culture*, pp. 235-236, 250-252.
11. See Edward Hoffman, *Despite All Odds: The Story of Lubavitch* (New York: Simon and Schuster, 1990).
12. As example, see: Elizabeth Stell Genne and William Henry Genne, eds., *Foundations for Christian Family Policy: The Proceedings of the North American Conference on Church and Family, April 30-May 5, 1961* (New York: National Council of the Churches of Christ in the U.S.A., 1961).
13. From J. Gary Knowles, Maralee Mayberry, and Brian D. Ray, "An Assessment of Home Schools in Nevada, Oregon, Utah, and Washington: Implications for Public Education and a Vehicle for Informed Policy Decisions; Summary Report," U.S. Department of Education Field Initiated Research Project (Grant #R117E 90220), submitted to U.S. Department of Education, December 24, 1991; and Brian D. Ray, *A Nationwide Study of Home Education in Canada: Family Characteristics, Student Achievement, and Other Topics* (Salem, OR: National Home Education Research Institute, 1994).
14. From an audio-visual presentation marking the community's twenty-fifth anniversary; presented October 25, 1998 at Heritage Homesteads, Elm Mott, Texas.

Index

Herbert Agar, 141
Southern Agrarians, 115
Wendell Berry, 185-86
Subsistence Homestead Program, 153-57, 172
Suburbs
  agrarianism failure and, 208-9
  Luigi Ligutti, 170-71
  rejection of, 170-71, 187-88
  value of, 170-71
  Wendell Berry, 187-88
Successful American Families (Zimmerman), 46-47

Taft, William Howard, 16
Tate, Allen, 100, 120
  agricultural background, 101
  economics, 103
  peasant model, 119
  religion, 117
Taxation
  single tax, 3
  Southern Agrarians, 111, 113-14
Technology
  agrarianism failure and, 204-7
  Carle C. Zimmerman, 48-49
  Herbert Agar, 132
  hostility to, 189-91
  Liberty Hyde Bailey, 14, 15, 20-21, 26, 27
  Louis Bromfield, 90-91, 95
  Luigi Ligutti, 161-62, 164-65, 171
  manhour decline, 3
  New Agrarian movement, 5
  Ralph Borsodi, 70
  religion and, 161-62, 171
  Southern Agrarians, 118
  steam-powered threshers, 3
  value of, 5, 14, 15, 20-21, 26, 27, 48-49, 70, 118, 132, 164-65
  Wendell Berry, 189-91
Tennessee Agrarians. *See* Southern Agrarians
This Ugly Civilization (Borsodi), 57, 58, 61-62, 65, 68, 70
Training of Farmers, The (Bailey), 12, 22
Twenty Four Hours (Bromfield), 89

University of Melbourne, 71-72
Unsettling of America, The (Berry), 190, 196

Until the Day Break (Bromfield), 93
Urbanization
  artistry and, 105
  Carle C. Zimmerman
    anti-urbanism, 35, 39
    reurbanization, 39, 46-48
  condemnation of, 35, 39, 89-90, 105, 130, 161
  Herbert Agar, 130
  Louis Bromfield, 89-90
  Luigi Ligutti, 161
  population and, 2-3
  Southern Agrarians, 105
U.S. Department of Agriculture, 48

Vanderbilt Agrarians. *See* Southern Agrarians

Wade, John Donald, 100
Wallace, Henry, 5, 16
War
  U.S. intervention
    Herbert Agar, 142-45
    Luigi Ligutti, 167
    Wendell Berry, 179-80
Warren, Robert Penn, 101
Watch With Me (Berry), 198
Who Owns America? A New Declaration of Independence (Agar), 133
Wild is the River (Bromfield), 84, 90
Women. *See also* Fertility
  female image, 79-81
  feminism, 181-82
  Louis Bromfield, 79-81
  marriage, 182-83
  sexuality, 183-84
  Wendell Berry, 181-82, 183-84
Wood, Grant, 6
Wright, Frank Lloyd, 6

Young, Stark, 100, 117, 118

Zimmerman, Carle C.
  background, 32-34
    birthplace, 32
    parental, 32
    religious, 32
  beliefs of
    anti-urbanism, 35, 39
    Christianity, 31-32
    decentralization, 49
    education, 50-51

CPSIA information can be obtained at www.ICGtesting.com
Printed in the USA
BVOW021900170613

323549BV00010B/316/P

9 780765 805904